Just Relax DBA

Arun Kumar Kubendiran
Mahendran Manickam
Sundaravel Ramasubbu
Gokulkumar Radhakrishnan

DOYENSYS
Technology Drives, We Lead

notionpress
.com

INDIA · SINGAPORE · MALAYSIA

Notion Press

Old No. 38, New No. 6
McNichols Road, Chetpet
Chennai - 600 031

First Published by Notion Press 2019
Copyright © Doyensys 2019
All Rights Reserved.

ISBN 978-1-64760-814-9

CONTENTS

INTRODUCTION

This book is about sharing the personal experience on day-to-day daily tasks for DBAs including both core and apps DBA. This will also have tips and tricks to help DBA trainees to do smart work in day to day daily tasks to save huge time.

As there are many ways to perform a single task, doing it smart way is the wise option for any DBA as his/her job is more hectic.

Another important thing is the quick way to perform a task. It can be pulling several log files of the same pattern, searching in a zip file, pulling a specific file from the zip file, uploading huge files to Oracle service request, finding a particular session in a database, analysing performance, getting erred job details for a specific time, etc. It could be any task but all that is needed from any DBA is quick and smart work.

This will have chapters on every area where DBA performs complicated tasks and involves huge timings. Also, this gives you many case studies on real-time activities and challenges.

Most importantly it will have "Best Practices" sections and/or "Do's and Don'ts" section that will help any DBA to start with any activity.

EBS PATCHING

Patching Oracle E-business suite is part of Oracle Apps DBA activities. Knowing to patch in depth will help DBAs to achieve many tasks easily. One can patch any Oracle component like E-business suite, SSO components, SOA suite, Hyperion etc. In this chapter, we have discussed many things in patching E-business suite application.

TOPIC 1	**Patching Nomenclature** - This discusses the various types of patches and nomenclature followed by Oracle to release a patch. This will give a clear idea about the patches for specific modules and its codelevel and codelines.
TOPIC 2	**Using Maintenance Mode effectively** - Enabling Maintenance Mode for patching activity may be common, but using it effectively will help customers to announce downtime activity during maintenance time. This topic shows step-by-step instructions to use maintenance mode effectively.
TOPIC 3	**Patch Impact Analysis** – Patch Impact Analysis is a must for every customer before applying to production. DBAs can perform patch impact analysis in two ways and this topic describes and discusses both.
TOPIC 4	**EBS Port Conflict In ADOP** – This is one of the failure scenarios in ADOP and this topic gives a solution.
TOPIC 5	**ADOP cutover problems in 12.2** – This topic just discusses the cutover problems in ADOP in detail with classic examples. Also, this provides the best practices for ADOP.

TOPIC

1

PATCHING NOMENCLATURE – MUST KNOW

As DBAs we need to be very clear on what patches are required to the database and when to get those applied. Many clients will look for basic information on what type of patches these are and how these patches are helpful for the organization. We must be ready to answer all client queries regarding the patches. Oracle has many patching terminologies and it has evolved over the years as well.

Let us discuss here in detail.

Below are the various types of patches and details.

Consolidated Name	Old Name	Description	Patch Source
Interim Patch	PSE, MLR, Exception release, One-Off, x-fix, Hotfix, Security One-Off	A patch containing one or more fixes made available to customers who cannot wait until the next patch set or new product release to get a fix.	This may be any patch in a My Oracle Support document or from a Service Request.
Diagnostic Patch	Diagnostic Patch, test Patch, Fix Verification Binary (FVB), e-fix	An interim patch created specifically to diagnose a problem and not to fix a bug.	This may be from a Service Request to help diagnose your issue after a defect has been filed but not fully resolved.

Bundle Patch (BP)	Maintenance Pack, Service Pack, MLRs, Cumulative Patch, Update Release, Bundle Patch	An iterative, cumulative patch that is issued between patch sets. Bundle patches usually include only fixes, but some may include minor enhancements. Examples are the Database Windows Bundles and SOA Bundle Patches.	This may be any patch in a My Oracle Support
Patch Set Update (PSU)	Patch Set Update (PSU)	A quarterly patch that contains the most critical fixes for the applicable product, allowing customers to apply one patch to avoid many problems. These will be documented in My Oracle Support documents and initially released from the Critical Patch Update program.	
		For example, Oracle WebLogic Server has a PSU delivered with the CPU program where the 5th digit, signifies that PSU release, e.g. 10.3.6.0.xx.	
Security Patch Update (SPU)	Critical Patch Update (CPU)	An iterative, cumulative patch consisting of security fixes. Formerly known as Critical Patch Update.	These will be documented in My Oracle Support documents and initially released from the Critical Patch Update program.

		SPUs are single patches for a single product or component to fix security vulnerability. These are cumulative for the same product or component they are released for, e.g. Oracle HTTP Server, noting other components installed together will have separate patches, e.g. OPMN and SSL installed with OHS. **The program name which delivers SPUs will still be called Critical Patch Update,** as defined below: Oracle's program for the quarterly release of security fixes. Patches released as part of this program may be Patch Set Updates, Security Patch Updates, and Bundle Patches. Regardless of the patch type, the patches are cumulative.	

As of November 2015 the version numbering for new Bundle Patches, Patch Set Updates and Security Patch Updates for Oracle Database, Enterprise Manager and Middleware products will start to change the format. The new format replaces the numeric **5th digit** of the bundle version with a **release date** in the form "**YYMMDD**" where:

- **YY** is the last 2 digits of the year
- **MM** is the numeric month (2 digits)
- **DD** is the numeric day of the month (2 digits)

Note that the "**release date**" is the release date of the main bundle / PSU / SPU. In some rare cases, for example, where the same bundle is released on multiple platforms, the patch for a specific platform may not be available until some days after the **"release date"**.

Some bundles may continue to use a numeric 5th digit in the short term but will transition to the new format over time.

The new version format makes it easier to see which bundle patches are from which time-frame, and in particular which patches are from the same Critical Patch Update release.

Examples

- "WebLogic Server PSU 12.2.1.0.**1**" will instead be called "WebLogic Server 12.2.0.1.**160119**"

- "Enterprise Manager Base Platform PSU 12.1.0.4.**6**" will instead be called "Enterprise Manager Base Platform PSU 12.1.0.4.**160119**"

- "Database PSU 11.2.0.4.9" will instead be called "Database PSU 11.2.0.4.**160119**"

- Oracle Applications patches are released in the following formats and these are exclusive only for Oracle E-business Suite.

Patches	Description
Individual bug fix	A patch that fixes an existing issue and fixes only that particular issue. Other fixes may or may not be included.
Product family release update pack (product family RUP)	A set of patches on a given codeline created for all products in specific product family for a specific point release. For example, R12.HR_PF.C.Delta.4
Release update pack (RUP)	A cumulative aggregation of product family release update packs on a given codeline created across Oracle E-Business Suite after the initial release. For example,

13

	12.1.1.
	Formerly known as a maintenance pack, it is now called a Release Update Pack with the short name of RUP. RUPs upgrade all products to higher codelevel. These point release upgrades can introduce substantial changes to the system and therefore need to be carefully planned. For example: RUP2 is equivalent to R12.0.2, RUP6 is equivalent to R12.0.6 etc.
Pre-upgrade patch	All upgrade-related, high-priority patches consolidated from all the products within a product family. Pre-upgrade patches are released as needed.
Consolidated upgrade patch	All upgrade-related patches consolidated from all the products in a product family. These patches are released as needed and are only available for upgrading a Release 12 system from one point release to another.
Recommended Patch Collection (RPC)	

There are different codelevels and codelines are followed starting from R12. Detailed information can be obtained from the reference notes below. Also, how frequent you should apply the patches, what to do if patches fail, how the patch details will be stored, how to check the latest information of patches: Answers to all these are available in the excellent MOS note below.

Oracle E-Business Suite Patching FAQ for Release 12 (Doc ID 459156.1)

TOPIC

2

USING MAINTENANCE MODE EFFECTIVELY

While performing any patching activity in R12, Users will be notified about the downtime well in advance. Still, some users who missed the sent downtime notifications will approach the DBA team about the downtime activities.

There is a way to avoid this situation where we can make an announcement when there is a patching activity in R12.

Prerequisite:

These steps will be useful when you have any maintenance with database availability.

Step 1:

Create a downtime Schedule using OAM before downtime.

Login to OAM as administrator and create a downtime schedule as follows.

Click on Sitemap --> Maintenance --> Maintain downtime schedules

Click on Schedule Downtime link

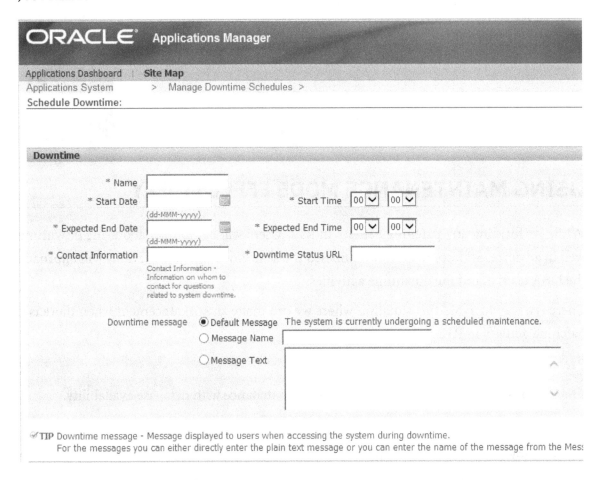

When you submit this message, it will create downtime_tls.html under $OA_HTML which will be called by downtime.html.

The downtime message should be created well in advance and if you create on the same date, you will get an error message as below.

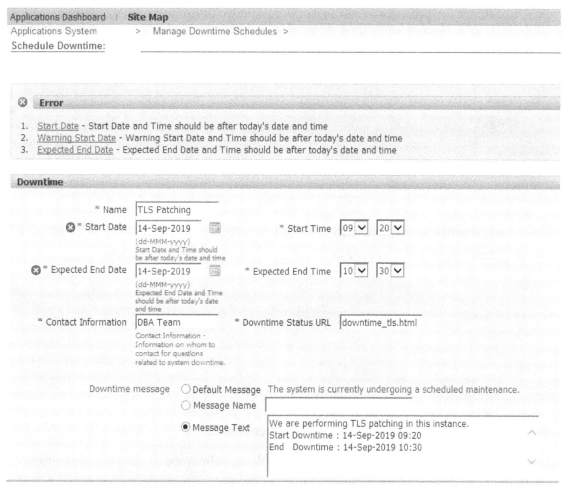

Once you create the downtime page, submit it.

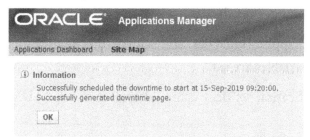

Review the downtime schedule upon submission. You can also view the downtime page and edit it if needed.

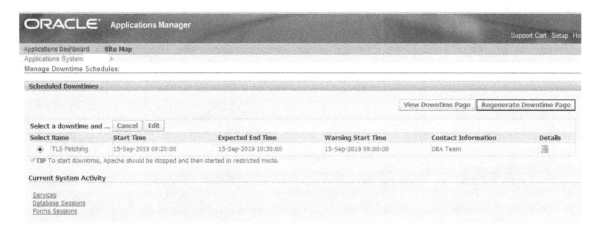

If the maintenance is planned well, you can configure the future downtime schedule as a warning message that will appear as below upon starting the applications.

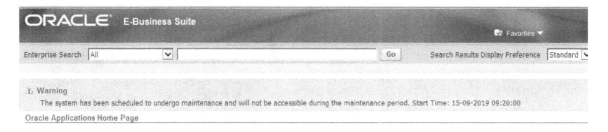

Step 2: Stop application and enable maintenance mode.

Stop all applications using adstpall.sh and enable maintenance mode using adadmin.

Step 3:

Configuring restricted mode Apache

1. Login to your applications tier and source the environment file so that all the environment variables are set.

2. Stop your application services using adstpall.sh from $ADMIN_SCRIPTS_HOME directory.

3. Run the command 'txkrun.pl -script=ChangeApacheMode' from the <FND_TOP>/bin directory:

4. This prompts for the following inputs:

5. Full path for the Applications Context file

6. Enter the mode for Apache. Type 'Restrict'

7. Confirmation of whether you have stopped your applications tier services [Default: Yes]

8. Once you enter the above details, the configuration script will perform sanity check and the change the apache values to restrict mode.

```
***********************************************
Sanity check to switch the mode to Restrict
***********************************************



*****************************************************************
Following context variables are in SYNC:
-------------------------------------------------
Variable: s_restricted_mode_comment(Value: #)
Variable: s_apache_mode(Value: NORMAL)
*****************************************************************

***************************************
Changing to RESTRICTED Mode...
***************************************
Updating context Variable s_restricted_mode_comment...
Updated context Variable s_restricted_mode_comment to
Updating context Variable s_apache_mode...
Updated context Variable s_apache_mode to RESTRICT


*****************************************************************
```

Now, start the apache (adapcctl.sh) and oacore service (adoacorectl.sh) so that users accessing the URL will get an announcement as below.

Scheduled Downtime Details

Start Time: 15-Sep-2019 09:20:00
Expected Up Time: 15-Sep-2019 10:30:00
For Updates: DBA Team

        We are performing TLS patching in this instance. Start Downtime : 15-Sep-2019 09:20
End Downtime : 15-Sep-2019 10:30

Current Status

Now, you can complete your list of activities including patching activity. Upon completion, you can revert all changes as below.

Changing Apache to NORMAL mode

1. Login to your applications tier and source the environment file so that all the environment variables are set

2. Stop your application services using adstpall.sh from $ADMIN_SCRIPTS_HOME directory.

3. Run the command 'txkrun.pl -script=ChangeApacheMode' from the <FND_TOP>/bin directory:

4. This prompts the following inputs:

   a. Full path for the Applications Context file

   b. Enter the mode for Apache. Type 'Normal'

   c. Confirmation of whether you have stopped your applications tier services [Default: Yes]

5. Once you enter the above details, the configuration script changes the apache values to normal mode.

Conclusion

The above steps are very useful for customers who need to display custom messages during the scheduled maintenance activity.

This will save time for the DBA team to reply to those users who missed the early notifications and prevent tickets in DBA queue.

TIP

The script below can be run quickly to enable maintenance mode instead of using adadmin.

```
SQL>apps/apps
SQL> @$AD_TOP/patch/115/sql/adsetmmd.sql ENABLE
```

TOPIC

3

PATCH IMPACT ANALYSIS

Oracle provides many patches for enhancements, bug fixes and upgrade and so on. Patch impact analysis is a must for every DBA to know about what files are impacted, untouched files and newly introduced files.

Various Methods

There are 2 methods by which this can be achieved.

- adpatch
- Patch wizard

1. adpatch

You can install patch with apply mode=no (by default it is yes).

apply=no mode will provide details of what the patch will perform during patching activity (like introducing new file, changing existing files and so on) but it will not apply the patch.

The syntax for using this mode is:

$ adpatch apply=no

The problem with this method is if you are applying patch set which involves 500+ objects, reading the log file (log file generated from adpatch) will be cumbersome because you will have to go through each object one by one and get the complete list of impacted objects.

2. Patch wizard

The Patch Impact Analysis screens are accessed from the Patch Wizard feature.

Use the following steps to generate and view patch impact analysis data.

Step 1: Configure Patch Wizard

- Create Patch Storage Area on the Apps Server (e.g.: /stage/patches/)

- Navigate to the Patch Wizard: Site Map > Maintenance (subtab) > Patching and Utilities (heading) > Patch Wizard (link).

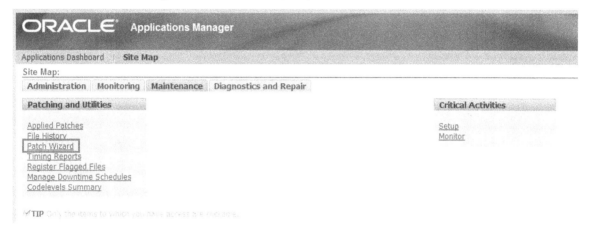

Select 'Patch Wizard'

Under Patch Wizard Tasks, Click the 1st option - 'Patch Wizard Preferences'

Task Name	Description	Tasks	Job Status
Patch Wizard Preferences	Set download, merge, and stage area preferences		
Define Patch Filters	Create custom patch filters		
Recommend/Analyze Patches	Submit requests for patch advice or analysis		
Download Patches	Submit requests to download patches		
Aggregate Patch Impact	Aggregate Patch Impact		

Here, enter the Linux path in the field called 'Staging Directory' = /stage/patches/

Leave other fields and click 'OK' at the bottom.

Create a directory called 'ad' under Patch Storage Area (/stage/patches) on the server.

This will complete the patching wizard configuration and it is a one-time setup.

Step 2: Analyse a Patch:

Under Patch Wizard Tasks, click 'Tasks' for the 3rd option - 'Recommend/Analyse Patches'

Now, select 'Analyse Specific Patches' > Enter the Patch number 'xxxxxxx' (make sure this patch is downloaded and placed on the server under Patch_Storage_Area/ad)

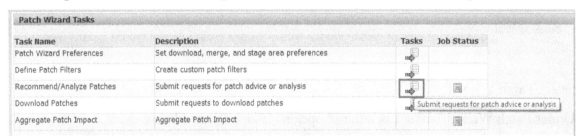

Provide the patch number under "Analyse Specific Patches" and press 'OK'. (Leave all other fields)

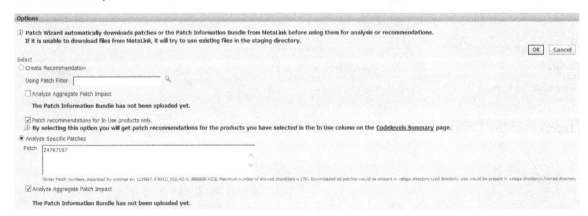

This will, in turn, submit a concurrent request to analyse our Patch

This patch submits the request set and upon its completion we get patch impact analysis in detail.

CONCURRENT_PROGRAM_NAME	DESCRIPTION
Submit Analyse Patches (Wrapper)	Patch Wizard Analyse Patches (Wrapper)
Analyse Impact Data	Analyse Data for Impact Analysis
Build JSP Dependency Tree	Build JSP Dependency Tree for Patch Impact Analysis
Compile Diagnostic Test Versions	Insert Java Diagnostic test version information into JTF_DIAGNOSTIC_CMAP table
Analyse Menu Tree Affected	Analyse Menu Tree Affected by a Patch
Analyse Impact Data 2	Analyse Impact Data 2
Aggregate Impact Analysis	Aggregate Impact for Recommended Patches
Patch Wizard Status Tracker	Tracks and sets the status of the request set

Step 3: To view the patch impact analysis, go to Patch wizard and under "Recommended Patches Results", select the patch.

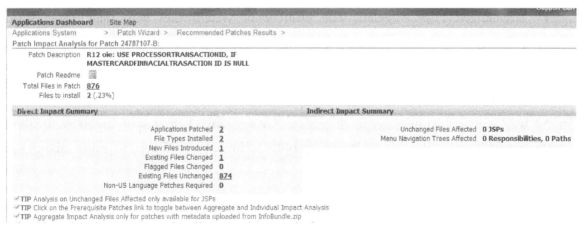

Direct patch impact includes:

- Applications Patched: The number of products that will have files updated. Click the number link to see details of each product affected, and how.

- File Types Installed: The number of different file types in the patch. Click the number link to see the file types and how they impact the system.

- New Files Introduced: The number of new files that will be introduced by the patch. Click the number link to details about each new file introduced.

- Existing Files Changed: The number of existing files in the system that will be changed by the patch. Click the number link to see the existing files changed and the new version numbers.

- Flagged Files Changed: The number of custom files that will be changed by this patch. Click the number link to identify the custom files changed by this patch.

- Existing Files Unchanged: The number of files unchanged because the version in the patch is older than the version in the system. Click the number link to see the files in the patch that are of the same or versions earlier than those currently in the system.

- Non-US Language Patches Required: If the patch supports multiple languages, click the number link to identify the other languages available.

Indirect summary information includes:

- Unchanged Files Affected: The number of system files with dependencies on patched files.

- Menu Navigation Trees Affected: The number of menu navigation trees that will be updated by the patch.

In this way, you will get detailed patch analysis for any patch before applying to the system. Patch impact analysis can be reviewed by both technical and DBAs to know about the impacted files.

This will help us to evaluate the amount of work or resources needed for testing purpose for any client.

In 12.1.3, there is a patch where we can get applied for this patch wizard which provides a button to export the impacted file details in csv format.

However, In Doyensys we use our own custom query to get the patch impact analysis report exported in csv format.

Tip: Use the query below to get the patch impact analysis report using SQL client.

```
Select b.APPLICATION_NAME Application,s.directory,s.filename,
DECODE(s.typeid, 'upgrade', 'Changed File', 'not applied',
'Unchanged File', 'new', 'New File') "Impact Type",
s.NEW_VERSION "Version in Patch",
s.OLD_VERSION "Version in APPL_TOP",
s.FILES_AFFECTED "Objects Affected"
From fnd_application_vl b,
FND_IMP_PSMaster2 s
Where s.app_short_name=b.APPLICATION_SHORT_NAME
And s.bug_no='24787107';
```

EBS PORT CONFLICT IN ADOP

In this blog, we are going cover the most common patching issue faced in EBS 12.2.X version patching.

As we already covered about ADOP (AD Online Patching Utility) in the earlier session, here we are going directly to the issue. ADOP FS_CLONE phase fails due to port conflict while running FS_CLONE after completing EBS and OAM integration and after completing a patch cycle resulting in FS_CLONE failing with the following error message.

> ERROR: The following required ports are in use:
>
> 7204: Managed Server Port 3
>
> Corrective Action: Free the listed ports and retry the adop operation.
>
> Completed execution: ADOPValidations.java

Problem Analysis

Port details in Run Edition Context file:

```
[run]$ cat $CONTEXT_FILE |grep -i 7204
    <oacore_server_ports oa_var="s_oacore_server_ports">oacore_server1:7203,oacore_server11:7204</oacore_server_ports>
    <oacore_nodes oa_var="s_oacore_nodes">                    7203,              7204</oacore_nodes>
appebsv                              /backup/dba/scripts
  [run]$ ls -rlt $CONTEXT_FILE
-rw-r--r-- 1         oinstall 116266 Mar  2 02:17        appebsv/fs2/inst/apps/              appl/admin/              ml
```

Port details in Patch Edition Context file:

```
[run]$ cat /      /appebsv/fs1/inst/apps/              /appl/admin/              .xml|grep -i 7204
    <oacore_server_ports oa_var="s_oacore_server_ports">oacore_server1:7201,oacore_server11:7204</oacore_server_ports>
    <oacore_nodes oa_var="s_oacore_nodes">              .com:7201,        .com:7204</oacore_nodes>
```

Port 7204 is used by the Run file system and at the same time, Patch file system also refers to the same Port Number for one of the managed servers.

Solution

1. Mention new port number for the managed server in Patch edition

2. Newly mentioned port number should be the same in the following patch edition configuration files

3. config.xml ($EBS_DOMAIN_HOME/config/)

4. apps.conf/mod_wl_ohs.conf in ($IAS_ORACLE_HOME/instances/EBS_web_DOYEN_OHS1/config/OHS/EBS_web_DOYEN/)

5. Disable EBS_LOGON trigger

6. Connect to RUN edition

7. Connect as system

8. Disable the EBS_LOGON trigger

```
[    _[run]$ sqlplus system/$SYSTEM_PWD

SQL*Plus: Release 10.1.0.5.0 - Production on Fri Mar 2 05:10:18 2018

Copyright (c) 1982, 2005, Oracle.  All rights reserved.


Connected to:
Oracle Database 12c Enterprise Edition Release 12.1.0.2.0 - 64bit Production
With the Partitioning, Real Application Clusters, Automatic Storage Management, OLAP,
Advanced Analytics and Real Application Testing options

SQL>
SQL>
SQL>
SQL>
SQL> select name from v$database;

NAME
---------


SQL>
SQL>
SQL> alter trigger ebs_logon disable;

Trigger altered.
```

Run Autoconfig from Patch edition

```
[      ]@                       :
[      ]_[run]$ . EBSapps.env patch

  E-Business Suite Environment Information
  ------------------------------------------
  RUN File System          :  /          /fs2/EBSapps/appl
  PATCH File System        :  /          /fs1/EBSapps/appl
  Non-Editioned File System : /          /fs_ne


  DB Host: prd1db01.ohdc.com  Service/SID:


  Sourcing the PATCH File System ...

appebsv@                   :/
[      ]_[patch]$ cd $ADMIN_SCRIPTS_HOME
```

```
[      ]patch]$ ./adautocfg.sh
Enter the APPS user password:
The log file for this session is located at: /          /inst/apps/         /admin/log/03010511/adconfig.log
AutoConfig is configuring the Applications environment...

AutoConfig will consider the custom templates if present.
    Using CONFIG_HOME location          /appebsv/fsl/inst/apps/5
    Classpath                  :         /appebsv/fsl/FMW_Home/Oracle_EBS-appl/shared-libs/ebs-appsborg/WEB-INF/lib/ebsAppsborgManifest.jar;/u01/app/appebsv/fsl/EB
Sapps/comn/java/classes

    Using Context file          :         /appebsv/fsl/inst/apps/5           /appl/admin/
Context Value Management will now update the Context file

    Updating Context file...COMPLETED

    Attempting upload of Context file and templates to database...COMPLETED
Configuring templates from all of the product tops...
    Configuring AD_TOP.......COMPLETED
```

```
AutoConfig completed successfully.
[      ]@                  /          /fs1/inst/apps/              /admin/scripts
[      ]_[patch]$ exit
```

Enable EBS_LOGON trigger.

```
[      ]_[run]$ sqlplus system/$SYSTEM_PWD

SQL*Plus: Release 10.1.0.5.0 - Production on Fri Mar 2 05:17:37 2018

Copyright (c) 1982, 2005, Oracle.  All rights reserved.


Connected to:
Oracle Database 12c Enterprise Edition Release 12.1.0.2.0 - 64bit Production
With the Partitioning, Real Application Clusters, Automatic Storage Management, OLAP,
Advanced Analytics and Real Application Testing options

SQL> alter trigger ebs_logon enable;

Trigger altered.
```

Start FS_CLONE again and verify.

TOPIC

5

ADOP CUTOVER PROBLEMS – EBS 12.2

Adop (Ad online patching utility) is used in R12.2 to apply the patches online without any downtime. It is the new utility to apply patches in online patching mode. It is in Perl script and called adpatch internally to apply the patch. It is not recommended to apply the patches directly using adpatch in R12.2

For online patching to work, Oracle Apps make use of 11g database feature called "Edition-Based Redefinition". Under this feature, on the Applications side, there will be two file systems, one called the patch and the other called the run file system. Both are identical and services will be running out of run file system. During the patching process, patches are applied to the patch file system, which does not require any downtime. For the patch changes to come into effect, the patch file system is switched as a run file system and vice versa, and services are restarted. In essence, downtime will be only for the time during which services are restarted.

Here we are going to talk about the Cutover phase challenge. This phase configures the patch file system as a new run file system and patch edition of the database as a new run edition. Restart application services from the new run file system of Apps. This is where downtime is required.

We know that we can abort and cleanup the patching works till we run the cutover phase (adop phase=cutover).

This blog will be about recovering and aborting a patch cycle even during a cutover.

Problematic scenarios in ADOP Cutover

The methods described here can be implemented in problematic scenarios such as a failed cutover and as a last resort.

If a cutover error occurs, you should first check the error message and try to determine if the problem can be fixed easily, or (as is true in many cases) cutover can be made to succeed simply by running the command again. Restoring to a point before cutover via Flashback recovery should only be done when the error cannot easily be fixed and continues to fail on subsequent cutover attempts.

So, to roll back the system to a point before the patching cycle was started, we can use Oracle Database's Flashback feature. We can go back to our restore point that we created just before we ran the cutover phase. Note that while creating a restore point, it is recommended to stop application services.

We must create this restore point when

1. We are ready to perform cutover.

2. All concurrent managers have been shut down cleanly.

3. There are no current database transactions being performed by any third-party applications.

In order to be able to use flashback restore points, we must enable the flashback in the database tier.

1. We must be in archive log mode.

2. We must set our retention to a sufficient value.

   Alter system set db_flashback_retention_target=120 (in minutes)

   Activate flashback. Alter database flashback on.

Okay, once we activate the flashback, we can create a restore point; so, just before the cutover phase, we create our restore point as follows:

```
SQL>alter system switch logfile;
System altered.
```

```
SQL>create restore point BEFORE_CUTOVER guarantee flashback
database;
Restore point created.
SQL>alter system switch logfile;
System altered.
```

So we created our Restore point. Now suppose we have encountered a problem in the cutover phase, and want to restore our database just before the cutover to able to do this.

We first shutdown our database and startup in mount mode as follows;

```
SQL>shutdown immediate
Database closed.
Database dismounted.
ORACLE instance shut down.
SQL>startup mount
ORACLE instance started.
```

Then we issue the following command to restore our database to the restore point.

```
SQL>flashback database to restore point BEFORE_CUTOVER.
```

Flashback complete.

Then we open our database in read-only mode and check if everything is clear.

Alter database open-read-only;

Lastly, we shut down and startup our database with open-reset-logs option.

```
SQL>shutdown immediate
Database closed.
Database dismounted.
ORACLE instance shut down.
SQL>startup mount
ORACLE instance started.
Total System Global Area 2142679040 bytes
Fixed Size 1346140 bytes
Variable Size 520095140 bytes
Database Buffers 1593835520 bytes
Redo Buffers 27402240 bytes
```

```
Database mounted.
SQL>alter database open resetlogs;
Database altered.

Once the database is altered, we can disable the flashback and
drop the restore point as follows:

SQL>alter database flashback off;
Database altered.
SQL>drop restore point BEFORE_CUTOVER;
Restore point dropped.
SQL>alter system set db_recovery_file_dest='';
System altered.
SQL>select FLASHBACK_ON from v$database;
FLASHBACK_ON
------------
NO
```

Okay, we have seen how to revert our database before the cutover phase, but we may also need to restore our applications file system before the cutover phase as well.

We can understand if there is a need for doing by looking to the cutover logs.

```
$NE_BASE/EBSapps/log/adop/<current_session_id>/cutover_<timestamp>
/ for your current session id.
```

Case 1 - If the log messages indicate that cutover failed before the file systems were switched:

If it is the case:

We just run adstpall.sh and clean the running services. Then we restart them using adstrtal.sh. Then we continue with aborting the patch cycle and doing a cleanup.

Case 2 - If the log messages indicate that cutover failed after the file systems were switched:

If this is the case, we need to shut down the application services and switch the file systems.

Perl $AD_TOP/patch/115/bin/txkADOPCutOverPhaseCtrlScript.pl \

```
-action=ctxupdate \
```

```
-contextfile=<full path to new run context file> \
-patchcontextfile=<full path to new patch file system context
file> \
-outdir=<full path to out directory>
```

Lastly, start up all services from the old run file system (using adstrtal.sh on UNIX).

Best Practices

1. We must be in archive log mode.

2. We must create this restore point when we are ready to perform cutover.

Reference

Erman Arslan's Oracle Blog: EBS 12.2 -- Recovering Cutover.

https://ermanarslan.blogspot.com/2014/07/ebs-122-recovering-cutover-problems.html

EBS CLONING

Cloning is a method of building a copy of production database. As Oracle e-business suite has a lot of modules, cloning of production instance is needed so that developers can test the bug fixes; enhancements and testing of new features can be performed in a cloned instance. Cloning is not as easy as copying of production files to the target server and it needs some set of standard procedures to be followed.

Oracle provides such standard recommended methods to copy the production instance called Rapid clone. In this chapter, we will discuss Rapid clone and cloning issues. Also, we will cover the post-cloning activities.

TOPIC 1	**Pre-clone – Deep dive** – This discusses in depth the pre-clone steps which will be very interesting in Rapid clone procedure.
TOPIC 2	**Clone without source apps password** – This topic discusses the method of cloning when there is no source apps password. It has all the steps to set the apps password and other credentials in the target environment.
TOPIC 3	**EBS post-cloning automation** – This discusses the steps to be followed after every cloning in the target environment. The scripts are also provided wherever necessary and those can be used to automate post-cloning activities.
TOPIC 4	**EBS 12.2 cloning and ports** – This gives an insight about EBS release 12.2 ports and cloning issues with examples.
TOPIC 5	**Common errors and mistakes in Rapid clone** – This discusses top errors and mistakes in Rapid clone and it is much-needed information for every new EBS customer.

PRE-CLONE - DEEP DIVE

Every production instance will be cloned to a non-production instance for various purposes. It can be for code deployment testing, performance testing, test bug fixes, etc.

Cloning becomes very easy using Rapid clone in E-business suite. You have to run pre-clone in source and post-clone configuration in Target instance.

Did you ever have a chance to look at what pre-clone does in Source in detail? Well, if not, you will know about pre-clone activities at the end of this topic.

Preparing the Database Tier on the Source System is performed by running the adpreclone.pl script generated by AutoConfig:

```
cd $ORACLE_HOME/appsutil/scripts/$CONTEXT_NAME
perl adpreclone.pl dbTier
```

Then enter the APPS password when prompted.

Example Screen output:

```
Copyright (c) 2002 Oracle Corporation
Redwood Shores, California, USA
Oracle Applications Rapid Clone
     adpreclone Version 120.20.12010000.5
Enter the APPS User Password:
Running:
perl /u02/DOYEN/12.1.0.2/appsutil/bin/adclone.pl
java=/u02/DOYEN/12.1.0.2/jdk/jre mode=stage
stage=/u02/DOYEN/12.1.0.2/appsutil/clone component=dbTier
method=CUSTOM
dbctx=/u02/DOYEN/12.1.0.2/appsutil/DOYEN_ch19.xml showProgress
```

```
APPS Password:

Beginning database tier Stage - Thu Sep 19 21:40:04 2019

/u02/DOYEN/12.1.0.2/jdk/jre/bin/java -Xmx600M -
DCONTEXT_VALIDATED=false -
DOracle.installer.oui_loc=/u02/DOYEN/12.1.0.2/oui -classpath
/u02/DOYEN/12.1.0.2/lib/xmlparserv2.jar:/u02/DOYEN/12.1.0.2/jdbc/l
ib/ojdbc6.jar:/u02/DOYEN/12.1.0.2/appsutil/java:/u02/DOYEN/12.1.0.
2/oui/jlib/OraInstaller.jar:/u02/DOYEN/12.1.0.2/oui/jlib/ewt3.jar:
/u02/DOYEN/12.1.0.2/oui/jlib/share.jar:/u02/DOYEN/12.1.0.2/oui/jli
b/srvm.jar:/u02/DOYEN/12.1.0.2/jlib/ojmisc.jar
Oracle.apps.ad.clone.StageDBTier -e
/u02/DOYEN/12.1.0.2/appsutil/DOYEN_ch19.xml -stage
/u02/DOYEN/12.1.0.2/appsutil/clone -tmp /tmp -method CUSTOM      -
showProgress
APPS Password:
Log file located at
/u02/DOYEN/12.1.0.2/appsutil/log/DOYEN_ch19/StageDBTier_09192140.l
og
     -      67% completed
Completed Stage...
Thu Sep 19 21:40:30 2019
```

This process prepares all the necessary scripts, templates and code needed to reconfigure the Database Tier, and places them into a clone stage area.

This clone stage area is copied to the target during the *copy* phase, where the scripts are executed on the target machine as part of the *configuration* phase.

A log file is generated by the adpreclone.pl script:

```
$ORACLE_HOME/appsutil/log/$CONTEXT_NAME/StageDBTier_<Timestamp>.
log
```

The log file contains details of the pre-clone stage, including the files that were copied, database connection information, and if required, details on starting the database and listener.

The log file contains the version of the java class file that was used.

This version should be checked with the latest cloning patch to ensure the latest code is being used.

The clone stage of DB tier consists of:

- **bin** directory containing the configuration scripts for use on the target system:

  - ➤ *adclone.pl - the main cloning script*

  - ➤ *adcfgclone.pl - used to configure the Target system, this is called adclone.pl*

  - ➤ *adclonectx.pl - used to clone a Source XML file manually*

  - ➤ *adchkutl.sh - checks for the existence of required O/S utils, cc, make, ar and ld*

- **context** directory containing the context file templates:

  - ➤ *CTXORIG.xml - a copy of the source context file, and is used during the creation of the Target Context file*

  - ➤ *$CONTEXT_NAME.xml - a copy of the source context file*

  - ➤ *adxdbctx.tmp - a copy of $ORACLE_HOME/appsutil/template/adxdbctx.tmp, and is used during the creation the Target Context file*

- **data** directory containing the driver file and templates for the recreation of the control files : *(Also used by the Applications Management Pack Cloning to store compressed datafile zip files)*

  - ➤ **addbhomsrc.xml** - information relating to the datafile mount points on the source

  - ➤ **data.drv** - driver file used to instantiate the templates within adcrdb.zip (Also used by the Applications Management Pack Cloning to uncompress the datafiles)

  - ➤ **adcrdb.zip** - contains the following files related to the recreation of the Control files:-

    - o *adcrdb.sh - template of the control file shell script*

    - o *adcrdbclone.sql - template of SQL script used to recreate the control files*

- o ***dbfinfo.lst*** - *list of the datafiles on the source database*

- **dbts** directory used by Rapid Install and Applications Management Pack Cloning to store dbTechStack (RDBMS ORACLE_HOME) in zip files and their associated driver files

- **html** directory - empty, not used

- **jlib** directory containing the Rapid Clone java and jdbc libraries

- **java** directory containingRapidClone AD java code copied from $ORACLE_HOME/appsutil/java

  oui directory containing the oui libraries for creating/maintaining the central/local inventory copied from $ORACLE_HOME/oui

- **jre** directory containing the java runtime files

In addition to the clone stage area, the following files are also generated:

$ORACLE_HOME/appsutil/driver

- **preclone.drv** - *creates the registration driver regclone.drv*

- **regclone.drv** - *used during the configuration phase to create and run the registration scripts*

Preparing the Application Tier on the Source System is performed by running the adpre-clone.pl script generated by AutoConfig:

41

```
Cd $COMMON_TOP/clone
perl adpreclone.pl appsTier

Copyright (c) 2002 Oracle Corporation
Redwood Shores, California, USA
Oracle Applications Rapid Clone
Version 12.0.0
adpreclone Version 120.20.12010000.5

Running:
perl /u02/apps/apps_st/appl/ad/12.0.0/bin/adclone.pl
java=/u02/apps/tech_st/10.1.3/appsutil/jdk mode=stage
stage=/u02/apps/apps_st/comn/clone component=appsTier method=
appctx=/u02/inst/apps/DOYEN_ch19/appl/admin/DOYEN_ch19.xml
showProgress
APPS Password:
method defaulted to CUSTOM

Beginning application tier Stage - Thu Sep 19 22:21:39 2019

/u02/apps/tech_st/10.1.3/appsutil/jdk/bin/java -Xmx600M -
DCONTEXT_VALIDATED=false  -DOracle.installer.oui_loc=/oui -
classpath
/u02/apps/tech_st/10.1.3/lib/xmlparserv2.jar:/u02/apps/tech_st/10.
1.3/jdbc/lib/ojdbc14.jar:/u02/apps/apps_st/comn/java/classes:/u02/
apps/tech_st/10.1.3/oui/jlib/OraInstaller.jar:/u02/apps/tech_st/10
.1.3/oui/jlib/ewt3.jar:/u02/apps/tech_st/10.1.3/oui/jlib/share.jar
:/u02/apps/tech_st/10.1.3/oui/jlib/srvm.jar:/u02/apps/tech_st/10.1
.3/jlib/ojmisc.jar  Oracle.apps.ad.clone.StageAppsTier -e
/u02/inst/apps/DOYEN_ch19/appl/admin/DOYEN_ch19.xml -stage
/u02/apps/apps_st/comn/clone -tmp /tmp -method CUSTOM    -
showProgress

Logfile located at
/u02/inst/apps/DOYEN_ch19/admin/log/StageAppsTier_09192221.log

    \      80% completed
```

```
Completed Stage...
Thu Sep 19 22:23:36 2019
```

The clone stage area contains all the cloning code required to run RapidClone and is created as follows

Applications Tier: $COMMON_TOP/clone

This contains the following directories and scripts:

- **bin** directory containing the configuration scripts for use on the target system:

  - **adclone.pl** - the main cloning script

  - **adcfgclone.pl** - used to configure the Target system, this calls adclone.pl

  - **adclonectx.pl** - used to clone a Source XML file manually

  - **adchkutl.sh** - checks for the existence of required O/S utils, cc, make, ar and ld

  - **adaddnode.pl** - used when adding a node to an existing system. This script is used to add a new row(representing the new node) to AD_APPL_TOPS to ensure the Patch History data is applicable to all existing and new nodes

- **context** directory containing the context file templates :

  - **CTXORIG.xml** - a copy of the source context file, and is used during the creation of the Target Context file

  - **$CONTEXT_NAME.xml** - a copy of the source context file

  - **adxmlctx.tmp** a copy of $AD_TOP/admin/template/adxmlctx.tmp, and is used during the creation the Target Context file

- **appl** directory used only when merging, i.e. cloning from multi-node to single node

- **appsts** directory used by the Applications Management Pack Cloning to store at TechStack (Tools and Web ORACLE_HOMEs) in zip files and their associated driver files

- **html** directory - empty, not used

- **jlib** directory containing the Rapid Clone java and jdbc libraries

- **java** directory containingRapidClone AD java code *copied from $$JAVA_TOP*

- **oui** directory containing the oui libraries for creating/maintaining the central/local inventory copied from $IAS_ORACLE_HOME/oui

- **jre** directory containing the java runtime files

- In addition to the clone stage area, the following files are also generated:

  (**Tools 10.1.2 $ORACLE_HOME**)

$ORACLE_HOME/appsutil/clone

- **ouicli.pl** - perl script that runs OUI CLI for ORACLE_HOME native cloning

- **txkstubcfg1013.pl** - script creates the file "EBIZ_R12_README.txt" in a selected list of directories

- **adlnktools.sh** - script to relink RDBMS binaries

$ORACLE_HOME/appsutil/clone/driver

- **preclone.drv** - creates the registration driver regclone.drv

- **regclone.drv** - used during the configuration phase to create the registration scripts

$ORACLE_HOME/appsutil/clone/template

- **ftrace_cfg_1012.tmp**

- **adouitools.pl** - template for script that runs OUI CLI for **ORACLE_HOME native cloning**

- **adlnk806.sh** - template for script to relink tools home

  (**Web 10.1.3 $ORACLE_HOME**)

$IAS_ORACLE_HOME/appsutil/clone

- **ouicli.pl** - perl script that runs OUI CLI for ORACLE_HOME native cloning

- **txkstubcfg1013.pl** - script to create the file "EBIZ_R12_README.txt" in a selected list of directories

- **adlnkweb.sh** - script to relink Web home binaries

$IAS_ORACLE_HOME/appsutil/driver

- **pre-clone.drv** - creates the registration driver regclone.drv

- **regclone.drv** - used during the configuration phase to create the registration scripts

$IAS_ORACLE_HOME/appsutil/template

- **adouiweboh.pl** - template for script that runs OUI CLI for ORACLE_HOME native cloning

- **txkstubcfg1013.pl** - script creates the file "EBIZ_R12_README.txt" in a selected list of directories

- **apachectl_sh_1013_oh.tmp**

- **adlnkweboh.sh** - template for Script to relink Web home binaries

You may think about why we need to know all about the internal process of pre-clone activities. Well, the more you know about the internal process, the quicker you will be able to debug the errors in the process of cloning.

Every DBA must know about each and every step of automated things in detail even though automation saves time.

Reference

MOS - **Troubleshooting RapidClone issues with Oracle Applications R12.0 & R12.1 (Doc ID 603104.1)**

TOPIC

2

CLONE WITHOUT SOURCE APPS PASSWORD

My friend worked for one of the clients and they were running EBS 12.1.3 in single node. Since the client was very keen on protecting all production passwords from everyone, all passwords were known only to the client DBAs and not shared by anyone.

My friend, who was working as a third party to the customer, was responsible for non-productions administration including cloning from source backup. Production was completely managed by Client DBA team and they never shared the password to any third-party DBA team. The teams were allowed only to work in non-production areas and had access to production backups. To perform cloning from prod to non-production, as you know, we need apps password.

Now you may wonder how to perform clone from prod to non-production as client DBA team will never share the password to this third party DBA team. Can you think of any way to perform clone without production apps password? Pause here and think well for a few minutes… Still wondering?? If you still do not find a way, then this section is for you.

These steps describe the steps required to remove the Production EBS database credentials, such as database user (schema) password hashes and encrypted passwords.

After all these procedures, the clone copy of the database will have a password set as 'clone'. Once all passwords have been reset as 'clone', you can follow the regular way of changing password.

STEP - 1

```
$ export ORACLE_SID=<sid>
$ export ORACLE_HOME=<db-Oraclehome>
$ export PATH=$ORACLE_HOME/bin
$ unset TWO_TASK
Oracle$ sqlplus '/ as sysdba'
```

To clear all the credentials in the cloned copy of a production database, create and execute the following 3 steps.

REM Start the database clone for the first time

```
SQL> startup restrict
```

REM Clear all production credentials from the cloned database

```
SQL> update SYS.user$ set
 password =
translate(password,'0123456789ABCDEF','0000000000000000')
 where type#=1 and length(password) = 16
/
SQL> update APPLSYS.FND_ORACLE_USERID set
 ENCRYPTED_ORACLE_PASSWORD='INVALID'
/

SQL> update APPLSYS.FND_USER set
 ENCRYPTED_FOUNDATION_PASSWORD='INVALID',
 ENCRYPTED_USER_PASSWORD='INVALID'
/
SQL> commit;
SQL> shutdown
SQL> exit
```

STEP - 2

Re-establish Bootstrap Credentials for basic accounts (SYS, SYSTEM, APPLSYSPUB, APPLSYS, APPS, GUEST, and SYSADMIN

The database at the moment has no credentials. Now log on as "SYS" with operation system authentication. This will allow you to establish new credentials.

```
Oracle$ sqlplus '/ as sysdba'
```

Here is the script for step 2, including inline comments which explain what is done.

```
REM --- step2.sql
spool step2.lst

REM set a new password for a few initial database users

alter user SYS identified by CLONE;
alter user SYSTEM identified by CLONE;
alter user APPLSYSPUB identified by CLONE;
alter user APPLSYS identified by CLONE;
alter user APPS identified by CLONE;

REM Provide boot-strap info for FNDCPASS...
update APPLSYS.FND_ORACLE_USERID set
 ENCRYPTED_ORACLE_PASSWORD='CLONE'
 where ORACLE_USERNAME = 'APPLSYSPUB'
/
update APPLSYS.FND_ORACLE_USERID set
 ENCRYPTED_ORACLE_PASSWORD='ZG' ||
 'B27F16B88242CE980EF07605EF528F9391899B09552FD89FD' ||
 'FF43E4DDFCE3972322A41FBB4DDC26DDA46A446582307D412'
 where ORACLE_USERNAME = 'APPLSYS'
/

update APPLSYS.FND_ORACLE_USERID set
 ENCRYPTED_ORACLE_PASSWORD='ZG' ||
 '6CC0BB082FF7E0078859960E852F8D123C487C024C825C0F9' ||
 'B1D0863422026EA41A6B2B5702E2299B4AC19E6C1C23333F0'
 where ORACLE_USERNAME = 'APPS'
/
commit;

REM We run as SYS, now connect as APPS to run some plsql
```

```
connect APPS/CLONE

REM Every EBS database needs a GUEST user
select APPS.fnd_web_sec.change_guest_password( 'CLONE', 'CLONE' )
"RES"
 from dual;
commit;

REM Set GUEST credential in site level profile option
set serveroutput on
declare
 dummy boolean;
begin
 dummy := APPS.FND_PROFILE.SAVE('GUEST_USER_PWD', 'GUEST/CLONE',
'SITE');
 if not dummy then
 dbms_output.put_line( 'Error setting GUEST_USER_PWD profile' );
 end if;
end;
/
commit;

REM One more time for luck (avoid session caching of profiles)
connect APPS/CLONE

REM Set SYSADMIN password
select APPS.fnd_web_sec.change_password('SYSADMIN','CLONE') "RES"
 from dual;
commit;
exit.
```

It is important to verify that no errors are reported and that the two returned "RES" values are both "Y", which indicates success.

STEP -3

Step 3 - Prepare Scripts for Setting Additional Passwords

In this step, scripts are prepared to assign passwords to the other database users which were disabled in Step 1. Dynamically generated scripts are used to accomplish this because the sets of database users may differ between instances of EBS. Create the script below and run it as the Operating System user "Oracle":

```
$ sqlplus '/ as sysdba'
```

The comments in the script below explain what is done in step 3.

```
REM --- step3.sql

REM Prepare SQL and SHELL scripts to set more passwords later
spool step3.lst

REM Generate an SQL script to set a password for DB users not
managed with EBS

select 'alter user "'|| USERNAME ||'" identified by CLONE; '
 from SYS.DBA_USERS
 where USERNAME not in (select ORACLE_USERNAME from
APPLSYS.FND_ORACLE_USERID)
 and USERNAME not in ('SYS','SYSTEM');

REM Generate a shell script to set a password for all base product
schemas

select 'FNDCPASS apps/clone 0 Y system/clone ALLORACLE clone' from
dual;

REM Generate a shell script to set a password for non-EBS DB users
managed with EBS

select 'FNDCPASS apps/clone 0 Y system/clone ORACLE "' ||
 replace(ORACLE_USERNAME,'$','\$') || '" clone'
 from APPLSYS.FND_ORACLE_USERID
 where READ_ONLY_FLAG = 'X'
 and ORACLE_USERNAME in (select USERNAME from SYS.DBA_USERS);
```

```
REM Generate a shell script to set a password for
APPS/APPLSYS/APPM_mrc DB users

select 'FNDCPASS apps/clone 0 Y system/clone SYSTEM APPLSYS clone'
from dual;

REM Generate scripts for steps 4 & 5
spool off

HOST grep '^alter user ' step3.lst > dbusers4.sql
HOST grep '^FNDCPASS ' step3.lst > dbusers5.sh

exit

REM End of Script
```

NOTE: The script above calls the UNIX command "grep" to extract 2 sets of lines from the step3.lst spool file. If you are running Windows, the shell redirection will fail when attempted from within SQLplus. You can perform the failed step by going to a command prompt (using the HOST command from SQLplus).

Step 4 - Assign New Passwords to All Schemas Not Managed with EBS

```
$ SQLplus "/ as sysdba"
```

Now run the "dbusers4.sql" file:

```
SQL> spool step4.lst
SQL> start dbusers4.sql
SQL> Shutdown

SQL> Startup
```

Reference:

Removing Credentials from a Cloned EBS Production Database (Doc ID 419475.1)

EBS POST CLONING AUTOMATION

EBS Cloning – Automating Post cloning steps automation

EBS cloning automation is environment-specific because everybody uses different methods for Database restoration methods like Active duplicate, Rman restore, cold backup and use DR solution. For Apps tier, some of them use existing context file, or some of them refresh Database part alone not Apps tier.

But common post-cloning steps can be automated that can be used irrespective of the environment. In this chapter, we have decided to consolidate the common steps for Post-cloning

Before that, let us see the high-level steps involved in EBS cloning.

Source system preparation:

- ➤ Run adpre-clone.pl in Database tier
- ➤ Run adpre-clone.pl in Apps tier

Copy Database to the target system:

1. With backup
    - ➤ Hot
    - ➤ Cold
2. Without backup
    - ➤ Rman active duplicate

Configure Database tier

- Run adcfgclone.pl dbTechStack

- Create temporary tablespace if not exists

- Clear FND_NODES and *ADOP_VALID_NODES*

- Start the listener from $ORACLE_HOME/network/admin/ $CONTEXT_NAME/listener.ora

- Run autoconfig first time ($ORACLE_HOME/appsutil/bin/adconfig.pl)

Copy Application files to the target system

- BASE_LOCATION/apps folder to the Target system (INST_TOP not required to copy)

- RUN_BASE_LOCATION/fs1/EBSapps to the target system (Not required to any folder other than EBSapps under run file system)

Configure Apps tier

- Run adcfglcone.pl appsTier

Post Cloning steps

- Disable alerts

- Put Concurrent requests on hold

- Profile options setup

- Change Apps Password and Need to fix the password in Weblogic admin console

- Other Schema passwords

- Workflow configuration

- Recreate dba_directories

Let's look at each Post cloning step in detail and we assume that the Database tier and Application tier configuration part was completed before executing these scripts below.

Please test this in a lower environment or a lap before running this in an actual environment and discuss the impact of running the script below with EBS technical and functional team before running this.

Disable alerts: It's advised to disable alerts in Non-Production environment; this will avoid unnecessary conflict.

```
update alr_alerts set enabled_flag = 'N',
last_update_date = 'SYSADMIN',
last_updated_by = (select user_id fro fnd_users where username =
'SYSADMIN'),
where enabled_flag = 'Y';
commit;
```

Put Concurrent requests on hold: This will avoid running scheduled concurrent request to run in Non-PROD environment; so it's safe to put the requests on 'hold' and let the technical team decide which one to be run in a Lower environment.

```
UPDATE fnd_concurrent_requests SET hold_flag = 'Y' WHERE
phase_code = 'P' AND status_code in ('Q','I');
commit;
```

Profile options setup: This is important as some of the profile option values may refer to a PRODUCTION entity, and this will avoid any major confusion. I have mentioned only the Site Name profile option; you can modify the script as per your environment.

```
set serveroutput on;
DECLARE
stat boolean;
BEGIN
dbms_output.disable;
dbms_output.enable(100000);
stat := FND_PROFILE.SAVE('SITENAME', 'TEST - cloned from
PRODUCTION on 12-SEP-19 01:00:00', 'SITE');   --Enter the forms
description here
IF stat THEN
dbms_output.put_line( 'Stat = TRUE - Site Name profile updated' );
ELSE
```

```
dbms_output.put_line( 'Stat = FALSE - Site Name profile NOT
updated' );
END IF;
commit;
END;
/
```

Change Apps Password and Need to fix the password in Weblogic admin console: These are necessary steps as PRODUCTION Apps Schema credentials should be known only to Admins.

```
FNDCPASS apps/$1 0 Y system/$2 SYSTEM APPLSYS $APPS_PWD
Start Admin server:
$ADMIN_SCRIPTS_HOME/adadminsrvctl.sh start
perl $FND_TOP/patch/115/bin/txkManageDBConnectionPool.pl
When prompted, select 'updateDSPassword' to update the new APPS
password in the WLS Datasource.
```

Other Schema Password: Like Apps schema credentials, this is yet another important step to change module schema password. We have an option to change one password for all schemas or, we can explicitly change the password for each schema.

```
FNDCPASS apps/$1 0 Y system/$2 ALLORACLE $ALLSCHEMAPWD
FNDCPASS apps/$1 0 Y system/$2 ORACLE <Schema Name> <Schema Pwd>
```

Workflow configuration: By default after the refresh, PRODUCTION workflow configuration will be there in Non-PROD environment. It's important to update the workflow configuration and set mail status to SENT for all the notifications to avoid conflict.

```
bash-3.2$ cat workflow_setup.sql
PROMPT UPDATE SCRIPT TO SETUP WORKFLOW
PROMPT SMTP SERVER NAME --> <Smtp_server_name>
PROMPT IMAP SERVER NAME --> <imap_server_name>
PROMPT IMAP EMAIL ADDRESS --> <imap_email_Address>
PROMPT SMTP SERVER NAME - UPDATE
UPDATE fnd_svc_comp_param_vals
```

```
SET    parameter_value = nvl('&smtp_server_name', parameter_value)
WHERE  component_parameter_id = to_number(nvl('10079', '0'))
/
PROMPT OUTPUT THREAD COUNT - UPDATE
UPDATE fnd_svc_comp_param_vals
SET    parameter_value = nvl('&Outbound_Thread_Count',
parameter_value)
WHERE  component_parameter_id = to_number(nvl('10086', '0'))
/
PROMPT IMAP USER NAME - UPDATE
UPDATE fnd_svc_comp_param_vals
SET    parameter_value = nvl('&imap_mail_address',
parameter_value)
WHERE  component_parameter_id = to_number(nvl('10054', '0'))
/
PROMPT Reply-to-Address - UPDATE
UPDATE fnd_svc_comp_param_vals
SET    parameter_value = nvl('&reply_to_address', parameter_value)
WHERE  component_parameter_id = to_number(nvl('10089', '0'))
/
PROMPT
UPDATE fnd_svc_comp_param_vals
SET    parameter_value = nvl('&Inbound_Thread_Count',
parameter_value)
WHERE  component_parameter_id = to_number(nvl('10082', '0'))
/
PROMPT Inbound Server Name - UPDATE
UPDATE fnd_svc_comp_param_vals
SET    parameter_value = nvl('&Inbound_Server_Name',
parameter_value)
WHERE  component_parameter_id = to_number(nvl('10069', '0'))
/
Commt;
**Script to update Imap email password**
cat wfmlrpwupd_in.sql
REM This script encrypts and updates the Inbound password for
Workflow Mailer.
REM Usage: sqlplus apps/**** @wfmlrpwupd_in <clear_password>
<component_id>
```

```
REM Example: sqlplus apps/**** @wfmlrpwupd_in welcome1 10006
REM       where 10006 is the mailer's component id
set feedback off
set verify off
set serveroutput on
declare
  l_string1 varchar2(2000) := '&Email_Password';
  l_string2 varchar2(2000);
  l_comp_id number := 10006;
  errmsg    varchar(1000);
  retcode   number;
  l_component_name varchar2(240);
begin
  ECX_OBFUSCATE.ecx_data_encrypt(l_input_string => l_string1,
                                 l_output_string =>l_string2,
                                 errmsg => errmsg,
                                 retcode => retcode);

  if (retcode > 0) then
    dbms_output.put_line('Return Code: '||retcode);
    dbms_output.put_line('Error Message: '||errmsg);
  else
    begin
      SELECT component_name
      INTO   l_component_name
      FROM   fnd_svc_components
      WHERE  component_id = 10006
      AND    component_type = 'WF_MAILER';
      FND_SVC_COMP_PARAM_VALS_PKG.load_row(X_COMPONENT_NAME =>
l_component_name,
                                           X_PARAMETER_NAME =>
'INBOUND_PASSWORD',

                                           X_PARAMETER_VALUE =>
l_string2,
                                           X_CUSTOMIZATION_LEVEL
=> 'L',
                                           X_OBJECT_VERSION_NUMBER
=> -1,
                                           X_OWNER => 'ORACLE');
```

```
      dbms_output.put_line('Updated');
    exception
      when no_data_found then
        dbms_output.put_line('Component Not Found for ID
'||l_comp_id);
        dbms_output.put_line('Nothing updated');
    end;
  end if;
end;
/
```

Recreate DBA_DIRECTORIES: By default after the refresh, PRODUCTION dba_dicrectoreis information will be there in Non-PROD environment. It's important to update the dba_directories entries.

```
set lines 170
set pages 1000
select 'CREATE OR REPLACE DIRECTORY '||DIRECTORY_NAME||' AS
'||''''||REPLACE(DIRECTORY_PATH,'<SOURCE STRUCTURE>','<Target
Structure>')||''''||';' FROM dba_directories where DIRECTORY_PATH
like '%key word%';

** This will create SQL command to update DBA_Directories.
```

We haven't collated all post-cloning scripts as we believe still some more steps required to collate all these scripts as per the environment needs; also, we strongly believe still there are many more steps involved like DB link recreation, SSL-related post-cloning steps, SSO-related steps, etc. But the main agenda of this topic is to cover common basic post-cloning steps.

Hope you have learned some common and basic information about EBS post-cloning steps.

Happy Cloning!!!

Reference:

https://ebs-dba.com/wp/blog/2017/09/08/automating-ebs-clones/

TOPIC

4

EBS R12.2 – PORTS AND CLONING ISSUES

Inside EBS R12.2 Cloning

Cloning in R12.2 is more complex than in previous releases of the E-Business Suite. The introduction of Weblogic Server is the major reason for this.

An installation of EBS R12.2 now uses two port pools, a run pool and a port pool that for the most part must contain distinct ports. This becomes an issue when more than one server is configured on the same apps tier. Since an instance of oacore_server should be limited to about 200 processes, most companies will need multiple oacore_servers. For many companies, there will be sufficient capacity on the apps node to allow these servers to be added on the existing node without having to add an apps tier on another node. However, this is not possible if the port for the additional managed server is in the port pool for the patch environment. The current recommendation is to make the patch port pool at least 10% higher than the run port pool. For more information on adding managed servers see MOS Note 1905593.1.

The port issue becomes even more complex with cloning using Rapid Clone (MOS Note 1383621.1). Because adpreclone.pl packages an installation of the fusion middleware from the source, the production port pools will be required while the target apps tier is configured. This means that you need 4 port pools that are distinct across all the managed server ports.

If you use the same port pool and are using a pairs file (perl adcfgclone.pl component=appsTier pairsfile=<PAIRSFILE> addnode=yes dualfs=yes), you will receive an error message that just says pairs file validation failed.

If you are using a different port pool, but one which does not allow sufficient room for the WLS Managed Servers in between any of the four port pools, you will find the clone fails during either the RUN or PATCH configuration stages.

Best practices

My recommendation to avoid this issue is to set the production patch port pool far enough from the run port pool to allow for both production and clone target ports to be in the middle. Set the target patch port pool to be having the same gap. For example, in production use port pools of 0 and 20, in the target use 10 and 30. I also strongly suggest that the first time you configure a target, you run rapid clone by hand to generate the pairs file for use in future runs (as opposed to editing a pairs file from another clone).

Very and most common errors that we faced during EBS R12 cloning

Scenario 1:

Oracle APPS R12 Post Cloning issue - Form not launching

Most of the DBAs face this issue after the clone. After the successful cloning of R12, when opening the form, it was not being launched.

DBAs will waste their time in bouncing the application and running auto config again in both the tiers. But there is a simple way to fix the issue.

We need to clear the WebLogic cache once the clone is done.

We need to follow the steps below.

- Stop all APPS Tier services.

- Rename the directory "tldcache" under following directories.

  $/INST_NAME/inst/apps/INST_NAME_MACHINE_NAME/ora/
  10.1.3/j2ee/oafm

  $/INST_NAME/inst/apps/INST_NAME_MACHINE_NAME/ora/10.1.3/j2ee/o
  acore

  $/INST_NAME/inst/apps/INST_NAME_MACHINE_NAME/ora/10.1.3/j2ee/f
  orms

- Create the empty directory with the name "tldcache" under the above directories.

- Restart the APPS Tier services.

- Start the apps tier services and test the issue.

Scenario 2:

R12: Rapid Clone Issue: ouicli.pl INSTE8_APPLY 255.

During EBS rapid clone, I was facing error as mentioned below (i.e. RC-00110: Fatal: Error occurred while relinking of ApplyDBTechStack).

While I ran perl adcfgclone.pl dbTechStack at dbTier, after some time it failed as below.

-    0% completed

\   0% completed   RC-00110: Fatal: Error occurred while relinking of ApplyDBTechStack

ERROR while running Apply...

Thu Sep 12: 09:22 2017

ERROR: Failed to execute /doyen/test_8026/Oracle/appsutil/clone/bin/adclone.pl

ease check logfile.

After that, I checked ApplyDBTechStack_08311408.log for the root cause. Then I realized that this failure happened because PATH was not set as expected.

ApplyDBTechStack_5679537.log:-

[AutoConfig Error Report]

The following report lists the errors AutoConfig encountered during each phase of its execution. Errors are grouped by directory and phase.

The report format is:

```
<filename>  <phase>  <return code where appropriate>
[APPLY PHASE]
```

AutoConfig could not successfully execute the following scripts:

```
Directory: /doyen/test_8026/orahome/perl/bin/perl -I
/data03/UAT_8026/orahome/perl/lib/5.8.3 -I
/doyen/test_8026/orahome/perl/lib/site_perl/5.8.3 -I
/doyen/test_8026/orahome/appsutil/perl
/data03/UAT_8026/orahome/appsutil/clone
ouicli.pl  INSTE8_APPLY     255
AutoConfig is exiting with status 1
RC-50013: Fatal: Instantiate driver did not complete successfully.
/doyen/test_8026/orahome/appsutil/driver/regclone.drv
```

Solution

After setting the PATH as below, rerun the Perl and issue gets resolved. Export PATH=$ORACLE_HOME/perl/bin:$PATH

Scenario 3:

Synchronize the AD tables FND_NODES, ADOP_VALID_NODES, and

FND_OAM_CONTEXT_FILES in 12.2 when adop fails

Issue applies to R12.2.to 12.2.9

$ adop phase=prepare

Enter the APPS password:

Enter the SYSTEM password:

Enter the WLSADMIN password:

Validating credentials...

Initializing...

Run Edition context : /appl/admin/PROD_prodapp1.xml

Patch edition context: /appl/admin/PROD_prodapp1.xml

*******FATAL ERROR*******

PROGRAM: (/appl/ad/12.0.0/bin/adzdoptl.pl)

TIME: Mon Sep 5 05:09:11 2019

FUNCTION: ADOP::GlobalVars::_GetMandatoryArgs [Level 1]

ERRORMSG: adop is not able to detect any valid application tier nodes in ADOP_VALID_NODES table.

Ensure autoconfig is run on all nodes.

[STATEMENT] Please run adopscanlog utility, using the command

"adopscanlog -latest=yes" to get the list of the log files along with snippet of the error message corresponding to each log file.

adop exiting with status = 255 (Fail)

Cause:

adop phase=prepare

In this case, the fnd_nodes table has NULL for domain entry of this valid server.

Example Data Supporting the Conclusion

```
--------------

[table.applsys.fnd_nodes]
NODE      PLAT    D C A F W    NODE_NAME     SERVER_ADDRESS
DOMAIN WEBHOST                              VIRTUAL_IP     S
-------  -----    ----------   -------------  -------------------
---------  ----------  --------------------               -----
----------  --
12,127    227    N Y Y Y Y    DOYEN    ###.###.###.201      NULL
test.doyensys.com  NULL            Y
```

Solution:

Due to the method required for "cleaning out" / "re-synchronizing" the following tables, it is EXPECTED / REQUIRED that the Applications have been shut down.

The only thing running should be the Database Tier.

A full backup should be taken before any testing begins.

1. Backup the fnd_oam_context_files, fnd_nodes, and adop_valid_nodes tables, and if on AD/TXK 8 or higher; ad_nodes_config_status in the EBS env nodes:

```
sqlplus applsys/<pwd>
SQLPlus#> create table fnd_oam_context_files_bkp as select *
```

```
from fnd_oam_context_files;
SQLPlus#> create table fnd_nodes_bk as select * from fnd_nodes;
SQLPlus#> create table adop_valid_nodes_bk as select * from
adop_valid_nodes;
```

If on AD/TXK 8 or higher:

```
SQLPlus#> create table ad_nodes_config_status_bk as select * from
ad_nodes_config_status;
```

2. Truncate the following tables (Continue from step 1):

```
SQLPlus#> truncate table fnd_oam_context_files;
SQLPlus#> truncate table fnd_nodes;
SQLPlus#> truncate table adop_valid_nodes;
```

If on AD/TXK 8 or higher:

```
SQLPlus#> truncate table ad_nodes_config_status;
```

3. Run AutoConfig on the DB tier:

```
Source the <RDBMS_ORACLE_HOME> home.
Linux#> cd <RDBMS_ORACLE_HOME>/appsutil/scripts/<SID>_<HOSTNAME>/
Linux#> ./adautocfg.sh
```

4. Run Autoconfig on the run file system.

```
Linux#> source <EBS_BASE>/EBSapps.env run
Linux#> cd $ADMIN_SCRIPTS_HOME
Linux#> ./adautocfg.sh
```

5. Run Autoconfig on the patch file system

Before running Autoconfig on the patch file system the ebs_login trigger MUST be disabled.

After the successful completion of Autoconfig the ebs_login trigger MUST be re-enabled.

a. Disable the ebs_login trigger using the following SQL.

SQLPlus#> alter trigger ebs_logon disable;

b. At this time Run autoconfig with the patch env sourced

```
Linux#> source <EBS_BASE>/EBSapps.env patch
Linux#> cd $ADMIN_SCRIPTS_HOME
Linux#> ./adautocfg.sh
```

Confirm Autoconfig completes successfully

If there is more than one EBS node, repeat step 5.b on all EBS nodes.

c. Enable the ebs_login trigger using the following SQL.

```
Linux#> sqlplus system/<pwd>
SQLPlus#> alter trigger ebs_logon enable;
```

6. After Autoconfig has been run successfully on all nodes, run the following two (2) queries in order to verify the tables have been correctly populated:

Select node_id, platform_code, support_db D, support_cp C, support_admin A, support_forms F, support_web W, node_name, server_id, server_address, domain, webhost, virtual_ip, status from fnd_nodes order by node_id;

```
Select NAME,VERSION,PATH, STATUS from FND_OAM_CONTEXT_FILES;
```

Reference

R12.2 Cloning and Ports – Tips and Tricks from an Apps DBA.
https://ebs-dba.com/wp/blog/2017/09/04/r12-2-cloning-and-ports/

TOPIC

5

COMMON ERRORS AND MISTAKES IN RAPID CLONE

Rapid clone helps us to perform production clone quickly but most of the time many customers perform clone with mistakes without knowing Oracle recommendations. This topic discusses common technical myths or misunderstandings about the E-business suite cloning.

MISTAKE#1

Rapid clone is an optional method of cloning.

Recommendation: Rapid clone simplifies the process of your cloning E-business suite. Simply copying the files to the target environment and editing the context files manually and then running autoconfig is never supported and not recommended. Devising your own cloning method is a very dangerous strategy.

Always use rapid clone and if it does not work for you, fix it and then move on. For any customisations, always use context editor rather than performing manual changes in the context file.

MISTAKE#2

Pre-clone scripts in database and application need to be run only once in a source environment.

Recommendation: Pre-clone scripts need to be run every time you take a backup of the source environment. It is also a good practice to remove or rename the database tier $ORACLE_HOME/appsutil/clone and application tier $COMMON_TOP/clone before running the pre-clone script.

MISTAKE#3

Perform autoconfig customisations in target environment after cloning.

Recommendation: Autoconfig customisations will be migrated to the target environment while performing rapidclone. Any customization performed in the source template file will be managed in the target environment by autoconfig engine. Do not edit E-Business Suite configuration files manually. Any change will be lost when AutoConfig is next run. Always use context editor to edit the templates in the source, and those will reflect automatically in the target environment.

MISTAKE#4

Scheduling Standard purge programs not required in the target environment.

Recommendation: Most of the cloning will have source as a production environment. The production environment will have many things enabled like database audit, audit trail, workflow scheduling and standard purge programs.

Cloned environments will have these source data and those are not required in the target database. These can be safely purged using standard purge programs so that the target environment performance will improve tremendously.

MISTAKE#5

Utl dir and dba_directories will be recreated in the target environment.

Recommendation: Rapid clone performs cloning of database and application and changes the specific profile option values based on the target context values. It does not change the relative path of DBA_DIRECTORIES or utl directories.

We have to perform the change manually according to our target environment. Even we need to take care of changing the custom profile option values according to the target environment.

MISTAKE#6

Starting Workflow Notification mailer has no impact in a cloned environment.

Recommendation: While performing cloning, as part of post-cloning we will need to purge workflow tables (using purge programs) and also we need to close set the mail_status as 'SENT'. Most importantly, we need to identify and mask the email_address column in important EBS tables so that emails will not trigger to a customer after starting the notification mailer. Also, we should set 'override email address', as well as outbound and inbound email configuration correctly according to the cloned environment.

# Chapter 3

EBS AND DATABASE AUDIT

Auditing is very important for every customer wishing to meet compliances and security standards such as Sarbanes-Oxley (SOX), Payment Card Industry (PCI), FISMA, HIPAA, etc. Every application will be audited as part of the auditing either internally or by external audit firms.

What Can One Expect in this Chapter? Oracle applications have many features in audit used for reporting purpose. There are many ways to perform an audit and each depends on what needs to be audited at what level. Readers can learn here about Audit trial data as well as tracking web and html pages including database audit with examples.

What would be my takeaway? In this chapter, the reader will learn about the various ways to perform audit activities including generation of audit reports.

TOPIC 1	**Audit Trail Data** has detailed steps to perform auditing for selected tables and use them for reporting purposes like who modifiedit, when it was modified and what data was modified in the database.
TOPIC 2	**Audit Specific user** has steps to audit user actions to report on who modified the data using forms and when.
TOPIC 3	**Database Audit** has detailed steps to enable the database auditing and what level of data has to be audited.
TOPIC 4	**Tracking web and html pages** has steps in detail to capture the changes in Oracle Application Framework pages and to what extent those can be captured. It also discusses how to generate the reports and steps to view those reports.
TOPIC 5	**Things to be audited** will educate about what had to be audited in E-business suite and top 7 areas on EBS audit.

AUDIT TRAIL DATA

AuditTrail lets you keep a history of changes to your important data: what was changed, who changed it, and when. With AuditTrail, we can easily determine who changed its current value and when.

We can track information on most types of fields, including character, number and date fields.

An Audit Trail retains the history of changes to data. It includes the following information:

- What was changed

- Who changed it

- When the data changed

This captures information on underlying base tables when we modify the values in forms. This tracks which rows in the table get modified, by which user and at what time the user logged in to the forms.

Shadow Tables

Audit Trail stores the history of changes in "Shadow Table" of the audited table. It works on database triggers. We need to explicitly specify which table needs to be audited and on what columns.

All Audit Trail shadow tables contain:

o AUDIT_USER_NAME – the name of the Oracle ID that made the insertion o AUDIT_TIMESTAMP - the date/time when the insertion occurred

o AUDIT_TRANSACTION_TYPE

I - Insert

U – Update

D – Delete

L – Last

C – Current

How to enable an audit trail for a particular table?

Step 1 – List the tables and their columns which require auditing.

Define the tables.

Responsibility: System Administrator

Navigation: Security > Audittrail > Tables

Create a record as below:

```
User Table Name = HZ_CUSTOMER_PROFILES
Table Name = HZ_CUSTOMER_PROFILES
Application = Receivables

Columns:

CUST_ACCOUNT_PROFILE_ID
COLLECTOR_ID
```

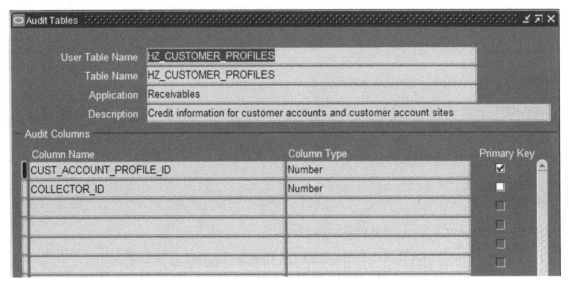

You must select the primary key and save it.

The primary key columns will always be saved. Add the columns that need to be audited.

Never add the following columns as user information is automatically added –

Creation Date

Created By

Last Update Login

Last Update Date

Last Updated By

Step 2- Define Audit groups.

Responsibility: System Administrator

Navigation: Security > Audittrail > Groups

Create a new group as below:

```
Application Name = Receivables
Audit Group = AR Collector Group
Group State = Enabled Requested

User Table Name:
HZ_CUSTOMER_PROFILES
```

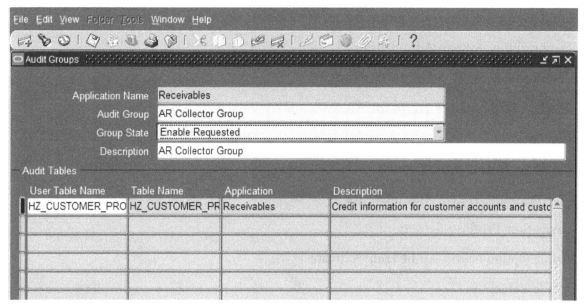

Add the tables to be audited.

Save the new audit group.

Step -3:

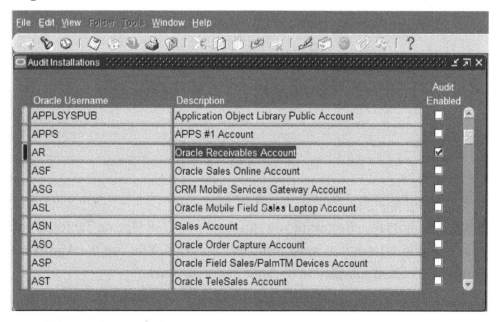

Install the Audit group.

Audit group is necessary to group the set of tables for smooth administration.

Responsibility: System Administrator

Navigation: Security > Audittrail > Install

Unselect all usernames except for AR

Step -4:

Enable Audit trail profile option.

Responsibility: System Administrator

Navigation: Profile > System

Profile Option Name: Audit Trail: Activate

Profile Value: Yes

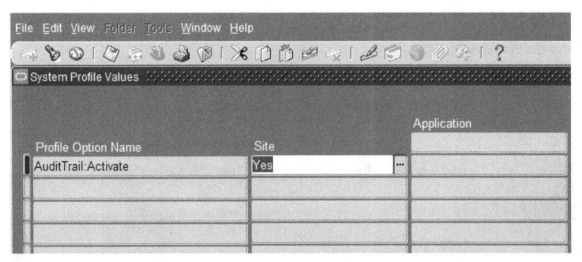

Step -5: Run AuditTrail Concurrent Request

Audit Trail definitions do not take effect until you run the AuditTrail Update Tables. If you change any of your definitions later, you must rerun this program. You run the AuditTrail Update Tables from the standard submission (Submit Requests) form:

This program creates database triggers on the tables in your audit groups for your installations. It also creates shadow tables, one for each audited table, to contain the audit data. If you make modifications to your audit definitions or disable your audit groups, the program drops or modifies the auditing triggers and shadow tables appropriately.

Submit the AuditTrail Update Tables concurrent request, as shown below.

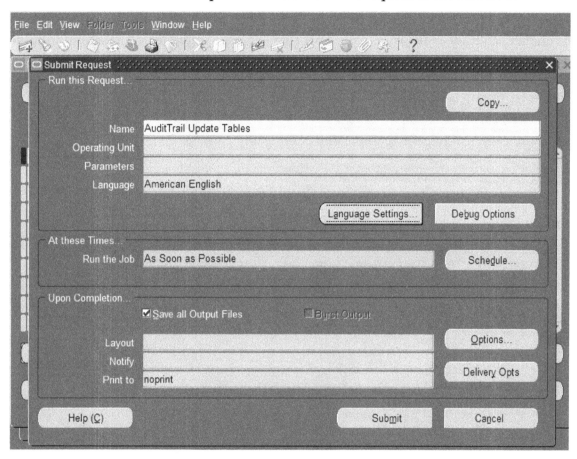

The program also creates special views you can use to retrieve your audit data for reporting.

This request should be completed normally and if the "AuditTrail Update Tables" program erred, you can use the queries below to delete the particular table and rerun it.

Delete from fnd_audit_tables where table_id not in (select table_id from fnd_tables where table_name in (' <table_name1>',' <table_name2>'));

Delete from fnd_audit_groups where GROUP_NAME not in ('<group name>');

Delete from fnd_audit_columns where table_id not in (select table_id from fnd_tables where table_name in ((' <table_name1>',' <table_name2>'));

After the successful completion of the program, it will create the required database triggers and shadow table as shown below. The shadow table will have the same name as the audited table appended with "_A". Two views will be created for each column with the names "_AC#" and "_AV#" where # is a sequential number.

Triggers:

	OWNER	TRIGGER_NAME	TRIGGER_TYPE		TRIGGERING_EVENT	TABLE_OWNER	BASE_OBJECT_TYPE	TABLE_NAME
1	APPS	HZ_CUSTOMER_PROFILES_AD	AFTER EACH ROW	DELETE	AR	TABLE	HZ_CUSTOMER_PROFILES
2	APPS	HZ_CUSTOMER_PROFILES_AC	BEFORE STATEMENT	DELETE	AR	TABLE	HZ_CUSTOMER_PROFILES
3	APPS	HZ_CUSTOMER_PROFILES_AU	AFTER EACH ROW	UPDATE	AR	TABLE	HZ_CUSTOMER_PROFILES
4	APPS	HZ_CUSTOMER_PROFILES_AT	BEFORE STATEMENT	UPDATE	AR	TABLE	HZ_CUSTOMER_PROFILES
5	APPS	HZ_CUSTOMER_PROFILES_AH	BEFORE STATEMENT	INSERT	AR	TABLE	HZ_CUSTOMER_PROFILES
6	APPS	HZ_CUSTOMER_PROFILES_AI	AFTER EACH ROW	INSERT	AR	TABLE	HZ_CUSTOMER_PROFILES
7	APPS	HZ_CUSTOMER_PROFILES_BRU	BEFORE EACH ROW	UPDATE	AR	TABLE	HZ_CUSTOMER_PROFILES

Shadow Table:

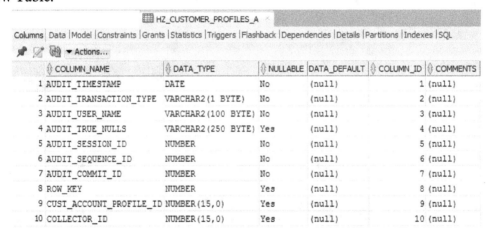

Views:

	OWNER	VIEW_NAME
1	APPS	HZ_CUSTOMER_PROFILES_AC1
2	APPS	HZ_CUSTOMER_PROFILES_AV1
3	APPS	HZ_CUSTOMER_PROFILES_AV2

Now, you have shadow tables and triggers for the table you audited. You can add as many tables as required to be audited and added to the respective groups.

How can we stop auditing the tables?

When you disable auditing, you should do any one of these below.

Variable	Description
Disable - Prepare for Archive	Copies the current values of all rows in the audited table into the shadow table, and then disables the auditing triggers. There is no longer any recording of any change. You should archive the shadow table before you purge it.
Disable - Interrupt Audit	Modifies the triggers to store one "final" row in the shadow table for each row that is modified in the audit table (remember that a given row in the shadow table represents the data in the audited row *before* an update). If a row in the table being audited is changed again (a second time), that change is not recorded. The shadow table grows slowly until it contains one row for each row in the table being audited. Then there is no longer any recording of any change.

Example:

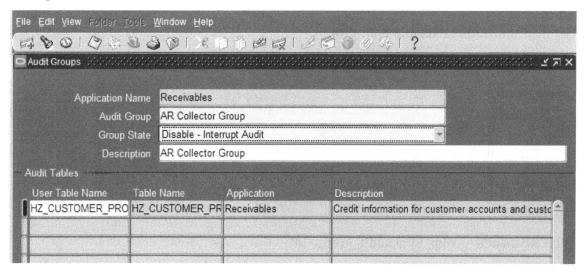

How can we purge the audit trail table?

There is no standard program to purge the shadow table rather we need to manually purge by setting the audit group to" Disable - Purge Table" and running the Audit Trail Update Tables report.

Variable	Description
Disable - Purge Table	Drops the auditing triggers and views and deletes all data from the shadow table.

In this topic, we have learned below:

> Setting up new tables and groups for auditing.

> Auditing tables and views.

> Disable Audit trail tables.

> Purge audit trail tables.

Tip - Useful Query

Get the list of audit tables and their groups.

SELECT b.group_name,

c.table_name,

a.state

FROM fnd_audit_tables a,

fnd_audit_groups b,

fnd_tables c

WHERE b.audit_group_id=a.audit_group_id

AND a.table_id =c.table_id;

Reference:

Overview of Audit Trails in Oracle E-Business Suite Applications (Doc ID 60828.1)

TOPIC

2

AUDITING SPECIFIC APPLICATION USER

Auditing specific application user in EBS

Oracle E-business suite supports auditing in the form of user activity and Database row changes.

Many organizations need to perform auditing frequently to meet compliances and security standards such as Sarbanes-Oxley (SOX), Payment Card Industry (PCI), FISMA, and HIPAA.

Oracle E-business suite provides a basic set of logging functionality. Most of the Oracle implementations do not leverage the built-in auditing features in E-business suite nor take full advantage of auditing features.

In this topic, we will see how to enable monitoring for a particular user, say SYSADMIN to track the sysadmin-related activities.

The goal is to take Step-by-step action for setting up an audit on an EBS Applications user SYSADMIN.

Sign-On: Audit Level allows you to select a level at which to audit users who sign on to Oracle Applications. Four audit levels increase in functionality: None, User, Responsibility, and Form. None is the default value, and means do not audit any user who signs on to Oracle Applications.

Auditing at the User level tracks:

> ➢ Who signs on to the system

> ➢ The number of times users log on and off

Auditing at the Responsibility level performs the User level audit functions and tracks:

> The responsibilities users choose

> How much time users spend using each responsibility

Auditing at the Form level performs the Responsibility and User level audit functions, and also tracks:

> The forms users choose

> How much time users spend on each form

Setup Audit for SYSADMIN:

Login to E-business suite and navigate to

System Administrator -> Profile -> System

Find "**Sign-On: Audit Level**" at the user level for SYSADMIN.

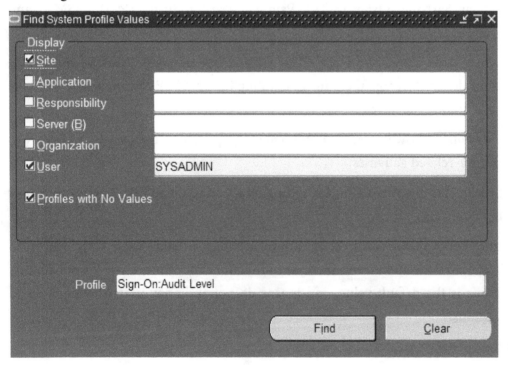

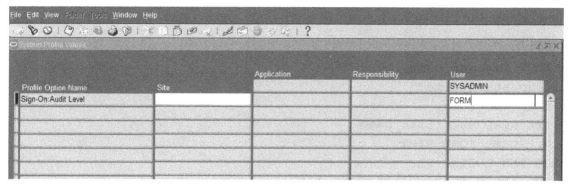

Set value as 'FORM' at the user level and save it.

Retrieve reports on SYSADMIN activities:

There are two ways to retrieve the reports of auditing user.

Option 1:

Oracle E-Business Suite ships standard reports to access sign-on, unsuccessful sign-on, responsibility usage, form usage and concurrent request usage. Access these reports through the system administrator responsibility.

Signon Audit Concurrent Requests (shows who submitted what requests)

Signon Audit Forms(shows who accessed what forms)

Signon Audit Responsibilities(shows who accessed what responsibilities)

Signon Audit Unsuccessful Logins(shows who unsuccessfully attempted to sign on as another user)

Signon Audit Users (shows who signed on to Oracle E-Business Suite)

Option 2:

The system stores end-user access data in the following tables. Develop SQL scripts to query these tables to generate reports.

```
<APPLSYS>.FND_LOGINS
<APPLSYS>.FND_LOGIN_RESPONSIBILITIES
<APPLSYS>.FND_LOGIN_RESP_FORMS
<APPLSYS>.FND_UNSUCCESSFUL_LOGINS
FND_CONCURRENT_REQUESTS
ICX.ICX_FAILURES
```

For example, the SQL query below will give you a detailed report on SYSADMIN forms navigation which is equivalent to running "Signon Audit Forms" report.

```sql
SELECT fu.user_name,
    flrp.start_time,
    flrp.end_time,
    frt.RESPONSIBILITY_NAME,
    fft.USER_FORM_NAME
FROM FND_LOGINS FL,
    FND_LOGIN_RESPONSIBILITIES FLR,
    FND_LOGIN_RESP_FORMS FLRP,
    fnd_user fu,
    fnd_responsibility_tl frt,
    fnd_form_tl fft
WHERE FL.USER_ID          =FU.USER_ID
AND FLR.LOGIN_ID          =FL.LOGIN_ID
AND FLRP.LOGIN_RESP_ID    =FLR.LOGIN_RESP_ID
AND FLR.RESPONSIBILITY_ID=frt.RESPONSIBILITY_ID
AND frt.LANGUAGE          = 'US'
AND FLRP.FORM_APPL_ID     =ffT.application_id
AND FLRP.FORM_ID          =FFT.FORM_ID
AND fft.LANGUAGE          = 'US'
AND fu.user_name          ='SYSADMIN'
ORDER BY flrp.start_time DESC;
```

The report below can be run to get the same details using the standard concurrent program.

Usually, auditing at site level will enable auditing for a complete application. In planning your organization Sign-On Audit implementation, you should consider the additional system overhead required to monitor and audit your users as they access Oracle E-Business Suite. The more users you audit, and the higher the level of auditing, the greater the system overhead such as processing costs and disk space.

We should carefully evaluate what type of auditing is needed for this application and at what level to avoid system overhead.

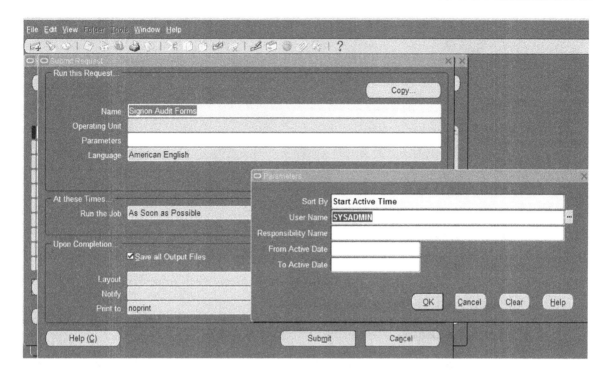

Reference

How to Audit an Oracle Applications User? (Doc ID 395849.1)

TOPIC

3

DATABASE AUDIT

Auditing is most important for every organization as audit reports are important to perform internal and external audits. Oracle E-business suite and database has many auditing features enabling Oracle applications to audit user level, table level, etc. We have seen a few important features in the last few topics.

Let us see about Oracle database auditing in detail here.

Database auditing is the process of recording, monitoring and reporting of the actions performed on a database. It allows the security auditors to observe whether the database users are using the database according to the established policies and that there are no policy violations. Database Auditing facilitates the analysis of the database activity patterns/trends and it can help in the process of gathering the historical data about a particular database user or activity.

Reasons for auditing:

➤ Enabling future accountability for current actions

➤ Preventing other users from inappropriate access.

➤ Investigating, monitoring and recording suspicious activities.

➤ Provide reports for auditors and for compliance.

How to enable database auditing?

Auditing feature is available in all types of editions. Connect as sysdba and follow the instructions.

Sqlplus / as sysdba

```
SQL> ALTER system SET audit_trail=db_extended scope=spfile;
SQL> Shutdown immediate
SQL> Startup
```

Set the auditing destination

alter system set audit_file_dest='/u01/app/db_1/DOYEN/admin/adump' scope=spfile;

System altered.

```
SQL> show parameter audit
```

```
NAME                                   TYPE          VALUE
-------------------------------------- ----------- -------------------
------------
audit_file_dest                        string
/u01/app/db_1/DOYEN/admin/adump
audit_sys_operations                   boolean       FALSE
audit_syslog_level                     string
audit_trail                            string        DB
unified_audit_sga_queue_size           integer       1048576
SQL>
```

The auditing is enabled by setting the AUDIT_TRAIL parameter to a value different than NONE followed by a restart of the database. The following table presents all the possible legal values for the AUDIT_TRAIL parameter:

NONE	Auditing is disabled
DB	The auditing is enabled and the audit data is written to the SYS.AUD$ table. If the database was started in read-only mode with AUDIT_TRAIL set to db, then Oracle Database internally sets AUDIT_TRAIL to os.
DB,EXTENDED	Behaves as DB but also populates the SQL_TEXT and SQL_BIND columns to the SYS.AUD$ table. If the database was started in read-only mode

	with AUDIT_TRAIL set to db, then Oracle Database internally sets AUDIT_TRAIL to os.
OS	The auditing is enabled. On Unix, the audit data is written to text files which are located in the directory specified via AUDIT_FILE_DEST. On Windows, the audit data will be sent to the Event Viewer.
XML	The auditing is enabled and the audit data is written to XML files which are located in the directory/folder specified via AUDIT_FILE_DEST. This is the case for Windows as well.
XML,EXTENDED	Behaves as XML but also populates the SQL_TEXT and SQL_BIND tags

Even though it records everything in sys.aud$, interpreting directly from this table is not understandable. You can use views below to read or interpret the actions.

DBA_AUDIT_EXISTS audit trail entries created by the AUDIT EXISTS command.

DBA_AUDIT_OBJECT or USER_AUDIT_OBJECT all/user audit trail records concerning objects.

DBA_AUDIT_SESSION or USER_AUDIT_SESSION all/user audit trail records concerning CONNECT and DISCONNECT.

DBA_AUDIT_STATEMENT or USER_AUDIT_STATEMENT all/user audit trail records concerning GRANT, REVOKE,AUDIT

DBA_AUDIT_TRAIL or USER_AUDIT_TRAIL all/user audit trail records.

Now, let see how to audit particular statements.

To set audit:

AUDIT [option] [BY user|SESSION|ACCESS] [WHENEVER {NOT} SUCCESSFUL]

For example:

```
SQL> audit select on dba_users by access whenever not successful;
Audit succeeded.
```

How to check what object are audited?

You can use DBA_OBJ_AUDIT_OPTS as below which shows what privileges are audited.

```
select * from dba_obj_audit_opts where object_name='DBA_USERS';
```

ry Result ×
SQL   All Rows Fetched: 1 in 3.98 seconds

OWNER	OBJECT_NAME	OBJECT_TYPE	ALT	AUD	COM	DEL	GRA	IND	INS	LOC	REN	SEL	UPD	REF	EXE	CRE	REA	WRI	FBK
SYS	DBA_USERS	VIEW	-/-	-/-	-/-	-/-	-/-	-/-	-/-	-/-	-/-	-/A	-/-	-/-	-/-	-/-	-/-	-/-	-/-

As you can see in the screenshot, DBA_USERS is audited against SEL (Select) option. You may wonder what -/A?

This means DBA_USERS is audited for unsuccessful login. In case, if you audit for successful as well, you will see as A/A. (successful / not successful).

ALT	Auditing ALTER WHENEVER SUCCESSFUL / UNSUCCESSFUL
AUD	Auditing AUDIT WHENEVER SUCCESSFUL / UNSUCCESSFUL
COM	Auditing COMMENT WHENEVER SUCCESSFUL / UNSUCCESSFUL
DEL	Auditing DELETE WHENEVER SUCCESSFUL / UNSUCCESSFUL
GRA	Auditing GRANT WHENEVER SUCCESSFUL / UNSUCCESSFUL
IND	Auditing INDEX WHENEVER SUCCESSFUL / UNSUCCESSFUL
INS	Auditing INSERT WHENEVER SUCCESSFUL / UNSUCCESSFUL
LOC	Auditing LOCK WHENEVER SUCCESSFUL / UNSUCCESSFUL
REN	Auditing RENAME WHENEVER SUCCESSFUL / UNSUCCESSFUL
SEL	Auditing SELECT WHENEVER SUCCESSFUL / UNSUCCESSFUL
UPD	Auditing UPDATE WHENEVER SUCCESSFUL / UNSUCCESSFUL
REF	Auditing REFERENCE WHENEVER SUCCESSFUL / UNSUCCESSFUL (not used)

EXE	Auditing EXECUTE WHENEVER SUCCESSFUL / UNSUCCESSFUL
CRE	Auditing CREATE WHENEVER SUCCESSFUL / UNSUCCESSFUL
REA	Auditing READ WHENEVER SUCCESSFUL / UNSUCCESSFUL
WRI	Auditing WRITE WHENEVER SUCCESSFUL / UNSUCCESSFUL
FBK	Auditing FLASHBACK WHENEVER SUCCESSFUL / UNSUCCESSFUL

Database auditing is a useful feature for auditing any tables to be monitored by its actions. This will help the audit team in the organization to closely monitor and identify the users on their actions against the important or audited tables. You should periodically purge all these tables to avoid performance issues in the database.

Useful information can be found in below MOS notes.

How to Truncate, Delete, or Purge Rows from the Audit Trail Table AUD$ (Doc ID 73408.1)

New Feature DBMS_AUDIT_MGMT to Manage and Purge Audit Information (Doc ID 731908.1)

TOPIC

TRACKING WEB AND HTML PAGES IN R12

Auditing feature in E-business suite allows capturing of information on not only the changes in the data at the form level, but also at web pages and OAF (Oracle Application Framework) pages. It also helps to track application usage statistics and perform Web site traffic analysis. In terms of performance, the data capture has negligible overhead.

At the Page Access Tracking administration UI, you can:

> Enable and disable Page Access Tracking

> Configure the granularity to which application context information is captured

> View reports on the gathered data

Examples of available reports:

> Access reports for a given application, responsibility and/or user across the Oracle Applications Framework, JTF, and Forms tech stacks

> Page Performance reports per mid-tier node

> Page access flow chart for a given user session

> Search reports based on several filter criteria

How to configure page access tracking in R12?

Step 1: Oracle Applications Manager: Site Map > Monitoring > Applications Usage Reports (Under Usage Tab) > Page Access Tracking and Sign-on Audit Configuration.

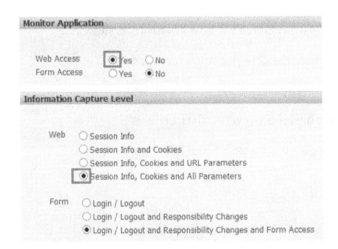

Step 2: Turning Page Access Tracking On or Off

On the Page Access Tracking Configuration page, you can enable or disable Page Access Tracking for your site. This is the master site-level switch for Page Access Tracking -- setting this field to **Off** overrides any other configurations.

Choose Web Access and capturing level as marked in Red.

On this Page Access Tracking Configuration page, you can choose how much data to collect by selecting one of the following combinations:

➢ Session Information

➢ See below for details.

➢ Session Information and Cookies

➢ This includes session information plus all incoming cookies.

➢ Session Information, Cookies, and URL Parameters

➢ This includes session information, all incoming cookies, and any GET parameters.

➢ Session Information, Cookies, and All Parameters

➢ This includes session information, all incoming cookies, any GET parameters, and any POST parameters.

"Session Information" refers to the following:

Page Information

➢ Timestamp

➢ JSP name (for example, jtflogin.jsp)

➢ JSP execution time, in milliseconds

Server Host Information

➢ Hostname

➢ Apache port

➢ Jserv port

➢ Request method (POST, GET, PUT, HEAD, etc.)

➢ Return status (OK, Error, or Exception)

Session Context

➢ Application ID

➢ Responsibility ID

➢ User ID

➢ Language ID

➢ Session ID

Client Browser Information

➢ Client language

➢ HTTP header

➢ User-agent

➢ Protocol

➢ Referer

➢ Authorization type

Client Language Information

➢ Character encoding

➢ Language

➢ Character set

Step 3: (Optional)Configuring Logging for Responsibilities or Users

Optionally, you can configure logging according to user or responsibility. To do so, use Oracle Forms to set up the profile JTF_PF_ENABLED.

Step 4: Choosing the Applications to Log

On the Page Access Tracking Configuration page, use the shuttle to move applications between the Disabled and Enabled lists. Only enabled applications will be logged. (Alternatively, this step can be performed through Oracle Forms by setting up the JTF_PF_ENABLED profile.)

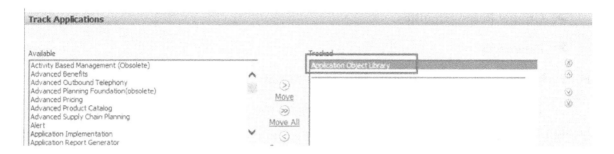

To apply the configuration changes that you have made, restart all the JVMs that use or will use Page Access Tracking.

How to view the page accessing report?

You can view the page accessing report in the OAM but generally, it does store information in stage data. A concurrent program called "**Page Access Tracking Data Migration**" submitted to migrate the data from the staging table to the database. The recommendation is to run the concurrent program once a day during off business hours for the reports to be up-to-date.

After the Concurrent Program completes, you should be able to view the latest data reports and statistics in the Oracle System Administrator Console. The page is located at **Oracle Applications Manager:** Site Map > Monitoring > Applications Usage Reports > Page Access Tracking and Sign-on Audit Reports.

If this concurrent program is taking too much of time, probably you are hitting a bug and that can be resolved by applying patch 17046728.

What is the information viewable?

Application Usage

This includes:

> Number of Page Hits

> Sessions

> Unique Users

> Unique Applications

> ➢ Unique Responsibilities

> ➢ Languages

For each of these statistics, you can drill down to view the respective Details page.

To see a graph of a complete session page flow, click an individual session ID on the Session Details page. The graph indicates which tech stack each access belongs to. If during a session a user accesses both JSPs and Forms across tech stacks (Oracle Applications Framework and/or Oracle Forms), the Session Details page shows the complete flow across the tech stacks, from login to logout.

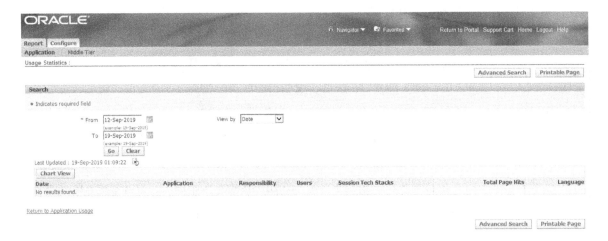

Middle Tier Usage

This includes:

> ➢ Hostname

> ➢ Server-Port

> ➢ Number of JVMs

> ➢ Average Page Execution Time

> ➢ Page Hits

> ➢ Page Failures

To define a specific date range, click **Edit**.

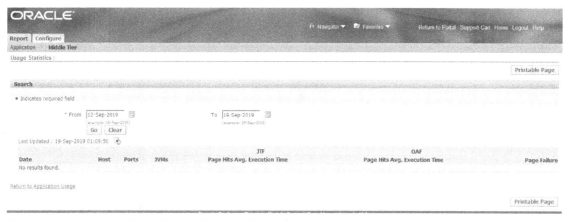

How can we purge the information and how frequently?

The amount of data recorded by Page Access Tracking depends on what applications, responsibilities and users have tracking turned on, the tracking level selected and the user traffic. On a regular basis, the System Administrator should purge the Page Access Tracking repository. The frequency of data purge also depends on how much historical tracking data is needed in the UI reports.

Use the following procedure to schedule the concurrent program "**Page Access Tracking Purge Data**" using Concurrent Manager:

- Log in to Oracle Forms through the Personal Home Page.

- Double-click **Requests**.

- Click **Submit a New Request**.

- Select **Single Request.**

- Click **OK.**

- In the Name field, enter **Page Access Tracking Purge Data**.

- Press the Tab key to select **Page Access Tracking Purge Data.**

- Schedule and submit the request.

Sometimes, R12 Page Access Tracking Purge Data Concurrent Program Does Not Purge Data. There is currently no option to force purge all Page Access Tracking Data in the JTF_PF_REPOSITORY table. The current behaviour is to purge data that has been migrated but keep non-migrated data. For those who have this issue, it can be got resolved by applying patch 16445598.

This feature in the E-business suite is very useful for all clients who intend to audit almost every user access in detail. These can be regularly printed and exported in a separate repository for a periodical review.

Useful Reference:

Page Access Tracking in Oracle Applications Release 12 (Doc ID 402116.1)

Printable Page: Different from the Page Access Tracking Page or "No results found" (Doc ID 2269969.1)

E-Business Suite: Page Access Tracking Data Migration Takes Many Hours to Complete (Doc ID 1575898.1)

R12 Page Access Tracking Purge Data Concurrent Program Does Not Purge Data (Doc ID 1587638.1)

TOPIC

5

TOP SEVEN ORACLE E-BUSINESS SUITE AREAS TO BE AUDITED

In this chapter, we are going to look at the areas where we need to perform Audit to keep E-Business suite system in security compliance.

Audit – It helps to identify the security breaches in the E-Business suite system, and this helps in identifying an area of improvement.

We are going to discuss the critical best practices we follow in Doyensys to perform an audit on EBS application on a regular basis, and this audit covers some portion of Database level audit as well.

Let us talk about it one by one and a solution is provided wherever possible.

Security Patch

Oracle strongly recommends applying the latest security patches in all E-Business suite application tier technology stack along with Database Oracle Home. For example, if you take EBS 12.2, security patches need to be applied to the technology stack components below.

- Database Oracle Home.

- Forms and Reports 10.1.2.3 Oracle Home.

- Oracle Fusion Middleware 11.1.1.9 Home.

- Oracle WebLogic Server 10.3.6.0 Home.

Script to find installed patches on E-Business Technology stack home

```
REM ---------------------------------------------------------------
--------------
REM Run as application OS user
REM Usage: ./EBScpupatches.sh
REM
REM This script will show whether CPU patches applied in apps tier
in R12.1.X.
REM
REM ---------------------------------------------------------------
--------------
#!/bin/bash
. $1
$ORACLE_HOME/OPatch/opatch lsinventory|grep -i "CPU"
$IAS_ORACLE_HOME/OPatch/opatch lsinventory|grep -i "CPU"


REM ---------------------------------------------------------------
--------------
REM
REM Usage: ./EBScpupatches.sh
REM This script will show whether CPU patches applied in apps tier
and Weblogic tier in R12.2.X
REM
REM ---------------------------------------------------------------
--------------

#!/bin/bash
#set -x
for i in run patch
do
. $1 $i
$ORACLE_HOME/OPatch/opatch lsinventory|grep -i "CPU"
$IAS_ORACLE_HOME/OPatch/opatch lsinventory|grep -i "CPU"

export ORACLE_HOME=$ORACLE_HOME/../../FMW_Home/webtier
export PATH="$ORACLE_HOME/oui/bin:$ORACLE_HOME/OPatch:$PATH"
$ORACLE_HOME/OPatch/opatch lsinventory
done
```

APPS and SYSADMIN password

When we write a proactive script to check service status we tend to hardcode the password within the script, if somebody shares across the script through email or some other way, the password will be visible to everyone. So it's recommended not to hardcode the password in scripts. Recommended options:

1. Separate credentials for monitoring solution and create Oracle wallet for that user to connect to the database without entering the password.

2. Call the password as a variable from the environment file.

System Administrator Privilege

User holding system administrator's responsibility privilege can maintain, change and even modify application data; so it's recommended to review whether users do need system administrator privileges, as per best practices suggested to create separate responsibility allocating the specific application functionality.

Script to find Users who have System administrator responsibility

```
SELECT fu.USER_ID,fu.USER_NAME,frvl.responsibility_name
FROM fnd_user_resp_groups_direct furgd, fnd_responsibility_vl
frvl, fnd_user fu
WHERE furgd.responsibility_id = frvl.responsibility_id
AND fu.user_id = furgd.user_id
AND(to_char(furgd.end_date) is null
OR furgd.end_date > sysdate)
AND frvl.end_date is null
AND frvl.responsibility_name = 'System Administrator'
and fu.end_date is NULL;
```

Oracle E-Business Applications – Default password

EBS application installation comes with default accounts which are much known to all. So it's recommended to change the password for default accounts. GUEST user is one of the default accounts; for this Oracle has provided a specific document to change the password.

```
select USER_NAME "Apps Users - Default Passwords" from (
          select
fnd_web_sec.validate_login('AME_INVALID_APPROVER','WELCOME') R,
'AME_INVALID_APPROVER' USER_NAME from dual
union ALL select fnd_web_sec.validate_login('ANONYMOUS','welcome')
R, 'ANONYMOUS' USER_NAME from dual
union ALL select fnd_web_sec.validate_login('APPSMGR','C') R,
'APPSMGR' USER_NAME from dual
union ALL select fnd_web_sec.validate_login('ASGADM','ASGADM') R,
'ASGADM' USER_NAME from dual
union ALL select fnd_web_sec.validate_login('ASGADM','welcome') R,
'ASGADM' USER_NAME from dual
union ALL select fnd_web_sec.validate_login('ASGUEST','welcome')
R, 'ASGUEST' USER_NAME from dual
union ALL select
fnd_web_sec.validate_login('AUTOINSTALL','DATAMERGE') R,
'AUTOINSTALL' USER_NAME from dual
union ALL select fnd_web_sec.validate_login('GUEST','ORACLE') R,
'GUEST' USER_NAME from dual
union ALL select
fnd_web_sec.validate_login('IBEGUEST','IBEGUEST2000') R,
'IBEGUEST' USER_NAME from dual
union ALL select fnd_web_sec.validate_login('IBE_ADMIN','MANAGER')
R, 'IBE_ADMIN' USER_NAME from dual
union ALL select fnd_web_sec.validate_login('IBE_GUEST','WELCOME')
R, 'IBE_GUEST' USER_NAME from dual
union ALL select
fnd_web_sec.validate_login('IEXADMIN','COLLECTIONS') R, 'IEXADMIN'
USER_NAME from dual
union ALL select
fnd_web_sec.validate_login('IRC_EMP_GUEST','WELCOME') R,
'IRC_EMP_GUEST' USER_NAME from dual
union ALL select
fnd_web_sec.validate_login('IRC_EXT_GUEST','WELCOME') R,
'IRC_EXT_GUEST' USER_NAME from dual
union ALL select fnd_web_sec.validate_login('MOBADM','C') R,
'MOBADM' USER_NAME from dual
union ALL select fnd_web_sec.validate_login('MOBDEV','C') R,
'MOBDEV' USER_NAME from dual
```

```
union ALL select
fnd_web_sec.validate_login('MOBILEADM','MOBILEADM') R, 'MOBILEADM'
USER_NAME from dual
union ALL select fnd_web_sec.validate_login('MOBILEADM','welcome')
R, 'MOBILEADM' USER_NAME from dual
union ALL select
fnd_web_sec.validate_login('OP_CUST_CARE_ADMIN','OP_CUST_CARE_ADMI
N') R, 'OP_CUST_CARE_ADMIN' USER_NAME from dual
union ALL select
fnd_web_sec.validate_login('OP_SYSADMIN','OP_SYSADMIN') R,
'OP_SYSADMIN' USER_NAME from dual
union ALL select fnd_web_sec.validate_login('PORTAL30','PORTAL30')
R, 'PORTAL30' USER_NAME from dual
union ALL select
fnd_web_sec.validate_login('PORTAL30','portal30_new') R,
'PORTAL30' USER_NAME from dual
union ALL select
fnd_web_sec.validate_login('PORTAL30_SSO','portal30_sso_new') R,
'PORTAL30_SSO' USER_NAME from dual
union ALL select fnd_web_sec.validate_login('SYSADMIN','SYSADMIN')
R, 'SYSADMIN' USER_NAME from dual
union ALL select
fnd_web_sec.validate_login('WIZARD','????UE:?H0UA}?K') R, 'WIZARD'
USER_NAME from dual
union ALL select fnd_web_sec.validate_login('XML_USER','WELCOME')
R, 'XML_USER' USER_NAME from dual
) where R='Y'
order by 1
/
```

Oracle Database schemas – Default password

When we install Oracle E-Business suite module schemas like AP, AR, etc. the password is the same as user name. This default password will help unauthorized access and technical users can log in into the database with module user and modify the data. This is a major security breach and we should change the module password to a complex one.

Secure APPLSYSPUB account

APPLSYSPUB is a public schema that grants access to the Oracle application initial sign-on forms. This account is used by Oracle Applications to initially connect to the database and validate the given credential during login process. So we should not revoke or grant unnecessary privileges to APPLSYSPUB account

Use Secure Flag on DBC File

The Server Security feature of the Application Object Library supports authentication of application server machines and code modules in order to access the database. When the Server Security is activated, application servers are required to supply server IDs (like passwords) and/or code IDs to access a database server.

For database side the Oracle Database Security Assessment Tool (DBSAT) is a command-line tool focused on identifying how securely the database is configured, who are the users and what are their entitlements, what security policies and controls are in place, and where sensitive data resides with the goal of promoting successful approaches to mitigate potential security risks.

Hope this chapter covers critical areas to be audited for Secure E-Business suite application.

Reference: Master Note For Oracle Database Security Assessment Tool (DBSAT) (Doc ID 2484219.1)

Happy Auditing!!!

ORACLE APPLICATION TROUBLE-SHOOTING

In this chapter, we are going to discuss how to troubleshoot. Troubleshooting is a hectic process until you practice it. As a fresher most of the persons are lagging here because of uncertainty like where to start, how to approach. Troubleshooting is a skill that you refine over time. Each time you solve a problem, you increase your troubleshooting skills by gaining more experience. You learn how, when and where to combine steps to reach a solution quickly. The troubleshooting process is a guideline that is modified to fit your needs. We are going to explain how to troubleshoot in E-Business suit. Here we are given real-time issues which are faced by most of the application DBAs. It will be helpful for entry-level DBAs, and it will reduce your time.

We are more focusing on the cause-and-effect along with a solution, and best practice. Many of the steps given here in the chapter are live troubleshooting that we work for most of the Doyensys customers. You can also apply other different solutions to fix the issue. Here we are going to cover some useful troubleshooting tips that help Oracle APPS DBAs.

TOPIC 1	**ADOP Cutover Failed Scenario – 1 & 2:** These two chapters provide information on how to perform a clean abort of the patching cycle and restart the cutover phase in ADOP cycle with examples.
TOPIC 2	**Workflow Notification Mailer:** This chapter discusses in detail about the workflow notification mailer inbound and outbound configuration and step by step analysis during configuration issues.
TOPIC 3	**Trouble-shooting pending request in OPP:** An idea to trouble-shoot the long-running report waiting on Output Post Processor manager.

TOPIC 4	**Login issues in EBS:** Discussing the general login issue and how to fix common login issues.
TOPIC 5	**Forms services failure:** This chapter discusses in detail about the workflow notification mailer inbound and outbound configuration and step by step analysis during configuration issues.
TOPIC 6	**Role-Based Access:** Let's understand about the role-based access, a new feature in E-business release 12 with a classic example
TOPIC 7	**Find and analyse particular session in Oracle:** This will help anyone to quickly understand the behaviour of the Oracle session, which will help us to make quick decisions about the sessions. Also discussed how to perform analysis and interpret the wait events.
TOPIC 8	**Easy way to import user account from AD to Oracle EBS using the command line:** Manual method to pull user account from AD to Oracle EBS Import user account from AD to Oracle EBS
TOPIC 9	**Troubleshooting OATS:** This discusses the installation of OATS, a comprehensive testing solution for Oracle applications in detail.
TOPIC 10	**Apex XDB Security Issues:** Common issue of migrating apex from one database to another database.
TOPIC 11	**Oracle Connection Errors:** This error occurs due to the fact your connection to the Oracle server is either no longer available, or the server couldn't respond to the client's requests.
TOPIC 12	**Trouble Shooting OEM Target Down after agent upgrade from 12c to 13c:** This discusses about a bug in upgrading an agent from 12c to 13c while discovering the host using an upgraded agent.

TOPIC

1

ADOP CUTOVER FAILED SCENARIO – 1

Scenario – Cutover phase failed in the middle

In EBS 12.2 Oracle has introduced ADOP feature for patching solution. We all know the benefit of ADOP which are 1) user can be operational while applying the patch, 2) minimum downtime, 3) patch can be roll backed if it's failed in the middle, etc.

We will be able to abort the patching cycle before starting the cutover phase, but once you come to the cutover phase we could not abort the patching cycle and we had to complete cutover phase at any cost.

In this chapter, we are going to see a scenario where the cutover phase was failed in the middle and how we can fix this issue and complete the cutover phase.

Scenario:

Multi-node architecture with a shared file system.

Run File System: FS1

Patch File System: FS2

ADOP Status:

Prepare – Completed

Apply – Completed

Finalize – Completed

Cutover – Failed

There are various stages within cutover and each stage has its own code. If the cutover failed, the below query will tell us on which stage cutover phase was failed.

```
set pagesize 200;
set linesize 160;
col PREPARE_STATUS format a15
col APPLY_STATUS format a15
col CUTOVER_STATUS format a15
col ABORT_STATUS format a15
col STATUS format a15

select NODE_NAME,ADOP_SESSION_ID, PREPARE_STATUS , APPLY_STATUS
,CUTOVER_STATUS , CLEANUP_STATUS , ABORT_STATUS , STATUS
from AD_ADOP_SESSIONS
order by ADOP_SESSION_ID;

NODE NAME ADOP_SESSION_ID PR AP CUT CL AB OS
--------- --------------- -- --- -- -- -- --
PRIMARY   12               Y Y  4   N  X  F
SLAVE     12               Y Y  D   N  X  F
```

In the above scenario on primary node cutover went on till "FS CUTOVER COMPLETED" stage, on slave node cutover went on till "'FLIP SNAPSHOTS COMPLETED" stage and cutover failed.

```
cutover status
cutover_status='Y' 'COMPLETED'
cutover_status not in ('N','Y','X') and status='F' 'FAILED'
cutover_status='0' 'CUTOVER STARTED'
cutover_status='1' 'SERVICES SHUTDOWN COMPLETED'
cutover_status='3' 'DB CUTOVER COMPLETED'
cutover_status='D' 'FLIP SNAPSHOTS COMPLETED'
cutover_status='4' 'FS CUTOVER COMPLETED
cutover_status='5' 'ADMIN STARTUP COMPLETED'
cutover_status='6' 'SERVICES STARTUP COMPLETED'
cutover_status='N' 'NOT STARTED'
cutover_status='X' 'NOT APPLICABLE'
```

Solution:

Generally cutover log exists under $NE_BASE/EBSapps/log/adop/<session_id>. Check the log file and find the actual errors. In our scenario issue is cutover failed before the FS CUTOVER on slave node. So we perform FS CUTOVER manually on failed slave node; upon successful run the cutover again.

Now on Primary node:

Run File System: FS2

Patch File System: FS1

Now on Slave node

Run File System: FS1

Patch File System: FS2

Step to run FS CUTOVER manually:

1. Stop if any services are started.

2. Just source the environment in slave node ($EBS_BASE/EBSapps.env run), in our scenario in the slave node; current RUN file system is FS1. Now Perform FS Cutover using the syntax below.

```
Source Run edition
{ echo "SYSTEM_PWD; $APPS_PWD; $WL_PWD; }|perl
/appl_share/app/appltst1/fs1/EBSapps/appl/ad/12.0.0/patch/115/bin/
txkADOPCutOverPhaseCtrlScript.pl -
contextfile=/u01/app/appltst1/fs1/inst/apps/$CONTEXT_NAME/appl/adm
in/$CONTEXT_NAME.xml -
patchcontextfile=/u01/app/appltst1/fs2/inst/apps/$CONTEXT_NAME/app
l/admin/$CONTEXT_NAME.xml -sessionid=12 -
outdir=/appl_share/app/appltst1/fs_ne/EBSapps/log/adop/43/cutover_
20180910_014603/$CONTEXT_NAME -action=ctxupdate
```

1. Once FS CUTOVER successfully is completed, Login into primary node and Source Run edition again and run cutover; in our scenario on primary node current RUN file system is FS2.

```
{ echo $APPS_PWD; echo $SYSTEM_PWD; echo $WL_PWD; } | adop
phase=cutover
```

We hope this topic is useful and will give you an overall idea about how to handle if ADOP cutover phase failed in the middle.

TOPIC

2

ADOP CUTOVER FAILED SCENARIO – 2

Scenario – Cutover phase failed in the middle

In EBS 12.2 Oracle has introduced ADOP feature for patching solution. We all know the benefits of ADOP which are 1) user can be operational while applying the patch, 2) minimum downtime, 3) patch can be roll backed if it's failed in the middle, etc.

We were able to abort the patching cycle before starting the cutover phase, but once we came to the cutover phase we could not abort the patching cycle and we had to complete the cutover phase at any cost.

In this chapter, we are going to see a scenario where the cutover phase has failed in the middle and how we can fix this issue and complete the cutover phase.

Scenario:

Multi-node architecture with a shared file system.

Run File System: FS1

Patch File System: FS2

ADOP Status:

Prepare – Completed

Apply – Completed

Finalize – Completed

Cutover – Failed

There are various stages within cutover and each stage has its own code. If the cutover failed, the query below will tell us on which stage cutover phase has failed.

```
set pagesize 200;
set linesize 160;
col PREPARE_STATUS format a15
col APPLY_STATUS format a15
col CUTOVER_STATUS format a15
col ABORT_STATUS format a15
col STATUS format a15

select NODE_NAME,ADOP_SESSION_ID, PREPARE_STATUS,
 APPLY_STATUS, CUTOVER_STATUS, CLEANUP_STATUS, ABORT_STATUS,
STATUS
from AD_ADOP_SESSIONS
order by ADOP_SESSION_ID;

NODE NAME ADOP_SESSION_ID PR AP CUT CL AB OS
--------- --------------- -- --- -- -- -- --
PRIMARY   12              Y  Y   6  N  X  F
SLAVE     12              Y  Y   5  N  X  F
```

In the above scenario on primary node cutover phase is almost over, on slave node cutover went till "ADMIN STARTUP COMPLETED" stage and in the next phase, cutover has failed.

cutover status
```
cutover_status='Y' 'COMPLETED'
cutover_status not in ('N','Y','X') and status='F' 'FAILED'
cutover_status='0' 'CUTOVER STARTED'
cutover_status='1' 'SERVICES SHUTDOWN COMPLETED'
cutover_status='3' 'DB CUTOVER COMPLETED'
cutover_status='D' 'FLIP SNAPSHOTS COMPLETED'
cutover_status='4' 'FS CUTOVER COMPLETED'
cutover_status='5' 'ADMIN STARTUP COMPLETED'
cutover_status='6' 'SERVICES STARTUP COMPLETED'
cutover_status='N' 'NOT STARTED'
cutover_status='X' 'NOT APPLICABLE'
```

Solution

Generally cutover log exists under $NE_BASE/EBSapps/log/adop/<session_id>. Check the log file and find the actual errors. In our scenario, the issue is with Manager Server's port used by another process. So we cleared that process and freed up the port and restarted the cutover as mentioned below.

Now On Primary node:

Run File System: FS2

Patch File System: FS1

Now on Slave node

Run File System: FS2

Patch File System: FS1

1. Stop if any services are started.

2. Shutdown Middle tier on Primary and Slave, if it's running. It's safe to shutdown CM, but it is not required.

3. Login in to primary server, source Environment file (This time Run file system will be FS2 and the Patch file system will be FS1). Run the cutover again; this time cutover will not bring down or bring up any services. So it will be completed quickly.

```
{ echo $APPS_PWD; echo $SYSTEM_PWD; echo $WL_PWD; } | adop
phase=cutover
```

1. Restart Middle tier on Primary and Slave node.

We hope this topic is useful and will give you an overall idea about how to handle if ADOP cutover phase failed

WORKFLOW NOTIFICATION MAILER

Workflow Notification Mailer – Troubleshooting

Oracle Workflow supports the Simple Mail Transfer Protocol (SMTP) for outbound messages and the Internet Message Access Protocol (IMAP) for inbound messages.

Let us discuss here both Workflow inbound and outbound email issues. This can also be used as a guide by the Workflow Administrators to troubleshoot any inbound/outbound notification email issues.

Workflow Outbound Issues:

Outbound messages (Emails going out from Oracle) from workflow should be received to the override email address set in "Workflow Notification Mailer" in non-production or intended recipients in production. If those emails are not received, follow the steps below to troubleshoot and get those fixed.

What should you ask from the user?

Notification ID which got triggered in workflow

Type of notification like Purchase requisition/Expense details.

Who is expected to receive the email?

What should you check?

Step 1: Your notification mailer logs are the key file to check the outbound mailer issues.

```
ls -lt $APPLCSF/$APPLLOG/FNDCPGSC*.txt
```

Pick the last file with the latest timestamp and check the last 100 lines. It should not have any errors.

Step 2: You can also grep the keywords like "ERROR", "Problem", "UNEXPECTED" as these will return the core problem details quickly from the log file. However, you should read the log file line by line to understand the issue.

Step 3: Check all workflow mailer and agent listeners are up and running.

Ensure that the following Workflow Service Components are up and running as these are responsible for outbound processing.

Workflow Deferred Agent Listener

Workflow Deferred Notification Agent Listener

Notification Mailer

Step 4: Ensure all values related to outbound have been configured correctly according to the environment values. In a cloned environment, it should not have the production values.

The quickest way to check is to just navigate the "Workflow Notification Mailer" Configuration page step by step.

Edit the workflow notification mailer and check outbound server name is configured properly.

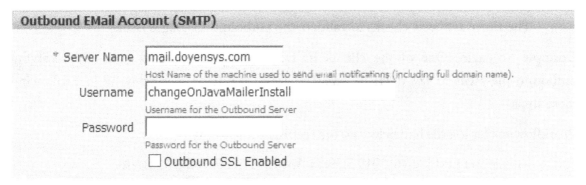

Check Outbound is set to 1 (Enabling outbound)

In the next step, check the test address is correctly updated.

Next step, HTML agent should have proper URL value.

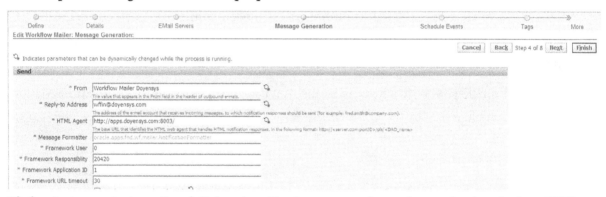

If the instance is in a Load Balancing Environment, then please check whether "WF Workflow Mailer Framework Web Agent and Application Framework Agent" Profile options are set correctly.

The above are basic checks to validate the outbound messages issues.

Example Scenario: One of the clients in Doyensys company had issues in receiving outbound messages to the override email address. We fixed it quickly by just following these steps.

Workflow mailer log file had below errors recorded repeatedly.

FNDCPGSC899414.txt:[Sep 6, 2019 5:39:35 AM EDT]:1567762775521:-1:-

```
1:apps.doyensys.com:172.20.1.11:-1:-1:1:20420:SYSADMIN(0):-
1:Thread[outboundThreadGroup1,5,outboundThreadGroup]:1785530491:66
24:1567743416727:63:UNEXPECTED:[SVC-GSM-WFMLRSVC-899414-10006 :
```

```
Oracle.apps.fnd.wf.mailer.NotificationFormatter.getFormattedMessag
es()]:Problem getting the HTML content ->
Oracle.apps.fnd.wf.mailer.NotificationFormatter$FormatterSAXExcept
ion: Problem obtaining the HTML content ->
Oracle.apps.fnd.wf.common.HTTPClientException: Unable to invoke
method HTTPClient.HTTPConnection. Get caused by: java.net.
ConnectException: Connection refused.
```

```
FNDCPGSC899414.txt:[Sep 6, 2019 5:40:35 AM EDT]:1567762835554:-1:-
1:apps.doyensys.com:172.20.1.11:-1:-1:1:20420:SYSADMIN(0):-
1:Thread[outboundThreadGroup1,5,outboundThreadGroup]:1785530491:66
24:1567743416727:63:UNEXPECTED:[SVC-GSM-WFMLRSVC-899414-10006 :
Oracle.apps.fnd.wf.mailer.NotificationFormatter.handleResEndTag]:
Problem obtaining the HTML content
Oracle.apps.fnd.wf.common.HTTPClientException: Unable to invoke
method HTTPClient. HTTPConnection. Get caused by: java.net.
ConnectException: Connection refused
```

These errors will appear if HTML agent URL is incorrect. Use the query below to quickly check the value and fix it.

```
SELECT e.profile_option_name Profile,
f.user_profile_option_name User_Profile_Name,
c.application_short_name,
decode(a.level_id,10001,'Site',10002,'Application',10003,'Resp',10
004,'User') LevelSet_At,
decode(a.level_id,10001,'Site',10002,c.application_short_name,
10003,b.responsibility_name,10004,d.user_name) LValue,
nvl(a.profile_option_value,'Is Null') Value
FROM fnd_profile_option_values a, fnd_responsibility_tl b,
fnd_application c, fnd_user d, fnd_profile_options e,
fnd_profile_options_vl f
WHERE f.user_profile_option_name in ('WF: Workflow Mailer
Framework Web Agent','Application Framework Agent')
AND  e.profile_option_id = a.profile_option_id
AND  e.profile_option_id = f.profile_option_id
AND  a.level_value = b.responsibility_id (+)
AND a.level_value = c.application_id (+)
```

```
AND a.level_value = d.user_id (+)
ORDER BY 1,2;
```

The above steps should resolve most of the outbound workflow issues. If you still have issues in outbound, you can check below if these are correct.

1. Check if the notification is present in the recipient/user's Worklist/Notifications page. If it does not exist, it means that the notification itself is not created and you need to check the corresponding workflow status. You may also query the notification from the wf_notifications table.

   SQL> select recipient_role, notification_id, status, mail_status from wf_notifications where recipient_role like '&user_name';

   The e-mail notification is sent only if all of the following is true.

   • Notification status is OPEN or CANCELED

   • Notification mail_status is MAIL or INVALID

2. Check the Recipient role has a valid e-mail address and notification preference MAIL%

   SELECT email_address, nvl(WF_PREF.get_pref(name, 'MAILTYPE'), notification_preference)
   FROM wf_roles
   WHERE name = '&recipient_role';

   The Recipient can receive email notification only if

   • notification preference is not set 'QUERY' / 'DISABLED' / 'SUMMARY' / 'SUMHTML' &

   • recipient has a valid email address

3. Run $FND_TOP/sql/wfmlrdbg.sql for notification id and check the status of the message in WF_DEFERRED and WF_NOTIFICATION_OUT queue.

   ➢ PROCESSED in WF_DEFERRED - The message is enqueued to WF_NOTIFICATION_OUT

➢ PROCESSED in WF_NOTIFICATION_OUT - The message is sent as e-mail

➢ READY in WF_DEFERRED - Check if Deferred Agent Listener is running

➢ READY in WF_NOTIFICATION_OUT

➢ Check if Notification Mailer is running

4. Finally, you try in solving the outbound email issues by recreating the mailer

```
    a. Stop Notification Mailer, rebuild Mailer Queue using
$FND_TOP/patch/115/sql/wfntfqup.sql. This
       will recreate WF_NOTIFICATION_OUT with new messages that
are eligible to be e-mailed.
    b. Bounce Workflow Mailer service.
```

Issue 2: Notification mailer not consuming emails and updating Oracle applications.

Usually, inbound messages are received to Oracle using emails from users. A user who receives an email (outbound email) for approving expense or purchase requisition will respond to using the available links in an outbound email. It can be "Approve" or "Reject" or "Need more information".

Upon responding to the email, the email will reach to an IMAP account and Oracle process will wait to read the unread messages from the Inbox. Based on the criteria, Oracle will decide to process or simply discard the email. If a valid email is processed, then it will be consumed in Oracle application and base tables are updated with necessary details.

This is designed for users to ease the way of approving the orders or expenses without logging into Oracle applications.

If any of these are not working, there are ways to debug it.

Step 1: Check inbound mailer is set to 1 (enabled).

Step 2: Check the responded email in IMAP account PROCESS or DISCARD folder.

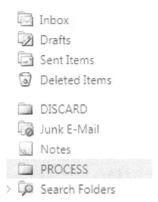

If a valid response email is moved to Discard folder, check if the same IMAP account details are shared by the multiple notification mailers from the different instance.

NOTE: It's recommended to use a dedicated IMAP account with each mailer.

Best Practices/tips:

1. Set the mailer parameter 'Processor Close on Read Timeout' to 'Y', i.e., select the checkbox for it.

2. Set the mailer parameter 'Expunge Inbox on Close' to 'Y', i.e., select the check-box for it.

3. Do not leave the mailer parameter 'NodeName' to the default value, i.e., WFMAIL but change it to a value as relevant for the instance type or name.

The above steps are effective ways of debugging workflow notification mailer which stopped working or intended functionality is not working properly.

TOPIC

TROUBLE-SHOOTING PENDING REQUEST IN OPP

Tips and Tricks to manage long-running report waiting on Output Post

Processor manager

One of our customers faced an issue which was concurrent report is stuck and waiting for Output Post Processor to process, that leads to CPU consumption and sometimes OPP JVM error with out of memory error and unable to process any requests.

We examined this issue with due diligence and found a way to rectify this issue.

Please note that in this content below you may see the word called "OPP" which refers to Output Post Processor concurrent manager.

In this chapter, we are going to see

1. How to find Long-running concurrent request waiting on OPP.

2. How to confirm whether a particular request is waiting for OPP to process.

3. How to cancel the long-running request.

Environment details:

1. OS -> Sun Solaris Sparc 5.11 64 Bit

2. DB Version -> 11.2.0.4

3. EBS Version -> R12.1.3

Step 1: Let's find the long-running concurrent request now. The query below will return query running for more than two hours.

```
SELECT fcp.user_concurrent_program_name cp_name
,fcr.request_id rqst_id
,ROUND (((SYSDATE - fcr.actual_start_date) * 60 * 24), 2)
runtime_min
,TO_CHAR (fcr.actual_start_date, 'DD-MON-YYYY
HH24:MI:SS')act_start_datetime
,DECODE (fcr.status_code, 'R', fcr.status_code) status
,fcr.argument_text
FROM apps.fnd_concurrent_requests fcr
,apps.fnd_user fu
,apps.fnd_responsibility_tl fr
,apps.fnd_concurrent_programs_tl fcp
WHERE fcr.status_code LIKE 'R'
AND fu.user_id = fcr.requested_by
AND fr.responsibility_id = fcr.responsibility_id
AND fcr.concurrent_program_id = fcp.concurrent_program_id
AND fcr.program_application_id = fcp.application_id
AND ROUND (((SYSDATE - fcr.actual_start_date) * 60 * 24), 2) > 120
ORDER BY fcr.concurrent_program_id ,request_id DESC;
```

Step 2: Now find the corresponding session matching session logon_time, respective module and program. This should exactly match with concurrent request actual start time.

```
set lines 200
col machine format a20
col username format a10
col event format a25
col module format a25
select
INST_ID,sid,serial#,username,machine,type,status,to_char(logon_tim
e,'DD-MON-YY HH24:MI:SS'),event,module,sql_id,prev_sql_id from
gv$session where status = 'ACTIVE' and type = 'USER' and
trunc(LOGON_TIME) = '&Date' order by 8;
```

SID	SERIAL#	USERNAME	TO_CHAR(LOGON_TIME,'DD-MON-	EVENT	MODULE	SQL_ID	PREV_SQL_ID
3875	49822	APPS	19-SEP-19 08:34:01	cell single block physica l read	rwrun@server_name.domain. com	608dutxggrz25	0dr2uccswl52g

Step 3: Now find the SQL_FULL text from v$sql, then we should find text like given below. This means this particular session is waiting on the Output Post Processor concurrent program.

```
Set long 2000
Select sql_fulltext from v$sql where sql_id = '&sql_id';
```

```
SQL> /

SQL_FULLTEXT
------------------------------------------------------------------------
select /*+ FIRST_ROWS(1) */  tab.rowid, tab.msgid, tab.corrid, tab.priority, tab
.delay,   tab.expiration , tab.exception_qschema,   tab.exception_queue, tab.cha
in_no, tab.local_order_no, tab.enq_time,   tab.time_manager_info, tab.state, tab
.enq_tid, tab.step_no,   tab.sender_name, tab.sender_address, tab.sender_protoco
l,   tab.dequeue_msgid, tab.user_prop, tab.user_data   from "APPLSYS"."FND_CP_GS
M_OPP_AQTBL" tab, "APPLSYS"."AQ$_FND_CP_GSM_OPP_AQTBL_I" iot  where (iot.subscri
ber# = :1 and iot.name = :2 and iot.queue# = :3)   and iot.msg_priority =
tab.priority and iot.msg_enq_time = tab.enq_time and iot.msg_step_no = tab.step_
no and iot.msg_chain_no = tab.chain_no and iot.msg_local_order_no = tab.local_or
der_no  and tab.corrid = :4 and tab.msgid = iot.msgid
```

Step 4: We can confirm whether this particular concurrent request is waiting on OPP manager by verifying the process from the operating system level. Select the process id of this particular session.

```
select process from v$Session where sid = '&sid';
```

```
SQL>
SQL> select process from v$session where sid = 3875;

PROCESS
------------------------------------------------------------------------
9203
```

Now go to the application server where CM is running and check for the process id; then we should be able to see the process as given below. This means this particular request is waiting only on OPP manager and not from the database level.

121

Step 5: Now finally we should cancel this request waiting on OPP manager and sometime it may not allow you to cancel from the front end. So let's follow the process to cancel the long-running request waiting on OPP manager.

1. See if you can kill the process_id from the application server.

2. Run the update statement to terminate the program and find out who is blocking you and kill the blocking session.

Hope this topic gave you an idea to troubleshoot the long-running report waiting on Output Post Processor manager.

Happy Troubleshooting!!!

TOPIC

5

LOGIN ISSUES IN EBS

EBS R12 Login page is not coming

Resolving the blank page issue in Oracle E-Business Suite while opening EBS R12 URL (http://test.doyensys.com:8000); so we have collected the most common root cause for a blank page.

> RFC 2068 Hypertext Transfer Protocol – HTTP/1.1

> JSP pages not compiled properly.

> Just after the clone.

> Archive log space is full.

> Java Cache issues between the multiple middle-tiers.

> Missing class files in the OA_HTML directory.

> The instance is very slow/inaccessible.

> Database Listeners are down.

Case 1: RFC 2068 Hypertext Transfer Protocol - HTTP/1.1

The request could not be understood by the server due to malformed syntax. The client should not repeat the request without modification.

Error code:

> From RFC 2068 Hypertext Transfer Protocol -- HTTP/1.1: 10.1.1 500 Internal Server Error

> From RFC 2068 Hypertext Transfer Protocol -- HTTP/1.1: 10.5.1 400 Bad Request

> ➤ From RFC 2068 Hypertext Transfer Protocol -- HTTP/1.1: 10.5.1 404 Not Found

If the server does not wish to make this information available to the client, the status code 404 (Forbidden) can be used instead. The 410 (Gone) status code SHOULD be used if the server knows, through some internally configurable mechanism, that an old resource is permanently unavailable and has no forwarding address.

An error occurs in the scenarios below:

> ➤ E-Business Suite R12 Login Page Enter Username/Password Fails with Error 'Exception Details. oracle.apps.fnd.framework.OAException'
>
> ➤ Error on Customer Creation Page. Selecting the LOV for GL code combinations throws an error
>
> ➤ User trying to do an export from forms, and was hit by the error below.

Cause: JSP files are got corrupted

Solution: Please follow the steps below to compile the jsp:

1. Open a telnet session to your environment
2. Source the instance
3. cd $OA_HTML
4. Compile all JSP
5. Restart all the application services

Compile all JSP

perl ojspCompile.pl --compile --flush -p 2

-p 2 (Number of parallel processes)

Case 2: JSP pages not compiled properly.

> ➤ Shutdown application services
>
> ➤ Clear persistence cache
>
> > o   rm -fr $INST_TOP/ora/10.1.3/j2ee/oacore/persistence/*
> >
> > o   rm -fr $INST_TOP/ora/10.1.3/j2ee/oafm/persistence/*

o rm -fr $INST_TOP/ora/10.1.3/j2ee/forms/persistence/*

➢ Compile JSP using the below command.

Compile all JSP

perl ojspCompile.pl --compile --flush -p 2

-p 2 (Number of parallel processes)

Case 3: Just after the clone.

➢ Shutdown opmnctl services

➢ Clear persistence cache

```
rm -fr $INST_TOP/ora/10.1.3/j2ee/oacore/persistence/*
rm -fr $INST_TOP/ora/10.1.3/j2ee/oafm/persistence/*
rm -fr $INST_TOP/ora/10.1.3/j2ee/forms/persistence/*
```

➢ Compile JSP using the below command.

```
Compile all JSP
perl ojspCompile.pl --compile --flush -p 2
-p 2 (Number of parallel processes)
```

Case 4: Archive log space is full.

Either delete old archive logs or temporarily move the archive log file to another location.

Case 5: Java Cache issues between the multiple middle-tiers.

Cause: This issue occurs only if you have more than one mid-tier and you had enabled Distributed Java Caching.

Error Message in the log file: Exception in a static block of jtf.cache.CacheManager. The stack trace is:

Oracle.apps.jtf.base.resources.FrameworkException:

IAS Cache initialization failed.

The Distributed Caching System failed to initialize on port: 78912.

The list of hosts in the distributed caching system is [node 1] [node 2].

The port [port no] should be free on each host running the JVMs.

At Oracle.apps.jtf.cache.IASCacheProvider.init(IASCacheProvider.java:214)

At Oracle.apps.jtf.cache.CacheManager.activateCache(CacheManager.java:1451)

In this scenario, s_java_object_cache_port value was listening on node 2 but not on node 1. So whichever connection went to node 1, it returned a blank page and occasionally it displayed 500 Internal Server error.

Solution: Autoconfig

Bring down opmn services on both the boxes.

Verify no process is listening for s_java_object_cache_port value. command: lsof -i tcp:[port number]

Change s_java_object_cache_port on all the nodes in the context file

Run autoconfig

Non-Autoconfig

s_java_object_cache_port value is referrenced in two places

1. $INST_TOP/ora/10.1.3/javacache/admin/javacache.xml

2. Profile option name JTF_DIST_CACHE_PORT

Change the port value to a new number and bounce opmnctl services. Don't forget to change it in $CONTEXT_FILE. (To take effect during next autoconfig)

Case 6. Missing class files in the OA_HTML directory.

1. We can see the error given below in OACORE application.log file

   javax.servlet.ServletException: Oracle.classloader.util.

   AnnotatedClassNotFoundException: Missing class: _AppsLocalLogin

Please perform the below steps:

☐ Shutdown the application services

☐ Compile the jsp's manually using the below command:

```
perl $FND_TOP/patch/115/bin/ojspCompile.pl -compile -flush -p 2
```
☐ Check whether all the jsp's are getting compiled successfully

- ☐ Restart the application services
- ☐ Clear the browser cache
- ☐ Try to open the R12 Login page

AppsLocalLogin?.jsp page was displaying errors

Solution:

- ☐ Edited the $IAS_ORACLE_HOME/Apache/Jserv/etc/jserv.properties
- ☐ Set wrapper.bin.parameters=-DLONG_RUNNING_JVM=false
- ☐ Add the line wrapper.bin.parameters=-DCACHEMODE=LOCAL
- ☐ Restarted Apache for these changes to take effect and retested the issue

Case 7: The instance is very slow or inaccessible.

First, check whether it happening only for particular users or all the EBS users.

In case it happened for all the users, then we have to look into the DB & Application performance.

In case it happened only for a particular user or user group then:

1. Local network connection
2. Browser cache
3. Crosscheck whether FND: Debug trace was enabled at the user level.

   Change the following values to 'No' for the user.

```
FND: Debug Log Enabled — No
FND: Debug Log Level — ( Blank )
FND: Debug Log Module — ( Blank )
SLA: Enable Diagnostics — No
FND Validation Level — None
```

Case 8: Database Listeners are down. Start the database listener to resolve this error.

Reference: RFC 2068 Hypertext Transfer Protocol -- | Oracle Community.
https://community.Oracle.com/thread/2389695

TOPIC

6

FORMS SERVICES FAILURE

Adoafmctl.sh Failed To Start Managed Process After The Maximum Retry Limit.

Most of the DBAs faced this error while starting Adoafmctl.sh failed once after clone or existing instance. There are many reasons for the failing services. Here we are going to cover a few of the scenarios that are most commonly faced by the DBAs.

Scenario 1: Adoafmctl.sh failed to start a managed process after the maximum retry limit

In version 12.1.3, IAS for Applications Technology when attempting to start oafm with $ADMIN_SCRIPTS_HOME/adoafmctl.sh start,

The following error occurs. The issue has the resulting business impact. Due to this issue, users cannot start OAFM service successfully.

11/09/19-05:23:11: adoafmctl.sh: Starting OPMN managed OAFM OC4J instance

opmnctl: starting opmn managed processes...

```
===================================================================
opmn id=xxxxxx.xxxxx.com:xxxx
 0 of 1 processes started.

ias-instance id=PROD_xxxxx.xxxxx.xxxxx.com
+++++++++++++++++++++++++++++++++++++++++++++++++++++++++++++++++++
-------------------------------------------------------------------
ias-component/process-type/process-set:
 default_group/oafm/default_group/

Error
--> Process (index=1,uid=189695577,pid=36855)
```

```
failed to start a managed process after the maximum retry limit
Log:
/doyen/inst/apps/TEST_xxxxx/logs/ora/10.1.3/opmn/default_group~oaf
m~default_group~1.log


11/09/19-05:24:46 :: adoafmctl.sh: exiting with status 204
====================================================================
```

After checking $LOG_HOME/ora/10.1.3/opmn/oafm_default_group_1/, and found below error message:

```
FileName = oafmstd.out
  11/09/19 05:23:01 Oracle Containers for J2EE 10g (10.1.3.5.0)
initialized
11/09/19 05:23:04 Shutting down...
11/09/19 05:23:24 INFO: SecuritySensitive.lookupException
Malformatted credentials for user ASADMIN. Please check your JAZN
repository; the password is not available for an indirect password
via application context (user: oc4jkeystoreadmin)
11/09/19 05:23:36 Fatal error: server exiting
11/09/19 05:23:39 INFO: SecuritySensitive.lookupException
Malformatted credentials for user ASADMIN. Please check your JAZN
repository; the password is not available for an indirect password
via application context (user: oc4jkeystoreadmin)
11/09/19 05:23:49 Fatal error: server exiting
11/09/19 05:24:05 INFO: SecuritySensitive.lookupException
Malformatted credentials for user ASADMIN. Please check your JAZN
repository; the password is not available for an indirect password
via application context (user: oc4jkeystoreadmin)
11/09/19 05:24:45 Fatal error: server exiting
FileName = oafmstd.out
```

> 11/09/19 05:23:01 Oracle Containers for J2EE 10g (10.1.3.5.0) initialized
>
> 11/09/19 05:23:04 Shutting down...
>
> 11/09/19 05:23:24 INFO: SecuritySensitive.lookupException Malformatted credentials for user ASADMIN. Please check your JAZN repository; the password is not available for an indirect password via application context (user: oc4jkeystoreadmin)
>
> 11/09/19 05:23:36 Fatal error: server exiting
>
> 11/09/19 05:23:39 INFO: SecuritySensitive.lookupException Malformatted credentials for user ASADMIN. Please check your JAZN repository; the password is not available for an indirect password via application context (user: oc4jkeystoreadmin)
>
> 11/09/19 05:23:49 Fatal error: server exiting
>
> 11/09/19 05:24:05 INFO: SecuritySensitive.lookupException Malformatted credentials for user ASADMIN. Please check your JAZN repository; the password is not available for an indirect password via application context (user: oc4jkeystoreadmin)
>
> 11/09/19 05:24:45 Fatal error: server exiting

Cause: The issue is caused by missing the exclamation mark (!) of user ASADMIN.

The issue can be checked with

```
$ORA_CONFIG_HOME/10.1.3/j2ee/oafm/config/system-jazn-data.xml
<user>
<name>ASADMIN</name>
<display-name>Default Apps SOA User</display-name>
<description>Used by SOAProvider for DB connection</description>
<credentials>asadmin</credentials>
</user>
```

Solution: First take backup of $ORA_CONFIG_HOME/10.1.3/j2ee/oafm/config/system-jazn-data.xml and then manually edit the system-jazn-data.xml file and change the following section for the ASADMIN user:

```
FROM:
    <user>
<name>ASADMIN</name>
<display-name>Default Apps SOA User</display-name>
<description>Used by SOAProvider for DB connection</description>
<credentials>asadmin</credentials>
</user>
TO:
<user>
<name>ASADMIN</name>
<display-name>Default Apps SOA User</display-name>
<description>Used by SOAProvider for DB connection</description>
<credentials>!asadmin</credentials>
</user>
```

NOTE: The change is adding the exclamation mark (!) "!" before the password.

Then try starting OAFM and check the results; the OAFM services will be up and running.

Best Practices:

1. It is mandatory to change ADADMIN password for only those using SOA in their environment; reset does not request to change the password.

2. Leave a comment line in the file that insists to add an exclamation mark (!) "!" before the password.

Scenario 2: While starting OPMNCTL services OC4J:oafm services were not starting up, it will be in the status "Init" for some time after timeout it will fail.

The following error occurs. The issue has the following business impact. Due to this issue, users cannot start OAFM service successfully.

Processes in Instance: TEST_doyen.doyen.doyensys.com

```
----------------------------------+-------------------+---------+-
ias-component                     | process-type      |     pid |
status    |           uid | memused |   uptime | ports
----------------------------------+-------------------+---------+-
OC4JGroup:default_group           | OC4J:oafm         |   88312 |
Init      | 1039750491 |    544712 |   0:05:21 | N/A
OC4JGroup:default_group           | OC4J:forms        |   77453 |
Alive     | 1039750490 |    620404 |   0:05:45 |
rmi:20505,jms:23505,ajp:22005
OC4JGroup:default_group           | OC4J:oacore       |   36770 |
Alive     | 1039750489 |    433284 |   0:09:02 |
rmi:20006,jms:23006,ajp:21506
OC4JGroup:default_group           | OC4J:oacore       |   16774 |
Alive     | 1039750488 |    157468 |   0:09:02 |
rmi:20005,jms:23005,ajp:21505
HTTP_Server                       | HTTP_Server       |   86727 |
Alive     | 1039750487 |    832264 |   0:05:43 |
https1:3333,http1:8003
```

After some time OC4J:oafm will be down.

Processes in Instance: SID_machine.machine.domain

```
--------------------+-------------------+---------+---------------
ias-component       | process-type | pid    | status
--------------------+-------------------+---------+---------------
OC4JGroup:default_group  | OC4J:oafm    | N/A | Down
```

Log:

```
$INST_TOP/apps/SID_machine/logs/ora/10.1.3/opmn/default_group~oafm
~default_group~1
```

Error

--> Process (index=1,uid=349189076,pid=15039)

time out while waiting for a managed process to start

12/09/19-06:13:11 :: adoafmctl.sh: exiting with status 152

Cause: Existing JSP Tag Library Cache content was preventing the TLD Cache for the map viewer app from initializing correctly.

Solution: To implement the solution test the following steps:

1. Clear the TLD cache:

2. Stop all middle-tier services.

3. Delete/backup the file:

$COMMON_TOP/_TldCache

4. Start OPMNCTL services and re-test.

The above steps will fix the issue; in some cases once after clearing cache file problem still exists.

For those environments, we have followed the steps below to fix the issue.

1. Stop all the application services.

2. Clear persistence cache.

```
rm -fr $INST_TOP/ora/10.1.3/j2ee/oacore/persistence/*
rm -fr $INST_TOP/ora/10.1.3/j2ee/oafm/persistence/*
rm -fr $INST_TOP/ora/10.1.3/j2ee/forms/persistence/*
```

3. Run autoconfig.

4. Start the application services

Best Practices:

1. Shutdown all the services completely, kill all died pid and defunct session before starting the services.

2. Clear persistence.

Reference:

Adoafmctl.sh Failed To Start A Managed Process After The ....
https://support.Oracle.com/knowledge/Oracle%20E-Business%20Suite/1599784_1.html

ROLE-BASED ACCESS

Role-based access – with example

There are times you might have noticed in R12 that users cannot view others report or program output.

This is because of RBAC (Role-Based Access Control) concept newly introduced in R12.

Here we can discuss in detail when trying to View a Concurrent Request Output as a user other than the user who submitted the request in R12 and also the solution for the same.

We need to know about RBAC before we learn about the problem.

To quickly know about RBAC, we need to learn about Function Security and Data Security.

Function Security

Function Security

Function Security Layer

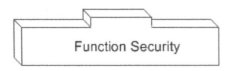

Function Security

Function security is the base layer of access control in the E-business suite. It restricts the user access to individual menus or menu functions but does not have control on retrieving the data.

For example, an organization could use function security to provide the sales team with necessary menus and menu functions for querying customer details. Note that it does not restrict the data in querying customers.

Data Security

Data Security Layer

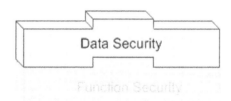

Data security is the next layer of access control as it is built on top of functional security as it provides control within E-business suite on the data a user can access. It restricts access to individual data that is displayed on the screen once the user has selected menu and menu options.

Role Based Access Control Layer

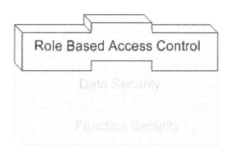

RBAC is the next layer and builds upon Data Security and Function Security. With RBAC, access control is defined through roles, and user access to Oracle E-Business Suite is determined by the roles granted to the user.

A role can be configured to consolidate the responsibilities, permissions, function security and data security policies that users require to perform a specific function.

Starting with R12, 'View Output' button greyed out when trying to view a concurrent request output file as privileges to report output files and log files generated by a concurrent program are controlled using Role-Based Access (RBAC) model.

Let's create a role in R12 so that users can view others' output. User should have the same responsibility which the other user used to submit that report.

As SYSADMIN user with "Functional Developer" responsibility, Search for object Concurrent Requests.

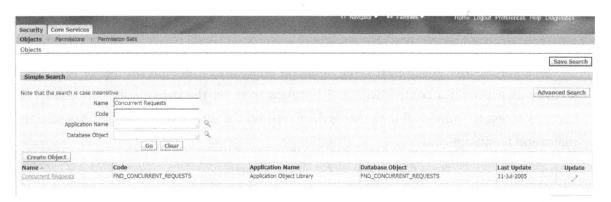

```
Click on Concurrent Requests.
Click on Object Instance Sets tab.
Click on Create Instance Set button.
Enter Name, Code and Description for new instance set as below.
Name        : Request Output Of The Same Responsibility
Code        :  FND_CONC_OUTPUT
Description     : Request Output Of The Same Responsibility
 - Enter the following for predicate:
&TABLE_ALIAS.request_id in (select cr.request_id from
fnd_concurrent_requests cr where
```

```
cr.responsibility_id = fnd_global.resp_id and
cr.responsibility_application_id =
fnd_global.resp_appl_id)
```

And then apply.

2. As the SYSADMIN user with "User Management", go to Roles and Role Inheritance tab.

Create a Role as below.

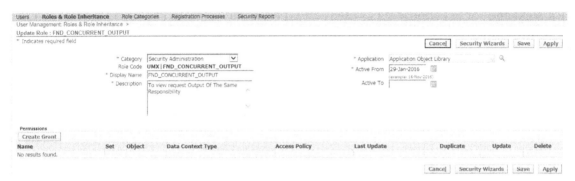

And then click 'SAVE'

And on the same page then create a Grant for the Role.

Enter Name and Description for the new Grant.

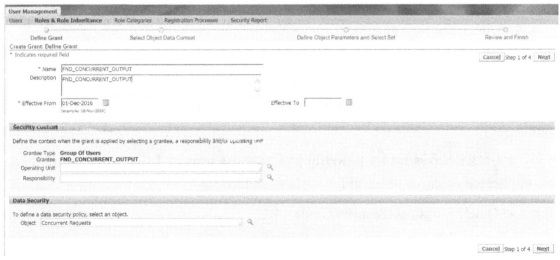

Click Next and provide the below details

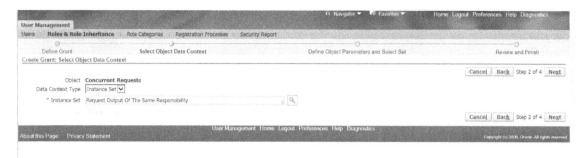

Click Next and for Set choose set as 'Request Operations'.

And then click Next and finish.

Now, you can assign this role to anyone who wants to view the users' output provided the responsibilities are available with them. These roles are very helpful for administrators or L3/L4 team so that they can work on any issues related to others' program.

Role-based access is very powerful and provides security for any organization and also complies with security policy at the application level.

Reference: Oracle E-business Security Guide – R12.

TOPIC

FIND AND ANALYSE A PARTICULAR SESSION IN ORACLE

Find and analyse a particular session in Oracle.

The subject might look trivial for seniors, but I have seen that most of the DBAs struggle to find a session if someone comes to you seeking help about that Oracle session. I have seen many DBAs struggle a lot when there are no tools available for them to monitor the database.

Let's say some applications team reaches you to find the Oracle session that application connected and asking to kill the session related to those applications.

If you rely on pure custom SQLs, here is the place to find how to use them and analyse those SQL sessions.

If you know SQL, then it might be easy to find any session from gv$session. Let's say if you don't have SQL, then you might need to look into the below columns in GV$session.

```
MACHINE - The name of the machine where the client is running.  If
you are connected to the database using your machine, then it will
show your machine name in this column.
MODULE - Name of the currently executing module.  It shows "SQL
Developer" if you connected to the database using "SQL Developer".
PROGRAM - OS program name.
OSUSER - OS username of the machine.
USERNAME - Oracle Username that connected.
CLIENT_IDENTIFIER - Client identifier of the session
PROCESS - OS process of the machine
```

LOGON_TIME - Logon time of the session.

You should get minimum details of the machine and username from the application team so that you can check against those columns in GV$Session.

Next step is to interpret the **module** and **program** for that particular process. For instance, for concurrent programs the **module** will be the short name of the concurrent program executable and **program** will show the manager short name.

Finally, the easiest way to find any process is just to grep the process number in the machine name and you can check whether it belongs to frmweb(forms) process or java (concurrent program) or anything else. The above columns are more than enough to interpret the session details.

For example,

```
applmgr@prodapp:~ $ ps -ef|grep 3324
applmgr   3324 12774  0 19:09?            00:00:09
/prod/apps/tech_st/10.1.2/bin/frmweb server webfile=HTTP-
0,0,1,default,10.130.65.28
```

By looking at this process, we could understand this process belongs to form sessions. (As it shows frmweb). Now, that is easy. How about the following one?

```
applmgr@prodapp:~ $ ps -ef|grep 26134
applmgr  18526 10890  0 21:09 pts/0     00:00:00 grep 26134
applmgr  26134     1  0 Sep06 ?         00:02:26
/prod/apps/tech_st/10.1.3/appsutil/jdk/bin/java -
DCLIENT_PROCESSID=26134 -server -Xmx384m -XX:NewRatio=2 -
XX:+UseSerialGC -DOracle.apps.fnd.common.Pool.leak.mode=stderr:off
-verbose:gc -
Ddbcfile=/prod/inst/apps/PROD_prodapp/appl/fnd/12.0.0/secure/PROD.
dbc -Dcpid=901581 -Dconc_queue_id=1140 -Dqueue_appl_id=0 -
Dlogfile=/prod/csf/applcsf/log/PROD_prodapp/FNDCPGSC901581.txt -
DLONG_RUNNING_JVM=true -DOVERRIDE_DBC=true -DFND_JDBC_BUFFER_MIN=1
-DFND_JDBC_BUFFER_MAX=2
Oracle.apps.fnd.cp.gsm.GSMSvcComponentContainer
applmgr@prodapp:~ $
```

By looking at the process, one may have much confusion on what this process about. Is this related to any java process or any other application process? Well if you read the process line by line, you could see -Dconc_queue_id= 1140. Looking at this, it gives us some hint about the concurrent manager related process. Let get these details from FND_CONCURRENT_QUEUES using the queue id. Now you will get the manager name.

```
SQL> select CONCURRENT_QUEUE_ID,CONCURRENT_QUEUE_NAME from
fnd_concurrent_queues where CONCURRENT_QUEUE_ID=1140;

CONCURRENT_QUEUE_ID CONCURRENT_QUEUE_NAME
------------------- -------------------------------
               1140 WFMLRSVC
```

Now, this does look like the short name of the concurrent manager. Well, let's query from FND_CONCURRENT_QUEUES_VL view which will give the concurrent manager name.

```
SQL> select USER_CONCURRENT_QUEUE_NAME , CONCURRENT_QUEUE_ID from
fnd_concurrent_queues_vl where CONCURRENT_QUEUE_ID=1140;
USER_CONCURRENT_QUEUE_NAME
CONCURRENT_QUEUE_ID
-------------------------------------------------- ----------------
Workflow Mailer Service                                        1140
```

There you go. This process belongs to "Workflow Mailer Service". If you still need to verify it, let us get that verified too from the front end.

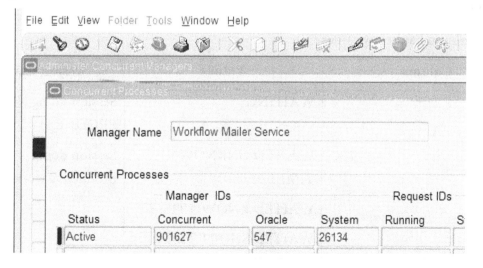

Once you interpret the session, you will be able to easily make some decision about the Oracle session or process for the next course of action. Now you have learned to identify the UNIX process and Oracle session.

Let us see what the Oracle session is doing in the database.

An Oracle Database session is always in one of three states:

1. **Idle.** Not doing anything—just waiting to be given some work.

2. **Processing.** Doing something useful—running on the CPU.

3. **Waiting.** Waiting for something, such as a block to come from disk or a lock to be released.

Idle	Session not doing anything and it is waiting to be given some work
Processing	Doing some productive work and it is running on CPU
Waiting	Waiting for something such as a lock on the object to be released.

Idle – The session is not slow; rather, it has nothing to do and it is simply idle.

Processing – It is neither waiting nor idle. It is doing some productive work.

Waiting – The session is waiting for some work to be completed such as a lock to be released so that this session can run.

Now, we understood the state of the session and that can be interpreted in STATE column in V$SESSION.

STATE column has below values

Column	Values	Session state
STATE	WAITING	Session doing NON PRODUCTIVE work
	WAITED UNKNOWN TIME WAITED KNOWN TIME WAITED SHORT TIME	Session doing productive work

To get meaningful details after referring the state column, you should combine with EVENT column to know about what the session is doing.

Event column will have many event details and give you information what the session is waiting for.

For example, STATE column is showing Waiting and EVENT column shows "enq: TX - row lock contention" which means it is waiting for some object lock to be released. Once released, it will start doing productive work.

Another example is STATE column showing "WAITED KNOWN TIME" and EVENT column shows "SQL*Net message from client" which means the session is doing productive work now and it was waiting for some data to be returned from the client.

Therefore, now you have almost all the details of the session. Ah! One thing is missing. How long has the session been waiting/waited and what is it doing? To get these details, we need to look into SECONDS_IN_WAIT column of GV$SESSION.

We must look at the STATE column first to identify the session is waiting or doing some work and then look at the SECONDS_IN_WAIT column to find the length of the wait time. When the session of the STATE column indicates any productive work (STATE column has other than WAITING), then we must look at the WAIT TIME in GV$SESSION. Note that WAIT TIME in GV$SESSION is shown in centiseconds (hundredths of a second). You must divide the WAIT TIME value by 100 to get timing details in SECONDS.

Let us tabulate the above discussion.

Column	Values	Session state	TIME
STATE	WAITING	Session doing NON-PRODUCTIVE work	SECONDS_IN_WAIT
	WAITED UNKNOWN TIME WAITED KNOWN TIME WAITED SHORT TIME	Session doing productive work	WAIT_TIME/100

Conclusion

In this article, we presented how to find a particular session and examine whether it is doing productive or non-productive work, as also, the length of the time of session doing productive or non-productive work. It is easy to understand any process of Oracle session and it is very crucial to analyse the Oracle session before taking any action on that particular session.

TOPIC

9

EASY WAY TO IMPORT USER ACCOUNT FROM AD TO ORACLE EBS USING A COMMAND LINE

Environment implemented with Oracle SSO for EBS login has not counted on this kind of issue. User account will migrate from AD to EBS using DIP configuration. DIP will sync the user account in a scheduled interval. Due to some technical reason, for some time the DIP will not sync some user account to EBS. It becomes a major headache to most of the DBAs. Here we have explained how to import the user account from AD to EBS using the command line.

Just 4four easy commands to import user account from AD to Oracle EBS. Search the user account in AD using LDAPSEARCH and create a template file with LDIF file format and import the LDIF file to Oracle Directory Services Manager (ODSM) using LDAPADD. Migrate user to Oracle EBS using Java command.

LDAPSEARCH

Use the command-line tool ldapsearch to search for specific entries in a directory. ldapsearch opens a connection to a directory, authenticates the user performing the operation, searches for the specified entry or using SAM account name, and prints the result in a format that the user specifies.

Syntax:

```
ldapsearch -h AD-host -p 389 -D
"CN=admin,CN=Users,DC=ch,DC=doyen,DC=com" -w "xxxxxx" -b
"CN=USERS,dc=ch,dc=doyen,dc=com" -s sub samaccountname="gokulr"
```

☐ This command searches the directory server myhost, located at port 389.

- ☐ The bind -D the user authenticating to the directory.

- ☐ The bind -b directory searched is the base DN designated.

- ☐ The bind -w Wallet location for one or two-way SSL authentication

- ☐ The bind -s search scope.

Example:

```
ldapsearch -h test.doyensys.com -p 389 -D
"CN=SSOTEST,CN=Users,DC=ch,DC=doyen,DC=com" -w "xxxxxx" -b
"CN=USERS,dc=ch,dc=doyen,dc=com" -s sub samaccountname="gokulr"
```

Create template using LDIF file format

Grep the AD search output and create a template file using LDIF format to load into ODSM.

```
dn:
cn=Radhakrishnan_Gokulkumar,cn=users,cn=adch,cn=users,dc=doyen,dc=
com
displayname: Radhakrishnan Gokulkumar
orclsamaccountname: gokulr
modifytimestamp: 20190801010710984
objectclass: inetorgperson
objectclass: organizationalperson
objectclass: posixAccount
objectclass: shadowAccount
objectclass: person
objectclass: top
createtimestamp: 20190801074650Z
uid: gokulr
mail: Gokulkumar.Radhakrishnan@doyensys.com
cn: Radhakrishnan_Gokulkumar
orclguid: 0701198420081991
physicaldeliveryofficename: CHENNAI,TN
krbprincipalname: gokulr@ch.doyensys.com
modifiersname: cn=orcladmin
creatorsname: cn=orcladmin
```

```
manager:
cn=Chockalingam_Somu,cn=users,cn=adch,cn=users,dc=doyen,dc=com
orclsourceobjectdn:
CN=Radhakrishnan_Gokulkumar,CN=Users,DC=ch,DC=doyen,DC=com
orclnormdn:
cn=radhakrishnan_gokulkumar,cn=users,cn=adch,cn=users,dc=doyen,dc=
com
orcluserprincipalname: gokulr
employeenumber: 10196
description: Principal Consultant
sn: Radhakrishnan
```

Import to ODSM using ldapadd

On confirmation that the user account exists in the AD the next step is to import the user account to Oracle Directory Services Manager (ODSM)

Syntax:

```
ldapadd -h {sso host} -p {port} -D  "cn=user" -w "password" -f
zzzzz.ldif
```

Example:

```
ldapadd -h testsso.doyensys.com -p 3060 -D "cn=ssoadmin" -w
"xxxxxx" -f gokulr.ldif
```

Using this command, user ssoadmin authenticates to the directory myhost, located at port 3060. The command then opens the file gokulr.ldif and adds its contents to the directory

Migrate User to EBS:

Copy the LDIF file from ODSM server to Oracle EBS Application server and execute the java command below to create the user account in EBS. Login into the application and verify the user in EBS.

Syntax:

Java Oracle.apps.fnd.oid.LDAPUserImport v -dbc {dbc file with path} –d –f {ldif file} –n uid -tcaRecord N -defresp

Example:

Java Oracle.apps.fnd.oid.LDAPUserImport -v -dbc $FND_SECURE/TEST.dbc -d -f /tmp/gokulr.ldif -n uid -tcaRecord N -defresp N

LDAPUserImport– Command line utility to read LDIF file (this file comes from OID containing users and their attribute). This is Java-class file available under $JAVA_TOP/Oracle/apps/fnd/oid

Best practices:

1. Apply the latest SSO patches to fix DIP sync issue.

2. Take comparisons report from AD to EBS to crosscheck whether all are in sync.

Reference:

LDAP Command-Line Tools - docs.Oracle.com.

https://docs.Oracle.com/cd/A97630_01/network.920/a96579/comtools.htm

TOPIC

10

TROUBLESHOOTING OATS

TROUBLESHOOTING COMMON ISSUES – ORACLE APPLICATION TESTING SUITE (OATS)

Oracle Application Testing Suite – is a comprehensive and integrated testing solution that helps you to define and manage the testing the application and validating the application functionality.

It includes the following products:

Oracle Functional Testing: Automated functional and regression testing of web applications. For functional testing of Oracle-packaged application like EBS, there is a separate product called "*Oracle Functional Testing Suite for Oracle Applications*".

Oracle Load Testing: Scalability, Performance and load testing of Web Applications.

Oracle Test Manager: Test process management, including test requirements management, test management, test execution and defect tracking.

In this chapter we are not going to show you the installation steps or how to set up; Instead of that, we are going to see some basic information about OATS, Log files location and Known issues which we have come across.

If you are logged in to the server where OATS is installed and if you want to see where OATS is installed, this is the command to find the OATS_HOME

```
cat /etc/rc.d/init.d/OracleATSServer |grep OATS_HOME|head -1
```

This is the list of application which comes by default when you install OATS. We have listed the URL details. Localhost will be replaced with hostname with a domain name.

Login page and default login details of Oracle Load Testing tool
http://localhost:8088/olt
administrator/master password (provided at the time of installation)

OATS console page and default login details
http://localhost:8088/console
oats/ master password (provided at the time of installation)

Login page and default login details of OTM
http://localhost:8088/otm
administrator/ master password (provided at the time of installation)

Login page and default login details of Admin
http://localhost:8088/admin
administrator/ master password (provided at the time of installation)

Before looking into the common issues, let us learn startup and shutdown sequence. We have included the sequence if you have root user credentials and if you don't have root user credentials.

If you have root access

Login as root

Shutdown sequence (DB Part excluded):
cd /etc/rc.d/init.d/
./OracleATSHelper stop
./OracleATSAgent stop
./OracleATSServer stop

Startup Sequence (DB Part excluded) :
cd /etc/rc.d/init.d/
./OracleATSServer start
./OracleATSAgent start
./OracleATSHelper start

If you don't have root access

Shutdown sequence (DB Part excluded):

cd $OATS_HOME/helperService/bin

```
./helperservice.sh stop

cd $OATS_HOME/agentmanager/bin
./agentmanager.sh stop

export MW_HOME=$OATS_HOME/wls
. $OATS_HOME/wls/wlserver/server/bin/setWLSEnv.sh
cd $OATS_HOME/oats/bin
./stopWebLogic.sh
```

Startup sequence (DB Part excluded):

```
export MW_HOME=$OATS_HOME /wls
. $OATS_HOME/wls/wlserver/server/bin/setWLSEnv.sh
cd $OATS_HOME/oats/bin
./startWebLogic.sh

cd $OATS_HOME/agentmanager/bin
./agentmanager.sh start

cd $OATS_HOME/helperService/bin
./helperservice.sh start
```

The first step in troubleshooting is to know the problem. To know the problem we should be familiar with the log file location. We have collated all log files location and listed below.

Installation log files

```
$OATS_HOME/logs/ (INSTALL_DIR will be provided at the time of
installation)

initConfig.log      - OatsConfigurationManager log
dbsetup.log         - Database setup log (creating
oats/olt/otm schemas and its log files)
config_ds.log   - Configuring data sources logs
unpack.log          - oats domain unpack log
storeUser.log   - creating the key file
deploy.log          - log files to deploy application called
OATS_EE
config_sec.log      - log deploy application called OATS_EE
```

```
ATSHelperInstall.log - ATSHelper install log
AgentInstall.log    - OATS agent install log
agentmanager_auth.log - Install OracleATSServer service logs
wls_oats.log        - oats run time log
```

OATS applications run time logs

```
$OATS_HOME/oats/servers/AdminServer/logs
AdminServer.log - Admin server log files.
oats.log - OATS application logs files. (OATS is the application which
deployed in the Admin servers)
```

Common Issues:

Issue 1: When we try to start OracleATSServer as root user and get the error below.

```
[root@ip-172-31-31-75 init.d]# ./OracleATSServer start
```

OracleATSServer dead but pid file exists

Solution:

1. Clear /var/run/OracleATSServer.pid file as root and start OracleATSServer again.

   ```
   rm -rf /var/run/OracleATSServer.pid
   ```

2. Start the OATS services again

   ```
   [root@hostanme init.d]# ./OracleATSServer start
   ```

Issue 2: When you restart OATS, sometimes we will be able to open the console but none of the applications olt, otm and admin URL is working and we are getting the error below.

Error 404--Not Found

From RFC 2068 Hypertext Transfer Protocol -- HTTP/1.1:

10.4.5 404 Not Found

Cause: oats_ee – Deployment might have stopped working: to check the status of application deployment

login to console

```
http://localhost:8088/console
```

1. On left-hand side, under Domain Structure, click Deployments

2. Now check name called oats_ee, Deployment State should be Active and Health should OK, if not:

3. Try to start the Deployment.

   Click checkbox of the Deployment (oats_ee) -> Start-> servicing all requests

   If the OATS_EE failed to start, then possible causes are given below.

4. Database connectivity.

5. Check any errors in the database.

6. Try connecting as oats/olt/otm in the database.

7. Check any error in the log

```
$OATS_HOME/oats/servers/AdminServer/logs
AdminServer.log and oats.log
$OATS_HOME/logs/
wls_oats.log
```

8. Still, if you see the issue, then another workaround would be to redeploy the oats_ee.

We have covered some basic information about OATS and common issues. Hope this information helped you to manage OATS application.

Happy Troubleshooting!!!

TOPIC

11

APEX XDB SECURITY ISSUES

APEX Application XDB security issue

In this chapter, we are going to see the issues faced while accessing apex after migrating the Apex application from one database to another database. We can come across this error even during the fresh installation of Apex.

Let us see the cause of the error and possible solutions:

"The server is asking for your user name and password". "The server reports that it is from XDB".

Environment details: DB Version: 12.1.0.2

Apex version: 5.1 and configured using PL/SQL gateway.

Cause: Since we have used Embedded PL/SQL Gateway (the default setup for Express Edition) then we will be connected as ANONYMOUS database user in Apex. By default access to XML DB repository will be denied. So it is important to enable access to XML DB repository to ANONYMOUS user. This can be achieved by running the PL/SQL block below. Also, it is recommended to check the local_listener parameter and account status of ANONYMOUS user.

Possible Solutions: Verify whether local_the listener parameter is set. If not, set this parameter and register.

```
SQL>Alter system register
```

Make sure DB user ANONYMOUS account is unlocked.

```
SQL> select username, account_status from dba_users where username =
'ANONYMOUS'
```

Enable anonymous access to the XML DB repository

```
CONN sys/password AS SYSDBA
SET SERVEROUTPUT ON
DECLARE
l_configxml XMLTYPE;
l_value VARCHAR2(5) := 'true'; -- (true/false)
BEGIN
l_configxml := DBMS_XDB.cfg_get();
IF
l_configxml.existsNode('/xdbconfig/sysconfig/protocolconfig/httpconfig/al
low-repository-anonymous-access') = 0 THEN
-- Add missing element.
SELECT insertChildXML
(
l_configxml,
'/xdbconfig/sysconfig/protocolconfig/httpconfig',
'allow-repository-anonymous-access',
XMLType('' ||
l_value ||
''),
'xmlns="http://xmlns.Oracle.com/xdb/xdbconfig.xsd"'
)
INTO l_configxml
FROM dual;
DBMS_OUTPUT.put_line('Element inserted.');
ELSE
-- Update existing element.
SELECT updateXML
(
DBMS_XDB.cfg_get(),
'/xdbconfig/sysconfig/protocolconfig/httpconfig/allow-repository-
anonymous-access/text()',
l_value,
```

```
'xmlns="http://xmlns.Oracle.com/xdb/xdbconfig.xsd"'
)
INTO l_configxml
FROM dual;

DBMS_OUTPUT.put_line('Element updated.');

END IF;

DBMS_XDB.cfg_update(l_configxml);
DBMS_XDB.cfg_refresh;
END;
/
```

ORACLE CONNECTION ERRORS

Types of Oracle connection errors

Oracle NET Services provide enterprise-wide connectivity solutions in distributed, heterogeneous computing environments. Oracle Net Services ease the complexities of network configuration and management, maximizes performance, and improves network diagnostic capabilities.

In this chapter, we are going to see that database name resolves most Oracle connection issues. If your connection error requires more troubleshooting, refer to the five common connection errors listed below.

1. ORA-03113: end-of-file on communication channel

2. ORA-12154: Could Not Resolve The Connect Identifier Specified

3. ORA-12514: TNS listener does not currently know of service requested in connect descriptor: SERVICE value incorrect

4. ORA-12541: TNS: no listener: PORT value incorrect

5. ORA-12525: Listener Has Not Received Client's Request in Time Allowed

1. ORA-03113: end-of-file on communication channel

This message ORA-03113 indicates that an error has occurred on the database server. This error occurs due to the fact that your connection to the Oracle server is either no longer available, or the server couldn't respond to the client's requests. This is usually called an Oracle server issue or a networking issue. Check the ALERT_SID.log file on the server. An unexpected end of file was processed on the communication channel. This may be an indication that the communications link may have gone down at least temporarily, or it may indicate that the server has gone down. You can start troubleshooting by digging our Oracle server, Oracle Database, and Listener are each up and running. If everything is up and without errors, then try another client box, or at least make sure the error is happening for everyone.

100% Disk full on ORACLE_HOME or USER_DUMP_DEST location will indicate the same error.

Archive log desk 100% full, then we have to remove the old archive log file manually to start the DB again.

```
SQL> startup
ORACLE instance started.

Total System Global Area 4647483648 bytes
Fixed Size 2926472 bytes
Variable Size 2524738936 bytes
Database Buffers 108969664 bytes
Redo Buffers 17848576 bytes
Database mounted.
ORA-03113: end-of-file on communication channel
Process ID: 18757
Session ID: 753 Serial number: 46844
```

2. ORA-12154: Could Not Resolve the Connect Identifier Specified

This message ORA-12154 indicates that a connection to a database or other service was requested using a connect identifier, and the connect identifier specified could not be resolved into a connect descriptor using one of the naming methods configured. For example, if the type of connect identifier used was a network service name, then the network service name could not be found in a naming method repository, or the repository could not be located or reached. Perform the following:

3. Check the type of naming adapters listed in the NAMES.DIRECTORY_PATH parameter in the sqlnet.ora file. If none are configured, then use the adapters command to determine which adapters are in use. The following example shows

```
$ adapters ... Installed Oracle Net naming methods are
 Local Naming (tnsnames.ora)
Oracle Directory Naming
Oracle Host Naming
NIS Naming
```

The network service name given in the connect string should be defined for at least one of the naming methods.

4. Check the resolution path for each adapter for possible problems. For example, ensure that the name given in the connect string is correct and complete, using the full name of the network service if necessary.

Perform the steps depending on your naming methods:

a. ORA-12154: When using the Local Naming Method

b. ORA-12154: When using the Directory Naming Method

c. ORA-12154: When using the Easy Connect Naming Method

A. ORA-12154: When using the Local Naming Method

Perform the following steps when using the local naming method:

1. Verify that the tnsnames.ora file exists and is in the correct location. The location is either the ORACLE_HOME/network/admin directory or the directory specified by the TNS_ADMIN environment variable.

2. Verify there is an entry in the tnsnames.ora file for the name given in the connect string. This network service name should match the name in the tnsnames.ora file exactly if the name is simple and there is no NAMES_DEFAULT_DOMAIN in the sqlnct.ora file or the network service name is fully-qualified. If the network service name in the connect string is simple, then check the NAMES_DEFAULT_DOMAIN parameter in the sqlnet.ora file. Its value is appended to the network service name given in the connect string. This fully-qualified name should be the entry in the tnsnames.ora file.

3. If you are connecting from a login dialogue box, then verify that you are not placing an 'at' sign (@) before the connect network service name.

4. Activate client tracing, and repeat the operation.

B. ORA-12154: When using the Directory Naming Method

Perform the following steps when using the directory naming method:

Verify the ldap.ora file exists and is in the correct location. The following directories are searched for ldap.ora file in the order given. The ldap.ora file found will be used.

➢ The directory specified by the TNS_ADMIN environment variable.

➢ The ORACLE_HOME/network/admin directory.

➢ The directory specified by the LDAP_ADMIN environment variable.

➢ The ORACLE_HOME/ldap/admin directory.

Verify that the parameters defined in the ldap.ora file are correct, as follows:

➢ The DIRECTORY_SERVERS parameter defines the correct host and port for one or more valid LDAP servers.–The DEFAULT_ADMIN_CONTEXT parameter defines the location of the Oracle Context in this directory which should include the network service entry. If the ldap.ora file does not exist, then these parameters are resolved using automatic discovery.

➢ Verify that the LDAP server host and port are defined in DNS.

➢ Verify that the directory has the default Oracle Context defined.

➢ Use the ldapsearch utility or a directory administration tool to verify that the network service object exists in the Oracle Context at the location given by the value of the DEFAULT_ADMIN_CONTEXT parameter.

C. ORA-12154: When using the Easy Connect Naming Method

Verify that the hostname given is correct, and is defined in the local hostname resolution service, such as local hosts file, DNS, and so on.

D. ORA-12514: TNS listener does not currently know of service requested in connect descriptor: SERVICE value incorrect

This message ORA-12514 indicates that the listener received a request to establish a connection to a database or other service. The connect descriptor received by the listener specified a service name for a service (usually a database service) that is either not yet dynamically registered with the listener or has not been statically configured for the listener. This may be a temporary condition such as after the listener has started, but before the database instance has registered with the listener.

Perform the following steps

➢ Wait a moment, and then try to connect a second time

➢ Check which services are currently known by the listener by running the Listener Control utility STATUS or SERVICES command.

➢ Check that the SERVICE_NAME parameter in the connect descriptor specifies a service name known by the listener.

➢ Check for an event in the listener.log file.

E. ORA-12541: TNS: no listener: PORT value incorrect

These messages ORA-12541 indicate that the connection request could not be completed because the listener is not running.

Perform the following actions

➢ Ensure the supplied destination address matches one of the addresses used by the listener.

➢ Verify the listener is running at the address specified by the request.

➢ Ensure the listener is listening on the host and port specified by the request.

➢ Verify the client is pointing to the listener.

F. ORA-12525: Listener Has Not Received Client's Request in Time Allowed

This message ORA-12525 indicates that the client failed to complete its connect request in the time specified by the "INBOUND_CONNECT_TIMEOUT_listener_name" parameter in the listener.ora file.

This error may be a result of network or system delays, or it may indicate that a malicious client is trying to cause a denial-of-service attack on the listener.

If the error occurred due to system or network delays that are normal for the particular environment, then reconfigure the INBOUND_CONNECT_TIMEOUT_listener_name parameter in listener.ora to a larger value.

If you suspect a malicious client, then perform the following steps:

Locate the IP address of the client in the listener.log file to identify the source. Keep in mind that an IP address can be forged.

For example, the following listener.log file excerpt shows a client IP address of 192.0.1.110

```
18-SEP-2019 07:20:15
<unknown connect data>
(ADDRESS=(PROTOCOL=tcp)(HOST=192.0.1.110)(PORT=1521))
establish  <unknown sid>  12525
TNS-12525: TNS: listener has not received client's request in time
allowed
TNS-12604: TNS: Application timeout occurred
```

Restrict access to the client. You can configure parameters for access rights in the sqlnet.ora file.

Parameter	File	Description
INBOUND_CONNECT_TIMEOUT_listener_name	listener.ora	The time, in seconds, for the client to complete its connect request to the listener after the network connection had been established. If the listener does not receive the client request in the time specified, then it terminates the connection. In addition, the listener logs the IP address of the client and an ORA-12525: Listener Has Not Received Client's Request in Time Allowed error message to the listener.log file.

SQLNET.INBOUND_CONNECT_TIMEOUT	sqlnet.ora	The time, in seconds, for a client to connect with the database server and provide the necessary authentication information. If the client fails to establish a connection and complete authentication in the time specified, then the database server terminates the connection. In addition, the database server logs the IP address of the client and an ORA-12170: Connect Timeout Occurred error message to the sqlnet.log file. The client receives either an ORA-12547: TNS: lost contact, or an ORA-12637: Packet receive failed error message.

Example: Listener.ora: INBOUND_CONNECT_TIMEOUT_<listener_name>=240

sqlnet.ora: SQLNET.INBOUND_CONNECT_TIMEOUT=600

Reference: Introduction to Backup and Recovery - docs.Oracle.com.

https://docs.Oracle.com/cd/E11882_01/backup.112/e10642/rcmintro.htm

TROUBLE SHOOTING OEM TARGET DOWN AFTER AGENT UPGRADE FROM 12C TO 13C

Host Target Remains in Down Status in Enterprise Manager 13c Cloud Control and/or Host Metrics do not Collect (No Data Available)

By the time you upgrade your OEM Agent from 12c to 13c, you may notice that the physical host is up and running and when you discover that host in 13c OEM, the target will be in down status; this is due to a Bug which can be fixed with the workaround below.

Below are some of the behaviours of this issue

1. Enterprise Manager (EM) 13c Cloud Control (13.1 or 13.2) A host target (typically with an EM 13c Agent upgraded from 12c) either remains in DOWN status or is UP but does not collect any metrics.

2. All the charts on the Host target's homepage show "No Data Available".

3. The EM Agent which is monitoring the host shows a target status of Up.

4. Database targets on this host show a target status of Up.

5. Stopping and starting the upgraded EM 13c Agent will return the Host target status to up, but once the Host target is involved in a blackout, it is shown as down when the blackout is over.

What went wrong?

Bug 23046988 - Host Target status showing down

From the Host target's homepage, Host > Monitoring > Metric and Collection Settings

The Response metric has a comparison operator > (greater than) instead of = (equals), putting the target in CRITICAL state despite being up.

Normally, a target CRITICAL status is determined by: if Response = 0 mark target as CRITICAL where 0=DOWN and 1=UP

By having the wrong comparison operator, this becomes: if Response > 0 mark target as CRITICAL effectively reversing the logic and putting the target in the CRITICAL state when it's up.

Once the host target is in CRITICAL state, its metrics are no longer collected.

To obtain the state of the target:

```
<agent_inst>/bin/emctl getmetric agent <hostname>,host, Response
[Oracle@example ~]$ /u01/app/agent/agent_inst/bin/emctl getmetric agent
example.domain.com, host, Response
Oracle Enterprise Manager Cloud Control 13c Release 1
Copyright (c) 1996, 2015 Oracle Corporation. All rights reserved.

Status 1
Status 1 means the target is UP. If this shows 0, something else is
causing the host to show as Down, and this document is not applicable.
<agent_inst>/bin/emctl status agent target <hostname>,host
[Oracle@example ~]$ /u01/app/agent/agent_inst/bin/emctl status agent
target example.domain.com, host

Oracle Enterprise Manager Cloud Control 13c Release 1
Copyright (c) 1996, 2015 Oracle Corporation. All rights reserved.

-------------------------------------------------------------
Target Name: example.domain.com
Target Type: host
Current severity state
----------------------
Metric Column name Key State Timestamp
```

```
----------------------------------------------------------------
-------
DiskActivity DiskActivitybusy dm-0 CLEAR Sun Mar 03 18:54:42 MST 2019
... Response Statu n/a CRITICAL Sun Mar 03 19:07:08 MST 2019
```

It is this CRITICAL status that is causing the issue. If this says CLEAR, something else is causing the issue, and this document is not applicable.

How to Fix this Issue?

1. Download the workaround monitoring template *responsefix-host.zip* from (https://support.Oracle.com/epmos/main/downloadattachmentprocessor?parent= DOCUMENT&sourceId=2236697.1&attachid=2236697.1:RESPONSEFIXTEMPAL TE&clickstream=yes)

2. Import the template into EM Cloud Control as SYSMAN:

3. Enterprise > Monitoring > Monitoring Templates > Actions > Import

Step 1:

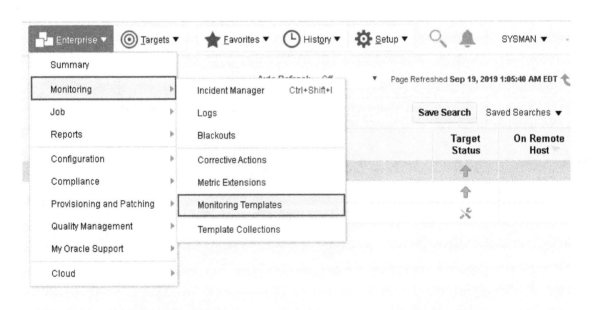

Step 2:

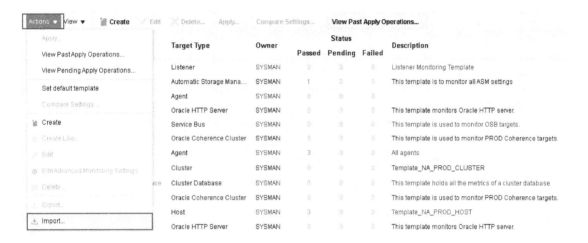

Step 3:

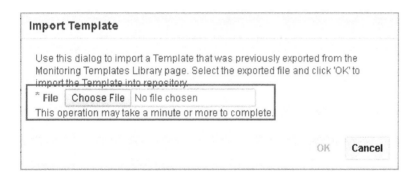

1. Apply the template to the problematic host target(s):
   - ☐ Select the responsefix template > Apply > (x) Template will only override metrics that are common to both template and target.

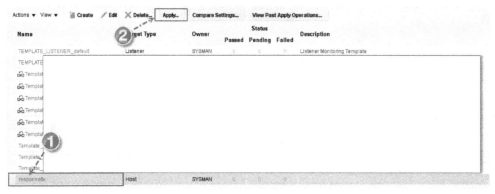

☐ **Destination Targets > Add > the host(s)**

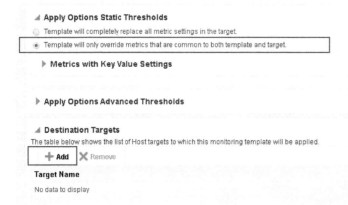

In most case the target status will be changed from down to up as soon as you add the host in the above step; if it is not changing the status you can go and restart the agent and upload the agent on the target host(s), which will fix the problem.

Reference: Oracle MOS Doc ID 2236697.1

BACKUP AND RECOVERY

Every Oracle database in an organization will have backup policies and backup methods. Every customer performs database recovery at some point in time. As a DBA, understanding these backup and recovery methods are necessary to devise a strategical backup approach for customers. This is very crucial to define one particular back method for all organization. Data of an organization is the most integral part of an organization. They all have extremely large amounts of data – user, system, etc. A DBA who has been assigned the job to protect this data should be aware of how important data is to an organization.

How do we make sure the data is always available to an organization?

Recovery Manager (RMAN) is an Oracle utility that can back up, restore, and recover database files. The product is a feature of the Oracle database server and does not require separate installation. RMAN uses database server sessions to perform backup and recovery. It stores metadata about its operations in the control file of the target database and, optionally, in a recovery catalogue schema in an Oracle database. RMAN has the ability to protect the database as a cold backup, hot backup of full RMAN or streaming backup is fully supported. DBAs can locate, recover and restore databases from backups that are stored in the disk or tape or cloud, using RMAN commands. RMAN can also be integrated with third-party backup software like Veritas NetBackup, Avamar, etc.

In this chapter, we are going to cover some basic methods of backups and recovery.

TOPIC 1	**Best Practices to improve backup and recovery performance**: This discusses the best practices of RMAN settings recommended by Oracle for better performance. Types of Backups: This chapter discusses types of backup. FULL BACKUP, INCREMENTAL BACKUP, DIFFERENTIAL INCREMENTAL BACKUP, & CUMULATIVE INCREMENTAL BACKUP
TOPIC 2	**Recover lost control file**: This will give you an idea about the control file and steps to recover both the control file and datafile from backup.
TOPIC 3	**Recover Dropped Tablespace Using Backup**: Human error is common and accidental tablespace drop may cost us huge. This discusses how to recover dropped tablespace from backup.
TOPIC 4	**Point in time Recovery**: This discusses the point in time recovery using SCN, time and log sequence which will help readers to quickly understand incomplete recovery.
TOPIC 5	**Standby database recovery by applying incremental**: This topic discusses the point in time recovery and gives a step-by-step example of recovering standby database using SCN backup.

TOPIC

1

BEST PRACTICES TO IMPROVE BACKUP AND RECOVERY PERFORMANCE

Backup and recovery process is one of the critical activities for Database Administrator and Performance of backup decided by many factors such as Hardware, disk speed, I/O and Media Manager Library if we choose Tape as a backup solution. Since many factors can affect the performance, finding a solution to a slow backup is a process of trial and error.

In this chapter, we are going to discuss the best practices to improve the RMAN backup performance.

As we mentioned above, to address slow backup is a trial-and-error method; so keep a record of backup timing with every change we do to address this performance issue. This will help us in making a decision.

Let us look at common factors that can improve the performance,

1. Best Practices to overcome RMAN Tape Performance Bottlenecks:

   a. BACKUP…VALIDATE command validate of a backup to tape performs the same disk reads as a real backup but will not perform any real disk I/O. If the actual time to take the backup to tape is higher, then backup validate of database backup taken in tape.

   b. Incremental Backup: Make sure we are taking incremental backup in the backup strategy. As we all know Incremental level 1 backups, write only the changed blocks from datafiles to tape, so that any bottleneck on writing to tape has less impact on your overall backup strategy.

2. RATE parameter:

This parameter controls the read bytes per second, and this help to free up disk bandwidth for other database operation. This parameter always affects backup performance and would like to suggest removing this parameter from "ALLOCATE CHANNEL" or "CONFIGURE CHANNEL" command if your backup is not going to Tape.

3. Disk I/O:

When an allocated channel reads from disk or writes to disk it uses either synchronous I/O or asynchronous I/O.

synchronous I/O – means server processes can perform only one task at a time.

asynchronous I/O – means, server processes can perform other work while waiting for the I/O to complete.

General suggestion to use asynchronous I/O for taking the backup: Sometimes Operating System may not support native async I/O; then use Oracle parameter DBWR_IO_SLAVES to enforce async I/O. When this parameter is set I/O buffers obtain SGA component LARGE_POOL; if LARGE_POOL is not configured, I/O buffers can be obtained from SHARED_POOL.

Suggestion:

a. Set DBWR_IO_SLAVES parameter to a nonzero value. Note that this is not a dynamic parameter.

b. Set BACKUP_TAPE_IO_SLAVES parameter to TRUE if you are using Tape as a backup solution.

c. Increase the processes parameter to a higher value.

d. Set LARGE_POOL_SIZE explicitly.

4. **Channel buffer size:**

RMAN channel buffer size managed by BLKSIZE and PARMS parameter in the channel configuration.

For Tape: Allocation Tape buffers play a major role in writing. By default, RMAN allocates four buffers for each channel for the tape writers. You can change this value BLKSIZE and PARMS parameter in the channel configuration.

For Disk: Allocation of Disk buffers major role in reading files from disk. Buffer calculation depends on how the files are multiplexes. See table below for general rules.

Level of Multiplexing	Input Disk buffer size
Less than or equal to 4	1MB channel buffer
Greater than 4 but less than or equal to 8	512 KB
Greater than 8	256 KB

5. RMAN other settings:

   a. **FILESPERSET** – This command specifies the maximum number of files in each backup set. This command plays a major role in RMAN multiplexing. The default value of FILESPERSET is 64, but we would like to suggest keeping lower values.

   b. **Number of channels** – This has to be calculated based on CPUs available in the database server. A general suggestion is to set the number of channels as four times the number of CPUs. For example, if the database server has 4 CPUs, then the number of channels can be 16. Please make sure we monitor CPU performance during the backup operation. If it is choking the server performance reduce this to some lower value and test.

6. Query v$views

   Both V$BACKUP_SYNC_IO and V$BACKUP_ASYNC_IO views will provide detailed information about backup processes.

   V$BACKUP_SYNC_IO – It contains rows when the I/O is synchronous to the process performing the backup.

   V$BACKUP_ASYNC_IO – It contains rows when the I/O is asynchronous to the process performing the backup.

Query to list Device type, Elapsed time, I/O rate achieved during the time of backup.

```
select device_type "Device", type, filename, to_char(open_time,
'mm/dd/yyyy hh24:mi:ss') open,
to_char(close_time,'mm/dd/yyyy hh24:mi:ss') close, elapsed_time ET,
effective_bytes_per_second EPS
from v$backup_async_io where close_time > sysdate - 1 order by close_time
desc;
```

The simplest way to identify the I/O bottleneck is to query V$BACKUP_ASYNC_IO or V$BACKUP_SYNC_IO for the datafile that has the largest ratio for LONG_WAITS divided by IO_COUNT.

```
select io_count , ready , short_waits , long_waits ,
long_waits/io_count , filename from v$backup_async_io ;
```

As mentioned at the beginning of this chapter, all these best practices are trial-and-error methods. So be extra cautious when you implement these best practices. Do monitor the system before and after the backup and come to a conclusion. Hope this document given some idea about improving the backup and recovery processes.

Reference: Advice on How to Improve RMAN Performance (Doc ID 579158.1)

http://cheatsheet4Oracledba.blogspot.com/2014/07/how-do-you-speed-up-restore-recovery-of.html

TOPIC

2

TYPES OF BACKUPS

Why Backup?

As a backup administrator, your primary job is making and monitoring backups for data protection. A backup is a copy of data of a database that you can use to reconstruct data. A backup can be either a physical backup or a logical backup.

Physical backups are copies of the physical files used in storing and recovering database. These files include datafiles, control files, and archived redo logs. Ultimately, every physical backup is a copy of files that store database information to another location, whether on disk or offline storage media such as tape.

Logical backups contain logical data such as tables and stored procedures. You can use Oracle Data Pump to export logical data to binary files, which you can later import into the database. The Data Pump command-line clients' expdp and impdp use theDBMS_DATAPUMP and DBMS_METADATA PL/SQL packages.

Physical backups are the foundation of any sound backup and recovery strategy. Logical backups are a useful supplement to physical backups in many circumstances but are not sufficient protection against data loss without physical backups.

Unless otherwise specified, the term backup as used in the backup and recovery documentation refers to a physical backup. Backing up a database is the act of making a physical backup. The focus in the backup and recovery documentation set is almost exclusively on physical backups.

While several problems can halt the normal operation of an Oracle Database or affect database I/O operations, only the following typically require DBA intervention and data recovery: media failure, user errors, and application errors. Other failures may require DBA intervention without causing data loss or requiring recovery from backup. For example, you may need to restart the database after an instance failure or allocate more disk space after statement failure because of a full datafile.

Disk Failures

Media failure is a physical problem with a disk that causes a failure of a read-from or write-to-a-disk file that is required to run the database. Any database file can be vulnerable to media failure. The appropriate recovery technique following a media failure depends on the files affected and the types of backup available. One particularly important aspect of backup and recovery is developing a disaster recovery strategy to protect against catastrophic data loss, for example, the loss of an entire database host.

Human error

User errors occur when, either due to an error in application logic or a manual mistake, data in a database is changed or deleted incorrectly. User errors are estimated to be the greatest single cause of database downtime. Data loss due to user error can be either localized or widespread. An example of localized damage is deleting the wrong person from the employees' table. This type of damage requires surgical detection and repair. An example of widespread damage is a batch job that deletes the company orders for the current month. In this case, drastic action is required to avoid an extensive database downtime.

While user training and careful management of privileges can prevent most user errors, your backup strategy determines how gracefully you recover the lost data when user error does cause data loss.

Application Errors

Sometimes a software malfunction can corrupt data blocks. In a physical corruption, which is also called a media corruption, the database does not recognize the block at all: The checksum is invalid, the block contains all zeros, or the header and footer of the block do not match. If the corruption is not extensive, then you can often repair it easily with block media recovery.

Data Archival

Data archival is related to data protection but serves a different purpose. For example, you may need to preserve a copy of a database as it existed at the end of a business quarter. This backup is not part of the disaster recovery strategy. The media to which these backups are written are often unavailable after the backup is complete. You may send the tape into fire storage or ship a portable hard drive to a testing facility. RMAN provides a convenient way to create a backup and exempt it from your backup retention policy. This type of backup is known as an archival backup.

RMAN Configurations

Using RMAN configuration we can configure the following parameters like retention policy, backup optimization, device type, auto backup, backup copies, backup encryption etc.

To view RMAN configurations

RMAN target /

```
SHOW ALL;

RMAN configuration parameters for database with db_unique_name PROD1 are:
CONFIGURE RETENTION POLICY TO RECOVERY WINDOW OF 3 DAYS;
CONFIGURE BACKUP OPTIMIZATION ON;
CONFIGURE DEFAULT DEVICE TYPE TO DISK; # default
CONFIGURE CONTROLFILE AUTOBACKUP ON;
CONFIGURE CONTROLFILE AUTOBACKUP FORMAT FOR DEVICE TYPE SBT_TAPE TO '%F'; # default
CONFIGURE CONTROLFILE AUTOBACKUP FORMAT FOR DEVICE TYPE DISK TO '%F'; # default
CONFIGURE DEVICE TYPE 'SBT_TAPE' PARALLELISM 2 BACKUP TYPE TO COMPRESSED BACKUPSET;
CONFIGURE DEVICE TYPF DISK PARALLELISM 1 BACKUP TYPE TO BACKUPSET; # default
CONFIGURE DATAFILE BACKUP COPIES FOR DEVICE TYPE SBT_TAPE TO 1; # default
CONFIGURE DATAFILE BACKUP COPIES FOR DEVICE TYPE DISK TO 1; # default
CONFIGURE ARCHIVELOG BACKUP COPIES FOR DEVICE TYPE SBT_TAPE TO 1; # default
CONFIGURE ARCHIVELOG BACKUP COPIES FOR DEVICE TYPE DISK TO 1; # default
CONFIGURE CHANNEL DEVICE TYPE 'SBT_TAPE' PARMS 'ENV=(OB_DEVICE=tape1)';
CONFIGURE MAXSETSIZE TO UNLIMITED; # default
CONFIGURE ENCRYPTION FOR DATABASE OFF; # default
CONFIGURE ENCRYPTION ALGORITHM 'AES128'; # default
CONFIGURE ARCHIVELOG DELETION POLICY TO NONE; # default
CONFIGURE SNAPSHOT CONTROLFILE NAME TO '/disk1/oracle/dbs/snapcf_ev.f'; # default
```

Different types of backup in RMAN

1. FULL BACKUP(INCONSISTENT AND CONSISTENT)
2. INCREMENTAL BACKUP
   a. LEVEL 0 INCREMENTAL BACKUP
   b. LEVEL 1 INCREMENTAL BACKUP
   c. DIFFERENTIAL INCREMENTAL BACKUP
   d. CUMULATIVE INCREMENTAL BACKUP

1. FULL BACKUP (INCONSISTENT):-

Full backup which backs up all the data blocks that contain data (ignores unused blocks) in the database, using full backup we can able to restore the database which might have minimal data loss, so it is also considered as an inconsistent backup.

BACKUP DATABASE

FULL BACKUP (CONSISTENT)

Full backup is that which backs up all the data blocks that contain data (ignores unused blocks);, for consistent backup we need to shut down the database and startup the database in mount stage and take full backup; in this case there won't be any data loss; so it is called s consistent backup.

BACKUP DATABASE;

1. INCREMENTAL BACKUP:-

An incremental backup is always the combination of level 0 and level 1 backup, an incremental backup will backup only those data that have changed since the previous backup; in this case, if we want to recover the database without any data loss, we need both the level 0 backup and level 1 backup.

A. LEVEL 0 INCREMENTAL BACKUP:-

Level 0 incremental backup is identically same as full backup, which will take the backup of each and every data block that contains data (ignores unused data blocks). The difference is that Level 0 is recorded as incremental backup in

RMAN, and it is the parent of level 1 incremental backup, using level 0 backup we can able to restore the database.

BACKUP INCREMENTAL LEVEL 0 DATABASE;

A. LEVEL 1 INCREMENTAL BACKUP:-

Level 1 incremental backup is always called as a dependent backup (depends on level 0 backup), because it will take the backup of data blocks changed since the previous backup.

Using level 1 backup we can recover the database.

BACKUP INCREMENTAL LEVEL 1 DATABASE

B. DIFFERENTIAL INCREMENTAL BACKUP:-

A differential incremental backup backs up all the data that changed since last incremental backup (which could be either level 0 backup or level 1 backup). In case of any data loss, we need both the level 0 and all the level 1 backups which we have taken previously.

BACKUP INCREMENTAL LEVEL 0 DATABASE

BACKUP INCREMENTAL LEVEL 1 DATABASE;

C. CUMULATIVE INCREMENTAL BACKUP:-

A cumulative incremental backup backs up all the data changed since most recent full backup (level 0 backup), in case of any data loss we need level 0 and the level 1 backup for the following day.

BACKUP INCREMENTAL LEVEL 0 DATABASE;

BACKUP INCREMENTAL LEVEL 1 CUMULATIVE DATABASE.

RMAN Best Practices:

1. Daily RMAN crosscheck: to ensure that backup pieces are available for restore.

2. Monthly restore validate with check logical: to confirm that a restore can be performed in the event of a disaster.

3. Quarterly Full Restore and Recovery: To test the DR strategy.

4. Use RMAN LOW or MEDIUM compression for optimal data transfers.

5. Increase PARALLELISM (until maximum network throughput is reached).

6. Refer to MOS Note 2078576.1 for performance investigation of backups.

7. Schedule archived logs' backup frequency to reduce RPO.

8. Run Installer once every two months to update to the latest RMAN SBT module.

9. Copy opc<SID>.orafile to other SIDs if same ORACLE_HOME is used by multiple databases.

10. Configure CONTROLFILE AUTOBACKUP ON.

11. This will enable the complete restoration of a database into a different host.

Reference: Introduction to Backup and Recovery - docs.Oracle.com.

https://docs.Oracle.com/cd/E11882_01/backup.112/e10642/rcmintro.htm

TOPIC

3

RECOVER LOST CONTROL FILE

Easy methods to Restore Control file and Datafile using RMAN

It is very important for all the DBAs to know about the restoration of any lost data in Oracle.

In this chapter, we going to cover the easiest way to recover control file/ datafile in Oracle.

First, we should know about the control file and datafile in Oracle.

What is a Control file?

A Control file is the key to the database, which is a small binary file that records the physical structure of the database. The control file includes information as below.

☐ DB name

☐ Names and locations of associated datafiles and redo log files

☐ The timestamp of the database creation

☐ The current log sequence number

☐ Checkpoint information

The control file must be available for writing by the Oracle Database server whenever the database is open. Without the control file, the database cannot be mounted and recovery is difficult.

The control file of an Oracle Database is created at the same time as the database. By default, at least one copy of the control file is created during database creation. On some operating systems the default is to create multiple copies. You should create two or more copies of the control file during database creation. You can also create control files later if you lose control files or want to change particular settings in the control files to restore the control file. It's mandatory to enable archive log because ARCHIVELOG mode enables the database to be backed up while it is online and is necessary to recover the database to a point in time later than what has already been restored.

What is a Datafile?

A tablespace in an Oracle database consists of one or more physical datafiles. A datafile can be associated with only one tablespace and only one database.

Oracle creates a datafile for a tablespace by allocating the specified amount of disk space plus the overhead required for the file header. When a datafile is created, the operating system under which Oracle runs is responsible for clearing old information and authorizations from a file before allocating it to Oracle. If the file is large, this process can take a significant amount of time. The first tablespace in any database is always the SYSTEM tablespace, so Oracle automatically allocates the first datafiles of any database for the SYSTEM tablespace during database creation. It's mandatory to enable archive log because ARCHIVELOG mode enables the database to be backed up while it is online and is necessary to recover the database to a point in time later than what has already been restored.

Here we are going to explain the simple scenario to restore the lost control file and datafile in Oracle.

Restoration of Control file

Unfortunately one of the DBA or OS team members deleted the control file physically from the OS when your database is live. Once the control file is lost the database's connection will be lost. When you try to start the database, it will throw the message below.

```
[oracle@trichydoyen ~]$ . .testdb.env
[oracle@trichydoyen ~]$ sqlplus / as sysdba

SQL*Plus: Release 12.2.0.1.0 Production on Wed Sep 11 13:45:18 2019

Copyright (c) 1982, 2016, Oracle.  All rights reserved.

Connected to an idle instance.

SQL> startup mount
ORACLE instance started.

Total System Global Area  734003200 bytes
Fixed Size                  8625032 bytes
Variable Size             599786616 bytes
Database Buffers          121634816 bytes
Redo Buffers                3956736 bytes
ORA-00205: error in identifying control file, check alert log for more info
```

Once we receive the above error message, bring down the database.

```
SQL> shut immediate
ORA-01507: database not mounted


ORACLE instance shut down.
SQL>
SQL>
SQL> exit
Disconnected from Oracle Database 12c Enterprise Edition Release 12.2.0.1.0 - 64bit Production
[oracle@trichydoyen ~]$ █
```

We have scheduled RMAN (Recovery Manager) Level 0 backup daily and control file backup. So it is easy to restore the control file using RMAN. RMAN will restore the latest control file from the backup set.

First we have started the database in nomount status as below.

```
SQL> startup nomount
ORACLE instance started.

Total System Global Area  734003200 bytes
Fixed Size                  8625032 bytes
Variable Size             599786616 bytes
Database Buffers          121634816 bytes
Redo Buffers                3956736 bytes
SQL> █
```

Now connect to the RMAN prompt for control file restore store.

```
[oracle@trichydoyen ~]$ rman target /

Recovery Manager: Release 12.2.0.1.0 - Production on Wed Sep 11 13:54:16 2019

Copyright (c) 1982, 2017, Oracle and/or its affiliates.  All rights reserved.

connected to target database: TESTDB (not mounted)
```

Execute the restore command below to restore the control file physically in the location. There are multiple options to restore the backup files. We can list the backup files, and we can choose the backup file that we want to restore with timestamp. But it is always better to restore with the latest control file backup. The auto-backup in RMAN does the job.

RMAN> restore controlfile from autobackup;

```
RMAN> restore controlfile from autobackup;

Starting restore at 11-SEP-19
using target database control file instead of recovery catalog
allocated channel: ORA_DISK_1
channel ORA_DISK_1: SID=35 device type=DISK

recovery area destination: /u01/app/oracle/fast_recovery_area/testdb
database name (or database unique name) used for search: TESTDB
channel ORA_DISK_1: AUTOBACKUP /u01/app/oracle/fast_recovery_area/testdb/TESTDB/autobackup/2019_09_11/o1_mf_s_1018708128_gqkg16qx_.bkp found in the recovery area
channel ORA_DISK_1: looking for AUTOBACKUP on day: 20190911
channel ORA_DISK_1: restoring control file from AUTOBACKUP /u01/app/oracle/fast_recovery_area/testdb/TESTDB/autobackup/2019_09_11/o1_mf_s_1018708128_gqkg16qx_.bkp
channel ORA_DISK_1: control file restore from AUTOBACKUP complete
output file name=/u01/app/oracle/oradata/testdb/control01.ctl
output file name=/u01/app/oracle/fast_recovery_area/testdb/control02.ctl
Finished restore at 11-SEP-19
```

Control file restored successfully; now we can mount the database.

```
RMAN> alter database mount;

Statement processed
released channel: ORA_DISK_1
```

Now we have restored the control file that we take a backup of at 10 a.m. The corruption happened around 1 p.m. So a lot of log switches may have happened in the time in between. We have to roll the database forward to apply generated archives.

We have recovered the database because I performed a couple of log switches after taking the backup of the full database through RMAN. So we have to roll the database forward to apply generated archives using recover database command in RMAN.

```
RMAN> recover database;

Starting recover at 11-SEP-19
Starting implicit crosscheck backup at 11-SEP-19
allocated channel: ORA_DISK_1
channel ORA_DISK_1: SID=41 device type=DISK
Crosschecked 18 objects
Finished implicit crosscheck backup at 11-SEP-19

Starting implicit crosscheck copy at 11-SEP-19
using channel ORA_DISK_1
Finished implicit crosscheck copy at 11-SEP-19

searching for all files in the recovery area
cataloging files...
cataloging done
```

```
List of Cataloged Files
=======================
File Name: /u01/app/oracle/fast_recovery_area/testdb/TESTDB/archivelog/2019_09_11/o1_mf_1_2_gqkg865f_.arc
File Name: /u01/app/oracle/fast_recovery_area/testdb/TESTDB/archivelog/2019_09_11/o1_mf_1_1_gqkg850z_.arc
File Name: /u01/app/oracle/fast_recovery_area/testdb/TESTDB/archivelog/2019_09_11/o1_mf_1_3_gqkg88dm_.arc
File Name: /u01/app/oracle/fast_recovery_area/testdb/TESTDB/autobackup/2019_09_11/o1_mf_s_1018708128_gqkg16qx_.bkp

using channel ORA_DISK_1

starting media recovery

archived log for thread 1 with sequence 1 is already on disk as file /u01/app/oracle/fast_recovery_area/testdb/TESTDB/archivelog/2019_09_11/o1_mf_1_1_gqkg850
z_.arc
archived log for thread 1 with sequence 2 is already on disk as file /u01/app/oracle/fast_recovery_area/testdb/TESTDB/archivelog/2019_09_11/o1_mf_1_2_gqkg865
f_.arc
archived log for thread 1 with sequence 3 is already on disk as file /u01/app/oracle/fast_recovery_area/testdb/TESTDB/archivelog/2019_09_11/o1_mf_1_3_gqkg88d
m_.arc
archived log for thread 1 with sequence 4 is already on disk as file /u01/app/oracle/oradata/testdb/redo01.log
archived log file name=/u01/app/oracle/fast_recovery_area/testdb/TESTDB/archivelog/2019_09_11/o1_mf_1_1_gqkg850z_.arc thread=1 sequence=1
archived log file name=/u01/app/oracle/fast_recovery_area/testdb/TESTDB/archivelog/2019_09_11/o1_mf_1_2_gqkg865f_.arc thread=1 sequence=2
archived log file name=/u01/app/oracle/fast_recovery_area/testdb/TESTDB/archivelog/2019_09_11/o1_mf_1_3_gqkg88dm_.arc thread=1 sequence=3
archived log file name=/u01/app/oracle/oradata/testdb/redo01.log thread=1 sequence=4
media recovery complete, elapsed time: 00:00:00
Finished recover at 11-SEP-19
```

Open the database using resetlogs command. Now the database opened successfully.

```
RMAN> alter database open;

RMAN-00571: ===========================================================
RMAN-00569: =============== ERROR MESSAGE STACK FOLLOWS ===============
RMAN-00571: ===========================================================
RMAN-03002: failure of sql statement command at 09/11/2019 15:01:22
ORA-01589: must use RESETLOGS or NORESETLOGS option for database open

RMAN> alter database open resetlogs;

Statement processed

    [oracle@trichydoyen ~]$ sqlplus / as sysdba

    SQL*Plus: Release 12.2.0.1.0 Production on Wed Sep 11 15:04:38 2019

    Copyright (c) 1982, 2016, Oracle.  All rights reserved.


    Connected to:
    Oracle Database 12c Enterprise Edition Release 12.2.0.1.0 - 64bit Production

    SQL> select name,open_mode from v$database;

    NAME      OPEN_MODE
    --------- --------------------
    TESTDB    READ WRITE
```

Restoring Datafile: One of the datafiles corrupted automatically; here we are going see how we can restore the datafile in a simple way using RMAN. SYSTEM. The datafile was corrupted as shown below. The database was in mount status.

```
[oracle@trichydoyen ~]$ sqlplus / as sysdba

SQL*Plus: Release 12.2.0.1.0 Production on Wed Sep 11 15:31:05 2019

Copyright (c) 1982, 2016, Oracle.  All rights reserved.

Connected to an idle instance.

SQL> startup
ORACLE instance started.

Total System Global Area  734003200 bytes
Fixed Size                  8625032 bytes
Variable Size             599786616 bytes
Database Buffers          121634816 bytes
Redo Buffers                3956736 bytes
Database mounted.
ORA-01157: cannot identify/lock data file 1 - see DBWR trace file
ORA-01110: data file 1: '/u01/app/oracle/oradata/testdb/system01.dbf'
```

Connect to the RMAN prompt the restore the lost datafile. Here we know that SYSTEM datafile was corrupted. So first we have to delete the datafile manually from the OS and restore using RMAN.

SYSTEM datafile is associated with SYSTEM tablespace; so we can restore SYSTEM tablespace to restore the SYSTEM datafile as shown below.

```
[oracle@trichydoyen ~]$ rman target /

Recovery Manager: Release 12.2.0.1.0 - Production on Wed Sep 11 15:31:51 2019

Copyright (c) 1982, 2017, Oracle and/or its affiliates.  All rights reserved.

connected to target database: TESTDB (DBID=2802028271, not open)

RMAN>

RMAN> run{
2> restore tablespace system;
3> recover tablespace system;
4> }
```

```
Starting restore at 11-SEP-19
using target database control file instead of recovery catalog
allocated channel: ORA_DISK_1
channel ORA_DISK_1: SID=41 device type=DISK

channel ORA_DISK_1: starting datafile backup set restore
channel ORA_DISK_1: specifying datafile(s) to restore from backup set
channel ORA_DISK_1: restoring datafile 00001 to /u01/app/oracle/oradata/testdb/system01.dbf
channel ORA_DISK_1: reading from backup piece /u01/app/oracle/fast_recovery_area/testdb/TESTDB/backupset/2019_09_11/o1_mf_nnndf_FULLCOLD1_gqkg02tx_.bkp
channel ORA_DISK_1: piece handle=/u01/app/oracle/fast_recovery_area/testdb/TESTDB/backupset/2019_09_11/o1_mf_nnndf_FULLCOLD1_gqkg02tx_.bkp tag=FULLCOLD1
channel ORA_DISK_1: restored backup piece 1
channel ORA_DISK_1: restore complete, elapsed time: 00:00:35
Finished restore at 11-SEP-19

Starting recover at 11-SEP-19
using channel ORA_DISK_1

starting media recovery

archived log for thread 1 with sequence 1 is already on disk as file /u01/app/oracle/fast_recovery_area/testdb/TESTDB/archivelog/2019_09_11/o1_mf_1_1_gqkg850
z_.arc
archived log for thread 1 with sequence 2 is already on disk as file /u01/app/oracle/fast_recovery_area/testdb/TESTDB/archivelog/2019_09_11/o1_mf_1_2_gqkhqpw
9_.arc
archived log for thread 1 with sequence 3 is already on disk as file /u01/app/oracle/fast_recovery_area/testdb/TESTDB/archivelog/2019_09_11/o1_mf_1_3_gqkhqpw
x_.arc
archived log for thread 1 with sequence 4 is already on disk as file /u01/app/oracle/fast_recovery_area/testdb/TESTDB/archivelog/2019_09_11/o1_mf_1_4_gqkhqpt
x_.arc
archived log file name=/u01/app/oracle/fast_recovery_area/testdb/TESTDB/archivelog/2019_09_11/o1_mf_1_1_gqkg850z_.arc thread=1 sequence=1
archived log file name=/u01/app/oracle/fast_recovery_area/testdb/TESTDB/archivelog/2019_09_11/o1_mf_1_2_gqkhqpw9_.arc thread=1 sequence=2
archived log file name=/u01/app/oracle/fast_recovery_area/testdb/TESTDB/archivelog/2019_09_11/o1_mf_1_3_gqkhqpwx_.arc thread=1 sequence=3
archived log file name=/u01/app/oracle/fast_recovery_area/testdb/TESTDB/archivelog/2019_09_11/o1_mf_1_4_gqkhqptx_.arc thread=1 sequence=4
media recovery complete, elapsed time: 00:00:01
Finished recover at 11-SEP-19
```

Now datafiles have been restored successfully. Open the database using the command below.

```
[oracle@trichydoyen ~]$ sqlplus / as sysdba

SQL*Plus: Release 12.2.0.1.0 Production on Wed Sep 11 15:31:05 2019

Copyright (c) 1982, 2016, Oracle.  All rights reserved.

Connected to an idle instance.

SQL> startup
ORACLE instance started.

Total System Global Area  734003200 bytes
Fixed Size                  8625032 bytes
Variable Size             599786616 bytes
Database Buffers          121634816 bytes
Redo Buffers                3956736 bytes
Database mounted.
```

RMAN> alter database open;

Best Practices:

a. Keep multiple control file for every database and keep in distributed location.

b. Enable auto backup ON for control file in RMAN.

c. Control file backup should be run at least once after any RMAN backup.

Reference: What is a Control File? - Oracle Help Center.

https://docs.Oracle.com/cd/B28359_01/server.111/b28310/control001.htm

TOPIC

4

RECOVER DROPPED TABLESPACE USING BACKUP

Recover a dropped Tablespace

Dropping a tablespace without a valid backup in the past will end up with a loss of huge data and the business as well; there are a few ways from which you can recover the tablespace which is being dropped accidentally. To recover from a case of a dropped tablespace, the TABLESPACE POINT IN TIME RECOVERY (TSPITR) method cannot be used.

When you drop a tablespace, the controlfile will no longer have any record of the tablespace which has been dropped. When you attempt to use "RMAN RECOVER TABLESPACE" command will return the **error RMAN-06019 – *"could not translate tablespace name"*** as shown below.

```
SQL> drop tablespace diamon01 including contents and datafiles;
Tablespace dropped.
testdb:/u01/Oracle/diag/rdbms/apex/apex/trace> rman target /
Recovery Manager: Release 10.2.0.4.0 - Production on Sat Aug 3 11:53:58
2019
Copyright (c) 1982, 2007, Oracle.  All rights reserved.

Connected to target database: TESTDB (DBID=2469552796)

RMAN> restore tablespace diamon01;
Starting restore at 03-AUG-19
using target database control file instead of recovery catalogue
allocated channel: ORA_SBT_TAPE_1
channel ORA_SBT_TAPE_1: sid=141 devtype=SBT_TAPE
channel ORA_SBT_TAPE_1: Data Protection for Oracle: version 5.5.1.0
allocated channel: ORA_DISK_1
```

```
channel ORA_DISK_1: sid=140 devtype=DISK
RMAN-00571: ===========================================================
RMAN-00569: =============== ERROR MESSAGE STACK FOLLOWS ===============
RMAN-00571: ===========================================================
RMAN-03002: failure of restore command at 08/03/2019 11:54:11
RMAN-20202: tablespace not found in the recovery catalog
```
When you drop a tablespace, you have two options to recover it:

1. You can do a point in time recovery of the whole database until the time when the tablespace was dropped and

2. You can clone the database from a valid backup, export the required tables from the tablespace which was dropped, recreate the tablespace and then import the tables from the newly cloned instance.

The first option will require an outage of the entire database and the entire database will be rolled back in time in order to recover the tablespace. The second option can be performed online, but we will need to factor in the disk space requirements to create a clone of the database from which the tablespace has been dropped.

Let us examine the first option using the example shown below:

In this example, CONTROLFILE AUTOBACKUP has been turned on and Flashback has been enabled for the database.

With Flashback enabled, the db_recovery_file_dest will have a sub-directory 'autobackup' as shown below for each day

```
ttestdb:/u02/oradata/testdb/TESTDB/autobackup/2019_08_03> ls -lrt
total 63040
-rw-r-----   1 Oracle   dba          6455296 Aug  3 10:22
o1_mf_s_693915680_57dlgcqh_.bkp
-rw-r----   1 Oracle   dba          6455296 Aug  3 11:49
o1_mf_s_693920955_57dqkw0j_.bkp
-rw-r-----   1 Oracle   dba          6455296 Aug  3 13:28
o1_mf_s_693926889_57dxcbdx_.bkp
-rw-r-----   1 Oracle   dba          6455296 Aug  3 14:18
o1_mf_s_693928526_57f094n9_.bkp
-rw-r-----   1 Oracle   dba          6455296 Aug  3 14:20
o1_mf_s_693930026_57f0fbo2_.bkp
```

When you drop the Tablespace, you are changing the structure of the database and since controlfile autobackup has been turned on, you will see another backup file has been created in the autobackup location in the flash recovery area on the disk.

```
SQL> drop tablespace diamond including contents and datafiles;
Tablespace dropped.
SQL> quit
Disconnected from Oracle Database 10g Enterprise Edition Release
10.2.0.4.0 - 64bit Production.
With the Partitioning, OLAP, Data Mining and Real Application Testing
options,
testdb:/u02/oradata/testdb/TESTDB/autobackup/2019_08_03> ls -lrt
total 75648
-rw-r-----    1 Oracle    dba          6455296 Aug   3 10:22
ol_mf_s_693915680_57dlgcqh_.bkp
-rw-r-----    1 Oracle    dba          6455296 Aug   3 11:49
ol_mf_s_693920955_57dqkw0j_.bkp
-rw-r-----    1 Oracle    dba          6455296 Aug   3 13:28
ol_mf_s_693926889_57dxcbdx_.bkp
-rw-r-----    1 Oracle    dba          6455296 Aug   3 14:18
ol_mf_s_693928526_57f094n9_.bkp
-rw-r-----    1 Oracle    dba          6455296 Aug   3 14:20
ol_mf_s_693930026_57f0fbo2_.bkp
-rw-r-----    1 Oracle    dba          6455296 Aug   3 14:38
ol_mf_s_693931114_57f1hbmo_.bkp
```

You can then shut down the database, startup in nomount mode and attempt to restore the controlfile from autobackup.

The most recent controlfile autobackup has been restored, but since this has been taken after the tablespace was dropped, the tablespace which has been dropped (DIAMOND) is not referenced in the control file that we just restored. If we try to restore and recover the database, the dropped tablespace will not be restored.

```
SQL> startup nomount;
ORACLE instance started.
Total System Global Area 264241152 bytes
Fixed Size            2083304 bytes
Variable Size          142607896 bytes
Database Buffers   113246208 bytes
Redo Buffers           6303744 bytes
```

```
RMAN> restore controlfile from autobackup;
Starting restore at 03-AUG-19
Using the target database control file instead of recovery catalogue
Allocated channel: ORA_DISK_1
Channel ORA_DISK_1: sid=156 devtype=DISK

Recovery area destination: /u02/oradata/testdb/
Database name (or database unique name) used for search: TESTDB
Channel ORA_DISK_1: autobackup found in the recovery area.
Channel ORA_DISK_1: autobackup found:
/u02/oradata/testdb/TESTDB/autobackup/2019_08_03/o1_mf_s_693931114_57f1hb
mo_.bkp
Channel ORA_DISK_1: control file restore from autobackup complete
Output filename=/u02/oradata/testdb/control01.ctl
Output filename=/u02/oradata/testdb/control02.ctl
Output filename=/u02/oradata/testdb/control03.ctl
Finished restore at 03-AUG-19

RMAN> alter database mount;
Database mounted
Released channel: ORA_DISK_1

RMAN> report schema;
...
List of Permanent Datafiles
===========================
File Size(MB) Tablespace          RB segs Datafile Name
---- -------- ------------------- ------- ------------------------
1    1230     SYSTEM              ***
/u02/oradata/testdb/system01.dbf
2    1700     UNDOTBS1            ***
/u02/oradata/testdb/undotbs01.dbf
3    370      SYSAUX              ***
/u02/oradata/testdb/sysaux01.dbf
4    280      USERS               ***
/u02/oradata/backup/bkp.04klgv2b
5    131      EXAMPLE             ***
/u02/oradata/testdb/example01.dbf
6    150      USERS               ***
/u02/oradata/backup/bkp.06klgv3k
```

```
9     100      USERS                 ***
/u02/oradata/backup/bkp.08klgv4i
```

We will need to restore a backup of the controlfile which contains records for the tablespace DIAMOND. We use the RESTORE CONTROLFILE FROM command to restore a specific controlfile autobackup.

```
RMAN> restore controlfile from
'/u02/oradata/testdb/TESTDB/autobackup/2019_08_03/o1_mf_s_693930026_57f0f
bo2_.bkp';

Starting restore at 03-AUG-19
Using channel ORA_DISK_1

Channel ORA_DISK_1: restoring control file
Channel ORA_DISK_1: restore complete, elapsed time: 00:00:02
Output filename=/u02/oradata/testdb/control01.ctl
Output filename=/u02/oradata/testdb/control02.ctl
Output filename=/u02/oradata/testdb/control03.ctl
Finished restore at 03-AUG-19

RMAN> report schema;

.....
List of Permanent Datafiles
===============================
```

File	Size (MB)	Tablespace	RB segs	Datafile Name
1	1230	SYSTEM	***	/u02/oradata/testdb/system01.dbf
2	1700	UNDOTBS1	***	/u02/oradata/testdb/undotbs01.dbf
3	370	SYSAUX	***	/u02/oradata/testdb/sysaux01.dbf
4	280	USERS	***	/u02/oradata/backup/bkp.04klgv2b
5	131	EXAMPLE	***	/u02/oradata/testdb/example01.dbf
6	150	USERS	***	/u02/oradata/backup/bkp.06klgv3k
7	**0**	**DIAMOND**	***	**/u02/oradata/testdb/diamond01.dbf**
9	100	USERS	***	/u02/oradata/backup/bkp.08klgv4i

The alert log will also show the time when the tablespace was dropped. We can also see that a controlfile autobackup has taken place after the tablespace was dropped.

Drop tablespace DIAMOND including contents and datafiles

Sat Aug 3 14:38:34 2019

Deleted file /u02/oradata/testdb/diamond01.dbf

Starting control autobackup

Control autobackup written to DISK device

```
handle
'/u02/oradata/testdb/TESTDB/autobackup/2019_08_03/o1_mf_s_693931114_57f1h
bmo_.bkp'
```

Completed drop tablespace diamond including contents and datafiles

Now you know the time the tablespace was dropped. You can now do a point in time recovery of the DATABASE in order to recover the tablespace which has been dropped.

```
RMAN> run {
2> set until time "to_date('03-AUG-2019 14:38:00','DD-MON-YYYY
HH24:Mi:SS')";
3> restore database;
4> recover database;
5> }
```

Executing command: SET until clause

Using target database control file instead of recovery catalogue.


```
Starting restore at 03-AUG-19
Allocated channel: ORA_SBT_TAPE_1
Channel ORA_SBT_TAPE_1: sid=159 devtype=SBT_TAPE
Channel ORA_SBT_TAPE_1: Data Protection for Oracle: version 5.5.1.0
Allocated channel: ORA_DISK_1
Channel ORA_DISK_1: sid=155 devtype=DISK

Channel ORA_DISK_1: restoring datafile 00004
Input datafile copy recid=14 stamp=693929215
filename=/u02/oradata/testdb/users01.dbf
Destination for restore of datafile 00004:
/u02/oradata/backup/bkp.04klgv2b
Channel ORA_SBT_TAPE_1: starting datafile backupset restore
Channel ORA_SBT_TAPE_1: specifying datafile(s) to restore from backup set
```

```
Restoring datafile 00001 to /u02/oradata/testdb/system01.dbf
Restoring datafile 00002 to /u02/oradata/testdb/undotbs01.dbf
Restoring datafile 00003 to /u02/oradata/testdb/sysaux01.dbf
Restoring datafile 00005 to /u02/oradata/testdb/example01.dbf
Restoring datafile 00007 to /u02/oradata/testdb/diamond01.dbf
Channel ORA_SBT_TAPE_1: reading from backup piece 0gkloo6p_1_1
Channel ORA_DISK_1: copied datafile copy of datafile 00004
Output filename=/u02/oradata/backup/bkp.04klgv2b recid=21 stamp=693932732
Channel ORA_DISK_1: restoring datafile 00006
Input datafile copy recid=13 stamp=693929146
filename=/u02/oradata/testdb/users02.dbf
Destination for restore of datafile 00006:
/u02/oradata/backup/bkp.06klgv3k
channel ORA_DISK_1: copied datafile copy of datafile 00006
Output filename=/u02/oradata/backup/bkp.06klgv3k recid=23 stamp=693932755
Channel ORA_DISK_1: restoring datafile 00009
Input datafile copy recid=10 stamp=693929108
filename=/u02/oradata/testdb/users03.dbf
Destination for restore of datafile 00009:
/u02/oradata/backup/bkp.08klgv4i
channel ORA_DISK_1: copied datafile copy of datafile 00009
Output filename=/u02/oradata/backup/bkp.08klgv4i recid=26 stamp=693932809
Channel ORA_SBT_TAPE_1: restored backup piece 1
Piece handle=0gkloo6p_1_1 tag=TAG20190803T113241
Channel ORA_SBT_TAPE_1: restore complete, elapsed time: 00:02:40
Finished restore at 03-AUG-19

Starting recover at 03-AUG-19
Using channel ORA_SBT_TAPE_1
Using channel ORA_DISK_1

Starting media recovery

Archive log thread 1 sequence 8 is already on disk as file
/u02/oradata/testdb/arch/arch.8.1.693662800.log
Archive log thread 1 sequence 9 is already on disk as file
/u02/oradata/testdb/arch/arch.9.1.693662800.log
Archive log thread 1 sequence 10 is already on disk as file
/u02/oradata/testdb/arch/arch.10.1.693662800.log
Archive log thread 1 sequence 1 is already on disk as file
/u02/oradata/testdb/redo01.log
```

```
Archive log thread 1 sequence 2 is already on disk as file
/u02/oradata/testdb/redo02.log
Archive log filename=/u02/oradata/testdb/arch/arch.8.1.693662800.log
thread=1 sequence=8
Archive log filename=/u02/oradata/testdb/arch/arch.9.1.693662800.log
thread=1 sequence=9
Archive log filename=/u02/oradata/testdb/arch/arch.10.1.693662800.log
thread=1 sequence=10
archive log filename=/u02/oradata/testdb/redo01.log thread=1 sequence=1
Archive log filename=/u02/oradata/testdb/redo02.log thread=1 sequence=2
Media recovery complete, elapsed time: 00:00:06
Finished recover at 03-AUG-19

RMAN>
RMAN> alter database open resetlogs;
Database opened
SQL> select file_name, bytes from dba_data_files where
tablespace_name='DIAMOND';

FILE_NAME                                      BYTES
------------------------------------------------------      -------------
-------------------------
/u02/oradata/testdb/diamond01.dbf        37748736
```

As the tablespace is being restored from a backup you need to open the database using *resetlogs* option allowing the logs to be reset. By now you can do recovery of the lost tablespace without losing any data (if the backup is very recent before dropping the tablespace). From Oracle 11g you can also do a point-in-time recovery which is discussed later in this chapter.

POINT-IN-TIME RECOVERY

Scenario 1: Point-in-time recovery scenarios

There are different cases where you can recover the database using point-in-time recovery method, but for this, you must be aware of the time when the database object was dropped: It may be a table or a tablespace. Consider that as a database administrator you are doing some activity and you accidentally dropped a tablespace called TEST which is very important for the application. For this, you need to restore the database before the TEST tablespace was dropped.

Let us recreate this scenario and see how to recover the dropped object.

```
SQL> drop tablespace test including contents and datafiles;
        Tablespace dropped.
```

Now you can refer the alert log for the exact timing when tablespace was dropped and you can start the database recovery as follows.

Alert log

Sun Feb 4 10:59:43 2019

```
drop tablespace test including contents and datafiles
Sun Feb 4 10:59:47 2019
Completed: drop tablespace test including contents and datafiles
SQL> shutdown abort
ORACLE instance shut down.
rman target / catalog rman/cat@risl64
Recovery Manager: Release 10.2.0.2.0 - Production on Sun Feb 4 11:02:48
2019
Copyright (c) 1982, 2005, Oracle.  All rights reserved.
Connected to target database (not started)
```

```
Connected to recovery catalog database
```

Now we know that the tablespace has dropped at Sun Feb 4 10:59:43 2019; so, we can restore the database till that time with the following command.

```
RMAN> run
{
startup nomount
Set until time "to_date ('04-02-19 10:58:00', 'DD-MM-YY HH24:MI:SS')";
restore controlfile;
alter database mount;
restore database;
recover database;
alter database open resetlogs;
}
Oracle instance started
Total System Global Area      268435456 bytes
Fixed Size                      2070448 bytes
Variable Size                 104859728 bytes
Database Buffers              155189248 bytes
Redo Buffers                    6316032 bytes
Executing command: SET until clause
Starting restore at 04-FEB-19
Allocated channel: ORA_DISK_1
Channel ORA_DISK_1: sid=157 devtype=DISK

Channel ORA_DISK_1: starting datafile backupset restore
.

.

.
Finished restore at 04-FEB-19

Database mounted
Released channel: ORA_DISK_1

Starting restore at 04-FEB-19
Starting implicit crosscheck backup at 04-FEB-19
Allocated channel: ORA_DISK_1
Channel ORA_DISK_1: sid=157 devtype=DISK
Crosschecked 18 objects
Finished implicit crosscheck backup at 04-FEB-19
```

```
Starting implicit crosscheck copy at 04-FEB-19
Using channel ORA_DISK_1
Finished implicit crosscheck copy at 04-FEB-19

Searching for all files in the recovery area
Cataloging files...
No files cataloged
Using channel ORA_DISK_1
.
Finished restore at 04-FEB-19
Starting recover at 04-FEB-19
Using channel ORA_DISK_1
Starting media recovery
Archive log thread 1 sequence 19 is already on disk as file
/u01/ORACLE/TEST/archivelog/2019_02_04/o1_mf_1_19_2wc0nztc_.arc
Archive log thread 1 sequence 20 is already on disk as file
/u01/ORACLE/TEST/redo02.log
Archive log
filename=/u01/ORACLE/TEST/archivelog/2019_02_04/o1_mf_1_19_2wc0nztc_.arc
thread=1 sequence=19
Archive log filename=/u01/ORACLE/TEST/redo02.log thread=1 sequence=20
Media recovery complete, elapsed time: 00:00:00
Finished recover at 04-FEB-19
Database opened
New incarnation of database registered in recovery catalog
Starting full resync of recovery catalog
Full resync complete
RMAN>
SQL> select name from v$tablespace;
NAME
--------------------------------
SYSTEM
UNDOTBS1
SYSAUX
USERS
TEMP
TEST
```

So, the tablespace TEST has been restored from the available backup as we found the time in which the tablespace was dropped. Once the restore is completed it is recommended to take a full backup of the database, to make sure we have a consistent backup after the recovery.

Scenario 2: Point in time recovery using RMAN (until a log sequence number)

Let us look at another scenario where we can recover the database using the log sequence number. This can be done by identifying the log sequence before the object is being dropped and restoring the database using that log sequence number.

Connect into the schema and check for the count of the objects.

```
SQL> conn scott/tiger
Connected.
SQL> select count(*) from myobjects;
  COUNT(*)
  ----------
   249410
```

Switch a logfile using the below alter statement so that the next log sequence will be generated and note down the current log sequence number.

```
SQL> conn / as sysdba
Connected.
SQL> alter system switch logfile;
System altered.
SQL> archive log list
Database log mode               Archive Mode
Automatic archival              Enabled
Archive destination             /u01/app/Oracle/testarch
Oldest online log sequence      12
Next log sequence to archive    14
Current log sequence            14
```

Now delete 'My objects' and commit the changes,

```
SQL> conn scott/tiger
Connected.
SQL> delete myobjects;
249410 rows deleted.
SQL> commit;
Commit complete.
```

The wrong DML statement was made AFTER 8:15 a.m. and we need to determine the log sequence that we need to recover until, use the below command to get the log sequence.

Select sequence#,first_change#, to_char(first_time,'HH24:MI:SS') from v$log order by 3

```
SQL> /

 SEQUENCE#  FIRST_CHANGE# TO_CHAR(
---------- -------------- --------
        13        2760463 07:49:36
        14        2761178 08:12:47
        15        2766622 08:18:49
```

Log sequence 14 was at 8:12 a.m. so we should recover to a log sequence before this which is sequence# 13.

Now Shutdown and start the database in mount state

```
SQL> shutdown immediate;
Database closed.
Database dismounted.
ORACLE instance shut down.
SQL> startup mount;
ORACLE instance started.


Total System Global Area  264241152 bytes
Fixed Size                  2070416 bytes
Variable Size             163580016 bytes
Database Buffers           92274688 bytes
Redo Buffers                6316032 bytes
```

Database mounted.

We know the sequence# to which the database is to be restored and recovered, let us restore the database to that sequence and recover the database using the RMAN command below.

```
RMAN> run {
2> set until sequence=13;
3> restore database;
4> recover database;
5> }
```

Executing command: SET until clause

```
Starting restore at 29-JAN-19
Allocated channel: ORA_DISK_1
```

```
Channel ORA_DISK_1: sid=154 devtype=DISK
Allocated channel: ORA_SBT_TAPE_1
Channel ORA_SBT_TAPE_1: sid=158 devtype=SBT_TAPE
Channel ORA_SBT_TAPE_1: Data Protection for Oracle: version 5.2.4.0

Channel ORA_DISK_1: starting datafile backupset restore
Channel ORA_DISK_1: specifying datafile(s) to restore from backup set
…
Channel ORA_DISK_1: reading from backup piece
/u01/app/Oracle/test.20190129.161.1.1.613122551
Channel ORA_DISK_1: restored backup piece 1
Piece handle=/u01/app/Oracle/test.20190129.161.1.1.613122551
tag=TAG20190129T074911
Channel ORA_DISK_1: restore complete, elapsed time: 00:00:16
Finished restore at 29-JAN-07

Starting recover at 29-JAN-07
Using channel ORA_DISK_1
Using channel ORA_SBT_TAPE_1
Starting media recovery
Archive log thread 1 sequence 13 is already on disk as file
/u01/app/Oracle/testarch/arch_1_13_613052894.dbf
Channel ORA_DISK_1: starting archive log restore to default destination
Channel ORA_DISK_1: restoring archive log
Archive log thread=1 sequence=12
Channel ORA_DISK_1: reading from backup piece
/u01/app/Oracle/test.20190129.162.1.1.613122577
Channel ORA_DISK_1: restored backup piece 1
Piece handle=/u01/app/Oracle/test.20190129.162.1.1.613122577
tag=TAG20190129T074937
Channel ORA_DISK_1: restore complete, elapsed time: 00:00:02
Archive log filename=/u01/app/Oracle/testarch/arch_1_12_613052894.dbf
thread=1 sequence=12
Archive log filename=/u01/app/Oracle/testarch/arch_1_13_613052894.dbf
thread=1 sequence=13
Media recovery complete, elapsed time: 00:00:01
Finished recover at 29-JAN-19
```

RMAN> sql 'alter database open resetlogs';

Sql statement: alter database open resetlogs

Confirm that the recovery has worked by querying myobjects.

```
SQL> select count(*) from myobjects;

  COUNT(*)
----------
    249410
```

Thus, the database is restored and recovered using 'set until' sequence and all the object that was dropped is recovered back. SET UNTIL TIME and SET UNTIL SEQUENCE are two different methods where you can recover the database after losing the object.

TOPIC

6

STANDBY DATABASE RECOVERY BY APPLYING INCREMENTAL

Recover Standby database using SCN Backup

Most of the time we will face gap issue in standby database, this may be due to various causes like poor network, or the size of the archive is too large or too many archives are generated etc., So, any of them may cause the standby database to go out of sync with its primary databases. If the gap is very small, say some 10-20 or more, we can SCP the file to the standby and can be recovered. If it is more than a day or a huge number of archives are missing, we cannot make the standby sync with primary. Then what is the solution for this?

We can resolve this issue by applying SCN based incremental backup to the standby dataset.

STEP 1: STANDBY SITE

Check for the minimum SCN number on the standby site.

```
SQL> select min (checkpoint_change#) from v$datafile_header order by 1;
MIN(CHECKPOINT_CHANGE#)
-----------------------
2091840345
```

STEP 2: PRIMARY SITE

Stop the logs being shipped from the primary to the standby database;

SQL> alter system set log_archive_dest_state_2=defer scope=both;

STEP 3: PRIMARY SITE

Let us take the SCN based backup from primary database using the SCN we took from the standby database. And, we'll take the standby controlfile backup from primary.

```
SQL> alter database create standby controlfile as
'/backup/Oracle/test/standby_control.ctl';
Database altered.
Exit
RMAN target /
RMAN> BACKUP INCREMENTAL FROM SCN 2091840345 DATABASE FORMAT
'/backup/Oracle/test/scn_backup_%U' tag 'TOSTANDBY';
```

STEP 4: PRIMARY SITE.

In this step we need to SCP the files from the primary site to the standby site if the backup mount point is not shared with primary and standby.

STEP 5: STANDBY SITE.

It's time to catalogue and recover the standby database with the incremental backup.

```
RMAN> CATALOG START WITH '/backup/Oracle/test/';
RMAN> RECOVER DATABASE NOREDO;
```

STEP 6: STANDBY SITE.

Keeping the datafile location of the standby database is advised if the location of the standby datafile is different than the primary.

```
SQL> spool datafile_path.txt
set lines 200
col name format a60
select file#, name from v$datafile order by file#;
spool off
```

STEP 7: STANDBY SITE.

Restore the standby control file which was backed up in step 3.

```
RMAN> SHUTDOWN IMMEDIATE;
RMAN> STARTUP NOMOUNT;
RMAN> RESTORE STANDBY CONTROLFILE FROM
'/backup/Oracle/test/standby_control.ctl';
```

STEP 8: STANDBY SITE.

Shut down the standby database and bring back to mount.

```
SQL> SHUTDOWN;
SQL> STARTUP MOUNT;
```

As we have restored the new controlfile from the primary database all the datafiles in the controlfile will be pointing the primary location (if the primary and standby datafile locations are different). So, we need to catalogue the standby datafiles to do the necessary rename operation as below.

Make sure to catalogue all the data mount points if you have more than one data top in your environment.

```
RMAN> CATALOG START WITH '+DATA/mystd/datafile/';
```

STEP 9: STANDBY SITE.

Switch the datafiles to their correct names at the **standby** site.

```
RMAN> SWITCH DATABASE TO COPY;
```

STEP 10: STANDBY SITE.

Let us clear all standby redo log groups:

```
SQL> ALTER DATABASE CLEAR LOGFILE GROUP [group number];
```

STEP 11: STANDBY SITE.

Start the MRP process on standby database and make sure the database is receiving and applying the current logs from the primary site.

```
SQL> RECOVER MANAGED STANDBY DATABASE DISCONNECT FROM SESSION;
```

Your standby database should now receive the archives form the primary site and apply it. In this chapter we demonstrated how to take SCN backup from the primary database and how to recover the standby database from the SCN backup. Following the above steps one by one will be more than enough to make your standby database Sync with the primary after a big archival gap.

PERFORMANCE TUNING

Performance means how well a person or machine does a piece of work or activity. Tuning means adjusting; when we relate these direct meanings with the Oracle database, it is adjusting an SQL query or activity in database activity so that the application runs smoothly.

With our previous experience from various customers, we have consolidated a few chapters on finding the problem on database performance perspective, analysing the impact of index rebuilding, how to copy and explain, plan across the environment and finally fragmentation

What Can One Expect in this Chapter?

If we know the problem, 50% of the actual performance problem is solved; so it's important to know where the bottleneck is. So we are mainly focusing to find the bottleneck instead of providing a direct solution. Each chapter is unique and talking about particular issues deeply and is provided scripts we have used and provided screenshots wherever it is required.

What would be my takeaway?

This chapter is designed to have a deep understanding of particular topics with working examples and scripts. After you complete these topics you will be able to understand the points mentioned below.

TOPIC 1	**Analyse Awr Report In Oracle:** To analyse the AWR (Automatic Workload Repository) report to understand the overall behaviour of the database for a certain time.
TOPIC 2	**CPU Overhead:** To answer "Is CPU configuration enough to handle the current load?" – With our experience, we have provided some calculations and real-time examples to answer the question.
TOPIC 3	**How To Migrate Explain Plan From One Database To Other Database And To Make Sure Optimizer Chose The Expected Plan:** Steps, with examples, are given to copy the good plan across the environment to address the performance issue like "A query works fine in the Lower environment and same query behaving differently in the production environment."
TOPIC 4	**Tuning Sql Statements Using Sql Tuning Advisor (Without Enterprise Manager):** Oracle Enterprise Manager provides direct option to run Tuning advisor against the SQL which has a performance issue, but what happens if we do not have OEM as a monitoring solution? We have explained the steps to run the tuning advisor from command prompt instead of running from Oracle Enterprise Manager or Grid control.
TOPIC 5	**Easy Steps To Identify And Remove Oracle Table Fragmentation:** In this same chapter, we are going to see how table defragmentation helps in performance enhancement but otherwise how an index-rebuild will impact the database performance after the activity at the macro level.
TOPIC 6	**Myths On Index Rebuild:** Myths on Rebuild – This reveals myths on Index rebuild and provides details with examples.

ANALYSE AWR REPORT IN ORACLE

What is Automatic Workload Repository (AWR)?

Automatic Workload Repository (AWR), a licensed feature of Oracle, is one of the best tools to monitor the performance issues. AWR is a collection of persistent system performance statistics owned by SYS. It resides in SYSAUX tablespace. By default, snapshots are generated once in every 60 min and maintained for seven days. An AWR report outputs a series of statistics based on the differences between pictures that may be used to investigate performance and other issues.

Generally, when AWR reports are asked by Admins, this could be related to the following typical scenarios:

☐ The performance has slowly degraded over time due to increased user activity

☐ The performance has slowly degraded over time due to increased or changing content

☐ The performance has become slower after a change of AppServer version or an AppServer patchset has been applied

☐ The performance has become slower after a change of Database version or a Database patchset has been applied.

How to generate the AWR report

Before we execute the AWR report we should know about the snapshot & types of AWR report.

At Doyensys office we used to collect AWR report for all clients on a regular basis and analysis the performance database and advise the key point to the clients in monthly meetings.

Snapshot: A snapshot is a staged copy of data in a Data Store that is used in one or more processes. Snapshot has a unique ID known as "snap_id". Snapshot detail can be found in "DBA_HIST_SNAPSHOT" view.

So before generating the **AWR Report** let's find the time interval for which we need an **AWR Report**.

Suppose we need **AWR Report** for 10-SEP-19. To achieve this we need snapshot ID for this data.

How to find Snap Id: Select from DBA_HIST_SNAPSHOT the view which has two fields **"BEGIN_INTERVAL_TIME"** and **"END_INTERVAL_TIME"**. These fields give the exact value for the time this snapshot belongs to.

From the table "DBA_HIST_SNAPSHOT "select your snap_id in the meantime for 10-SEP-19. In this case, starting snap_id is 1980 and it goes up to 1983.

DBA_HIST_SNAPSHOT tables information about the snapshots in the Workload Repository.

Various Types of AWR Reports

awrrpt.sql	Displays various statistics for a range of snapshots Ids.
awrrpti.sql	Displays statistics for a range of snapshot Ids on a specified database and instance.
awrsqrpt.sql	Displays statistics of a particular SQL statement for a range of snapshot Ids. Run this report to inspect or debug the performance of a particular SQL statement.
awrsqrpi.sql	Displays statistics of a particular SQL statement for a range of snapshot Ids on a specified SQL.
awrddrpt.sql	Compares detailed performance attributes and configuration settings

	between two selected time periods.
awrddrpi.sql	Compares detailed performance attributes and configuration settings between two selected time periods on a specific database and instance.

Steps to run AWR Report

1. Log in to database:

```
[Oracle@doyen ~]$ export ORACLE_SID=doyen
[Oracle@doyen~]$ sqlplus "/as sysdba"
```

2. Execute command for Report generation: Depending on the reasons for collecting the report, the default can be used, or for a more focused view, a short 10-15 minute snapshot could be used.

```
SQL> @$ORACLE_HOME/rdbms/admin/awrrpt.sql
```

3. Choose Report Type: It will prompt for AWR report type. This report can be generated in two types "HTML" and "TEXT". Default is HTML

Specify the Report Type:

Would you like an HTML report or a plain text report?

Enter 'html' for an HTML report, or 'text' for plain text.

Defaults to 'html'

Enter value for report_type: **HTML**

4. Snap details: You can give any value it will show you all snap ids and detail for the given no. of days.

Enter the value for num_days: **1**

5. Specify the Begin and End Snapshot Ids: Listing the last day's Completed Snapshots

```
Instance      DB Name       Snap Id   Snap Started        Snap Level
-----------   -----------   --------- ------------------- ------------------
------------------
DOYEN         DOYEN         1980  10 Sep 2019 00:00              1
                                 1981  10 Sep 2019  01:00
      1
```

```
                                     1982    10 Sep 2019   02:00
      1
```

Enter value for begin_snap:**1980**

Enter value for end_snap: **1982**

Here you need to give 'begin and end snap id.'

6. Specify Report Name: Default is awrrpt_1_begin_span_id_end_snap_id.html. Press enter for default name or give a new name.

Specify the Report Name: The default report file name is AWR_09SEP0000_10SEP0000.html. To use this name, press to continue; otherwise, enter an alternative.

Enter a value for report_name:

7. Report generated: Your report is generated at the present working directory.

Report is written to AWR_09SEP0000_10SEP0000.html

8. To get the report:

```
SQL> exit;
[Oracle@doyen]$ pwd
/home/Oracle
```

9. Read AWR Report:

Go to /home/Oracle, find the file as "AWR_09SEP0000_10SEP0000.html". This is your AWR report generated.

Now DBA has generated AWR Report. So, the next step is to analyse the AWR Report.

How to analyse AWR report

As you have generated AWR Report in Oracle, the next task is to analyse AWR Report in Oracle. By Reading AWR Report, you can easily solve issues like 'Slow database', 'high wait events', 'Slow query' and many more. Though it's a lengthy report, analysing or reading the relevant part of AWR Report can help to troubleshoot issues in an easy and fast manner.

Recommendations before getting an AWR Report.

1. *Collect Multiple AWR Reports:* It's always good to have two AWR Reports, one for a good time (when the database was performing well), second when performance was poor. This way Remote DBA can easily compare the good and bad reports to find out the culprit.

2. *Stick to a Particular Time:* "Database is performing slow" will not help any more to resolve performance issues. We have to have a specific time like Database was slow yesterday at 1 p.m. and continue till 4 p.m. Here, DBA will get a report for these three hours.

3. *Split Large AWR Report into Smaller Reports:* Instead of having one report for a long time like one report for 4 hours, it is better to have four reports, one for each hour. This will help to isolate the problem.

In case of RAC env. generate one report for each instance. Once, you have generated AWR report' it's now time to analyse the report. Since AWR report is a huge report and area to look into AWR also varies from problem to problem. Here, I am listing the most common area for a DBA to look into which will give a clear picture of the issue.

Steps to Analyse AWR Report

1. Database Details: After getting an AWR Report This is first and Top part of the report. In this part cross-check for database and instance and database version with the Database having a performance issue. This report also shows RAC=YES if it's an RAC database.

DB Name	DB Id	Instance	Inst num	Startup Time	Release	RAC
			1 04-Sep-19 05:09	12.1.0.2.0	YES

2. Host Configuration: This will give you a name, **platform CUP, socket** and **RAM,** etc. An <u>important thing to notice is the number of cores into the system.</u> In this example, there are 12 CUPs in **Cores.**

Host Name	Platform	CPUs	Cores	Sockets	Memory (GB)
	Linux x86 64-bit	64	32	4	251.90

3. Snapshot Detail: This is the detail about the snapshot taken, **Snap start time** and **end time**. The difference between them is known as "**Elapsed**". Here is a new term "**DB Time**".

	Snap Id	Snap Time	Sessions	Cursors/Session	Instances
Begin Snap:	51429	09-Sep-19 00:00:11	761	9.9	4
End Snap:	51453	10-Sep-19 00:00:10	838	10.4	4
Elapsed:		1,439.99 (mins)			
DB Time:		28,327.42 (mins)			

DB Time= session time spent in database.

DB Time= CPU Time + Non IDLE wait time.

You can find, DB time is very large as compared to Elapse time, which is not a concern. Check if you have taken a report for the time having a performance problem. If yes, fine; otherwise take a report for performance problem time.

Next is Cache Sizes, which is just detail about SGA components

4. Load Profile: Here are a few important stats for a DBA to look into. First is "DB CPU(s)" per second. Before that let's understand how DB CUPs work. Suppose you have 12 cores into the system. So, per wall clock second you have 12 seconds to work on CPU.

Load Profile

	Per Second	Per Transaction	Per Exec	Per Call
DB Time(s):	19.7	0.5	0.01	0.05
DB CPU(s):	12.7	0.3	0.00	0.03
Background CPU(s):	0.6	0.0	0.00	0.00
Redo size (bytes):	1,516,965.1	39,114.8		
Logical read (blocks):	4,465,933.3	115,153.6		
Block changes:	9,378.8	241.8		
Physical read (blocks):	12,975.6	334.6		
Physical write (blocks):	453.2	11.7		
Read IO requests:	1,364.1	35.2		
Write IO requests:	240.2	6.2		
Read IO (MB):	101.4	2.6		
Write IO (MB):	3.5	0.1		
IM scan rows:	0.0	0.0		
Session Logical Read IM:				
Global Cache blocks received:	1,213.9	31.3		
Global Cache blocks served:	1,185.4	30.6		
User calls:	400.2	10.3		
Parses (SQL):	237.4	6.1		
Hard parses (SQL):	3.1	0.1		
SQL Work Area (MB):	22.6	0.6		
Logons:	3.8	0.1		
Executes (SQL):	2,930.1	75.6		
Rollbacks:	1.8	0.1		
Transactions:	38.8			

So, if "**DB CPU(s)**" per second in this report > **cores** in (Host Configuration (#2)) means env is CPU-bound and either needs more CPUs or needs to further check if this is happening all the time or for just for a fraction of time. As per my experience, there are very few cases when the system is CPU-bound.

In this case, the machine has 12 cores and DB CPU(s) per second is 6.8. So, this is not a CPU-bound case.

Next stat to look at are **Parses** and **Hard Parses**. If the ratio of Hard Parse to Parse is high, this means Database is performing more of Hard Parse. So, needs to look at parameters like cursor_sharing and application level for bind variables etc.

5. Instance Efficiency Percentages:

In these statistics, you have to look at "**% Non-Parse CPU**". If this value is near 100% means most of the CPU resources are used into operations other than parsing, which is good for database health.

Buffer Nowait %:		99.99 Redo NoWait %:	100.00
Buffer Hit %:		99.97 In-memory Sort %:	100.00
Library Hit %:		99.76 Soft Parse %:	98.69
Execute to Parse %:		91.90 Latch Hit %:	98.07
Parse CPU to Parse Elapsd %:		65.36 % Non-Parse CPU:	99.77
Flash Cache Hit %:		0.00	

6. Top 5 Timed Foreground Events:

This is another most important stats to consider while looking at AWR Report for any database performance related issue. This has a list of top 5 foreground wait events.

Event	Waits	Total Wait Time (sec)	Wait Avg(ms)	% DB time	Wait Class
DB CPU		1.1M		64.3	
db file sequential read	62,520,608	208.6K	3.34	12.3	User I/O
direct path read	9,420,636	117.4K	12.46	6.9	User I/O
gc buffer busy acquire	17,178,243	48.8K	2.84	2.9	Cluster
enq: TX - row lock contention	7,599	33.1K	4357.48	1.9	Application
db file scattered read	2,260,711	18.5K	8.19	1.1	User I/O
gc cr block busy	3,318,810	18.3K	5.50	1.1	Cluster
gc cr multi block request	10,929,328	17.7K	1.62	1.0	Cluster
log file sync	2,426,484	16.6K	6.82	1.0	Commit
library cache lock	446,028	15.2K	34.01	.9	Concurrency

Here, first of all, check for **wait class.** If the wait class is User I/O, System I/O, Others, etc. this could be fine but if wait class has value "Concurrency" then there could be some serious problem. Next to look at is **Time (s)** which show how many times DB was waiting in this class and then **Avg Wait (ms)**. If **Time(s)** are high but **Avg Wait (ms)** is low then you can ignore this. If both are high or **Avg Wait (ms)** is high then this has to be further investigated.

In the above screenshot, most of the resources are taken by DB CPU = 64% DB time. Taking resource by DB CUP is a normal situation.

Let's take an example, in which event is "log file switch (checkpoint incomplete) " which has high **waits**, huge **Time (s)** and large values in **Avg Wait (ms)** and **wait class** is configuration. So, here you have to investigate and resolve log file switch (checkpoint incomplete).

Host CPU, Instance CPU and Memory Statistics are self-explanatory. Next is RAC Statistics: I did not find any issue in these stats most of the time.

7. Time Model Statistics: This is a detailed explanation of the system resource consumptions. Stats' order is by Time (s) and % of DB Time.

Statistic Name	Time (s)	% of DB Time	% of Total CPU Time
sql execute elapsed time	1,627,574.21	95.76	
DB CPU	1,093,422.05	64.33	95.98
inbound PL/SQL rpc elapsed time	21,992.31	1.29	
PL/SQL execution elapsed time	15,548.76	0.91	
parse time elapsed	13,278.10	0.78	
connection management call elapsed time	11,750.32	0.69	
hard parse elapsed time	11,031.99	0.65	
failed parse elapsed time	2,946.14	0.17	
hard parse (sharing criteria) elapsed time	2,321.53	0.14	
RMAN cpu time (backup/restore)	1,996.20	0.12	0.18
PL/SQL compilation elapsed time	404.21	0.02	
repeated bind elapsed time	111.78	0.01	
hard parse (bind mismatch) elapsed time	102.28	0.01	
sequence load elapsed time	27.74	0.00	
Java execution elapsed time	20.43	0.00	
DB time	1,699,645.37		
background elapsed time	137,841.08		
background cpu time	45,751.81		4.02
total CPU time	1,139,173.86		

A noticeable result Sum of all % of DB time is > 100%. Why is this so?

\Because this is cumulative time i.e. in this case, SQL execute elapsed time is taking 89% of DB time, which includes its subparts like parse time elapsed, hard parse elapsed time, etc. So, if you find hard parse time elapsed is taking more %, investigate further so on and so forth.

DBA has to look for stat which is taking abnormal % of DB time.

8. Operating System Statistics - Detail:

This is the information related to OS; what is the load status on System is shown here.

Snap Time	Load	%busy	%user	%sys	%idle	%iowait
09-Sep 00:00:11	27.90					
09-Sep 01:00:16	29.29	44.79	43.28	1.18	55.21	6.45
09-Sep 02:00:36	28.19	40.75	39.37	1.08	59.25	5.74
09-Sep 03:00:11	29.96	42.85	41.43	1.12	57.15	5.98
09-Sep 04:00:09	27.46	40.18	38.88	1.06	59.82	5.50
09-Sep 05:00:22	43.63	44.15	42.51	1.22	55.85	5.75
09-Sep 06:00:04	45.34	52.66	50.51	1.51	47.34	5.13
09-Sep 07:00:13	33.95	55.77	53.52	1.59	44.23	4.35
09-Sep 08:00:01	41.14	44.86	43.15	1.24	55.14	4.38
09-Sep 09:00:14	13.77	29.09	27.71	0.94	70.91	5.93
09-Sep 10:00:17	15.09	21.47	20.40	0.75	78.53	7.95
09-Sep 11:00:07	14.00	22.06	20.85	0.92	77.94	5.94
09-Sep 12:00:24	14.99	16.92	16.08	0.62	83.08	3.86
09-Sep 13:00:01	11.97	17.16	16.47	0.55	82.84	2.82
09-Sep 14:00:12	12.78	19.68	18.85	0.65	80.32	3.55
09-Sep 15:00:22	14.02	11.52	10.26	0.99	88.48	4.96
09-Sep 16:00:04	12.45	11.91	11.00	0.71	88.09	4.16
09-Sep 17:00:01	8.89	14.41	13.50	0.71	85.59	4.57
09-Sep 18:00:18	8.25	9.54	8.73	0.66	90.46	2.77
09-Sep 19:00:05	10.59	13.77	12.72	0.86	86.23	3.53
09-Sep 20:00:04	19.75	15.41	14.26	0.84	84.59	4.29
09-Sep 21:00:17	21.79	31.09	29.48	1.06	68.91	3.40
00 Sep 22:00:31	11.61	20.43	18.83	1.05	79.57	2.59
09-Sep 23:00:14	12.07	16.18	14.63	1.10	83.82	5.88
10-Sep 00:00:10	11.53	15.90	14.66	0.94	84.10	2.30

This report shows system is 62 and 70% idle at time of report taken. So, there is no resource crunch at system level. But if you found very high busy, user or sys % indeed this will lead to low idle %. Investigate what is causing this. OS Watcher is the tool which can help in this direction.

Next, a very crucial part of AWR report for a DBA is SQL Statistics which has all SQL query details executed during the report time interval.

SQL Statistics

- SQL ordered by Elapsed Time
- SQL ordered by CPU Time
- SQL ordered by User I/O Wait Time
- SQL ordered by Gets
- SQL ordered by Reads
- SQL ordered by Physical Reads (UnOptimized)
- SQL ordered by Executions
- SQL ordered by Parse Calls
- SQL ordered by Sharable Memory
- SQL ordered by Version Count
- SQL ordered by Cluster Wait Time
- Complete List of SQL Text

We will explore a few of them, to understand how to analyse these reports. Let's start with:

9. SQL Ordered by Elapsed Time: As explained by the name itself, this lists SQL queries ordered by **Elapsed time** into the reported time interval.

Elapsed Time (s)	Executions	Elapsed Time per Exec (s)	%Total	%CPU	%IO	SQL Id	SQL Module	SQL Text
692,451.08	691	1,002.10	40.74	97.40	2.36	f5cuuz6v0gmww		
670,115.87	696	962.81	39.43	97.79	2.60	frzqzm2n2b1gbs		
319,526.86	30	10,650.90	18.80	69.03	9.82	1mm32w3t67z2t		BEGIN DBMS...
64,480.75	67	962.40	3.79	9.37	84.95	a3kxyqjurdtp8	Oracle Enterprise Manager.Metric Engine	Insert into
59,375.07	261,448	0.23	3.49	78.97	0.01	7tmrnrinp8gb0		UPDATE
55,397.03	254,409	0.22	3.26	80.42	0.01	a2s7ft2tddcf		update
51,060.68	259,721	0.20	3.00	71.73	0.02	cud96m2vspd8n		UPDATE

In this report, look for query which has low **executions** and high **Elapsed time per Exec (s)** and this query could be a candidate for troubleshooting or optimizations. In the above report, you can see the first query has maximum Elapsed time but no execution. So you have to investigate this.

An Important point, if executions are 0, it doesn't mean the query is not executing; this might be the case when the query was still executing and you took AWR report. That's why query completion was not covered in Report.

10. SQL Ordered by CUP Time: In this report, SQL queries are listed on the basis of CPU taken by the query i.e. queries causing high load on the system. The top few queries could be the candidate query for optimization.

CPU Time (s)	Executions	CPU per Exec (s)	%Total	Elapsed Time (s)	%CPU	%IO	SQL Id	SQL Module	SQL Text
674,470.19	691	976.08	61.68	692,451.08	97.40	2.36	f5cuuz6v0gmww		SELECT CNT FROM (SELECT COUNT...
655,299.36	696	941.52	59.93	670,115.87	97.79	2.60	fzqgm2n2b1gbs		BEGIN
220,575.26	30	7,352.51	20.17	319,526.86	69.03	9.82	1mm32w2t67z2t		BEGIN
46,986.34	261,448	0.18	4.29	59,375.07	78.97	0.01	7tmrnrinp8gb0		UPDATE
44,551.51	254,409	0.18	4.07	55,397.03	80.42	0.01	a2s7ft2tfddcf		update
38,066.36	212,379	0.18	3.48	48,514.37	78.46	0.01	4z9dchiagmmay		update
36,619.24	259,721	0.14	3.35	51,060.68	71.73	0.02	cud96m2vspd8n		UPDATE

From the above stat, look for queries using the highest **CPU Times**. If a query shows **executions** 0, this doesn't mean the query is not executing. It might be the same case as in SQL queries ordered by Elapsed time. The query is still executing and you have taken the snapshot.

Best Practice:

Automatic AWR on a daily basis analyses and improves the performance of the database. By default, snapshots are generated once every 60 min and maintained for 7 days but keep history at least for 60 days or keep the data in other backup tables to review the historical capture. Present the actionable report taken based on the AWR report to the clients during monthly review.

Reference:

AWR Report in Oracle 11g - Ampersand Academy.

https://ampersandacademy.com/tutorials/Oracle-admin-1/awr-report-in-Oracle-11g

TOPIC

2

CPU OVERHEAD

It's always a challenging task for DBA to convince Customer that your hardware is not enough to handle the current load. So we have to fight hard to prove them. We want to do a simple calculation based on the data from AWR report to prove that CPU configuration is not enough to handle the load.

We all know the AWR report or statspack report help DBAs to understand what is happening in the database. If we figured them out correctly, our major portion of performance issue is solved because we know what the issue is.

In this chapter, we are going to see "DB CPU" and "DB Time" in AWR report and how we can interrupt to find the Average active sessions and how we can measure if Hardware CPU is correctly configured.

Explanations: DB CPU: DB CPU is the CPU consumption by Oracle Server processes+Oracle foreground sessions during snapshot interval time.

DB Time: Total time in database calls by foreground sessions which includes CPU Time, IO Time and non-idle wait time.

Average Active Session: Sum of Average activity overall sessions.

Scenario 1- when the database server is heavily loaded:

	Snap Id	Snap Time	Sessions	Cursors/Session
Begin Snap:	60963	11-Sep-19 10:30:21	1274	20.8
End Snap:	60964	11-Sep-19 11:30:40	1392	20.1
Elapsed:		60.32 (mins)		
DB Time:		1,541.44 (mins)		

Picture 2:

Wait Class	Waits	Total Wait Time (sec)	Avg Wait (ms)	% DB time	Avg Active Sessions
DB CPU		21,784		23.6	6.0
Application	8,836	5,035	569.80	5.4	1.4
User I/O	3,022,760	4,980	1.65	5.4	1.4

Picture 3:

Statistic Name	Time (s)	% of DB Time	% of Total CPU Time
sql execute elapsed time	90,438.86	97.79	
DB CPU	21,784.49	23.55	99.12
inbound PL/SQL rpc elapsed time	11,066.12	11.97	
PL/SQL execution elapsed time	8,122.25	8.78	
parse time elapsed	4,224.03	4.57	
hard parse elapsed time	4,083.93	4.42	
hard parse (sharing criteria) elapsed time	625.24	0.68	
PL/SQL compilation elapsed time	303.86	0.33	
connection management call elapsed time	199.64	0.22	
hard parse (bind mismatch) elapsed time	118.31	0.13	
Java execution elapsed time	18.73	0.02	
repeated bind elapsed time	3.43	0.00	
sequence load elapsed time	2.59	0.00	
failed parse elapsed time	0.81	0.00	
OLAP engine elapsed time	0.29	0.00	
OLAP engine CPU time	0.06	0.00	
DB time	92,486.65		
background elapsed time	2,060.69		

Picture 4:

Statistic	Value	End Value
AVG_BUSY_TIME	221,472	
AVG_IDLE_TIME	139,696	
AVG_IOWAIT_TIME	2,365	
AVG_SYS_TIME	14,683	
AVG_USER_TIME	206,611	
BUSY_TIME	14,185,544	
IDLE_TIME	8,951,438	
IOWAIT_TIME	162,936	
SYS_TIME	951,021	
USER_TIME	13,234,523	
LOAD	25	57
OS_CPU_WAIT_TIME	15,092,800	
RSRC_MGR_CPU_WAIT_TIME	0	
PHYSICAL_MEMORY_BYTES	182,536,110,080	
NUM_CPUS	64	
NUM_CPU_CORES	8	

Scenario 2- when database server works during night time and when only a scheduled job runs

Picture 5:

Snap Id	Snap Time	Sessions	Cursors/Session
Begin Snap: 61004	13-Sep-19 03:30:44	567	23.5
End Snap: 61005	13-Sep-19 04:30:56	569	23.7
Elapsed:	60.22 (mins)		
DB Time:	568.25 (mins)		

Picture 6:

Event	Waits	Total Wait Time (sec)	Wait Avg(ms)	% DB time	Wait Class
DB CPU		12.1K		35.5	
db file sequential read	1,232,239	3157.4	2.56	9.3	User I/O
SQL*Net message from dblink	459,035	322.3	0.70	.9	Network

Picture 7:

Statistic Name	Time (s)	% of DB Time	% of Total CPU Time
sql execute elapsed time	33,663.77	98.74	
DB CPU	12,113.59	35.53	99.02
PL/SQL execution elapsed time	6,469.82	18.98	
inbound PL/SQL rpc elapsed time	4,609.97	13.52	
parse time elapsed	443.93	1.30	
hard parse elapsed time	272.87	0.80	
connection management call elapsed time	27.25	0.08	
PL/SQL compilation elapsed time	15.16	0.04	
hard parse (sharing criteria) elapsed time	7.00	0.02	
sequence load elapsed time	1.01	0.00	
hard parse (bind mismatch) elapsed time	0.95	0.00	
repeated bind elapsed time	0.50	0.00	
Java execution elapsed time	0.02	0.00	
failed parse elapsed time	0.01	0.00	
OLAP engine elapsed time	0.00	0.00	
OLAP engine CPU time	0.00	0.00	
DB time	34,094.86		

Picture 8:

Statistic	Value	End Value
AVG_BUSY_TIME	42,536	
AVG_IDLE_TIME	317,557	
AVG_IOWAIT_TIME	3,440	
AVG_SYS_TIME	1,500	
AVG_USER_TIME	40,360	
BUSY_TIME	2,769,446	
IDLE_TIME	20,370,183	
IOWAIT_TIME	256,898	
SYS_TIME	139,198	
USER_TIME	2,630,248	
LOAD	9	5
OS_CPU_WAIT_TIME	2,898,900	
RSRC_MGR_CPU_WAIT_TIME	0	
VM_IN_BYTES	8,192	
VM_OUT_BYTES	0	
PHYSICAL_MEMORY_BYTES	186,831,077,376	
NUM_CPUS	64	
NUM_CPU_CORES	8	
NUM_LCPUS	64	
NUM_VCPUS	8	
GLOBAL_RECEIVE_SIZE_MAX	1,048,576	

Let's take some real-time example with AWR data on how to arrive average active session per second.

Average Active session in Scenario 1: DB Time /Elapsed => 1541.44/60.32 => 25.55

Average Active session in Scenario 2: DB Time /Elapsed => 568.25/60.22 => 9.43

In the Scenario 1 Average Active session is 25.55 whereas the number of CPU cores is 8. This indicates that the database server needs higher CPU configuration to handle the peak load or Database needs to be tuned on to reduce the average active session value to below the number of CPU cores.

In the Scenario 2 Average Active session is 9.43 whereas the number of CPU cores is 8. This indicates that the database server needs a slightly higher CPU configuration even to handle the scheduled jobs load.

In both the Scenarios it's evident that CPU core is under configured but still as a DBA we have room to tune the CPU intensive queries and check any Parsing activity as this CPU intensive operation.

Note: Please be advised that running AWR report and interrupting AWR history tables requires additional "Diagnostics Pack" license. Please be cautious before running the AWR report.

Hope you have got some idea about DB CPU and DB TIME statistic in AWR report.

Happy Performance Tuning!!!

Reference:

http://deepakbhatnagardba.blogspot.com/2015/12/what-elapsed-time-db-time-and-db-cpu.html

https://www.Oracle.com/technetwork/oem/db-mgmt/s317294-db-perf-tuning-with-db-time-181631.pdf

http://orasal.blogspot.com/2017/06/on-db-time-db-cpu-and-utilization.html

HOW TO MIGRATE EXPLAIN PLAN FROM ONE DATABASE TO OTHER DATABASE AND TO MAKE SURE OPTIMIZER CHOSE THE EXPECTED PLAN

The explained plan is the execution plan chosen by Oracle optimizer for select, update, insert and delete operation. An SQL statement execution plan is the sequence of operations Oracle performs to run the statement.

One of our customers has faced an issue like in DEVELOPMENT query is running fine but in PRODUCTION it's taking a lot of time. There are reasons like recent statistics collected on tables, recently tables might be heavily loaded and hardware configuration, etc. for the optimizer to pick a different plan for different database.

But in our case there is not much difference between DEV and PROD; so we have decided to copy the explained plan from DEVELOPMENT to PRODUCTION database.

There is more than one way to migrate the plan but here we are going to discuss some simple steps to migrate the plan. Please be advised that running the query mentioned below will touch the AWR tables and create profiles that required additional "Diagnostics Pack" license. Please be sure that you have this license before running this.

We have not used SQL Plan Management to manage the explain plan; so we have used other simple ways to migrate the plan and that is exactly we are going to discuss here.

We know the SQL_ID for the SQL query is having two different behaviours in two different databases. In case you want to find out sql_id if we know the sql_text we can easily query from these two tables.

☐ v$SQL -> if the query available in memory

☐ dba_hist_sqltext -> if the query not available in memory.

Now we have to create a profile for the SQL_ID by running coe_xfr_sql_profile.sql. You can get the script from by downloading sqlt from Oracle support. Please refer Doc ID 1614107.1 for downloading and we don't have to install this tool. Just download and unzip it locally on the server.

1. Run the script coe_xfr_sql_profile.sql and input the SQL_ID that will list the available plan for the SQL ID and average elapsed time in seconds.

2. Now you have to input expected PLAN_HASH_VALUE and this will create a file.

3. Copy the newly created file from DEVELOPMENT database server to PRODUCTION database server.

4. On PROD server login as sysdba and run that file. This will create a SQL_PROFILE for the problematic SQL_ID in PRODUCTION.

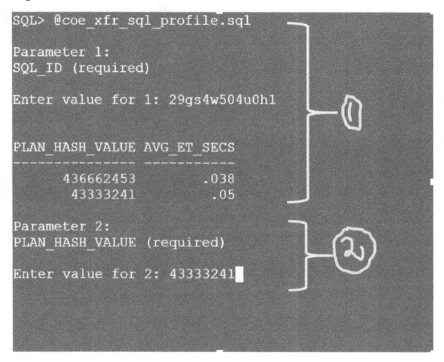

```
SQL> @coe_xfr_sql_profile.sql

Parameter 1:
SQL_ID (required)

Enter value for 1: 29gs4w504u0h1


PLAN_HASH_VALUE AVG_ET_SECS
--------------- -----------
      436662453        .038
       43333241         .05

Parameter 2:
PLAN_HASH_VALUE (required)

Enter value for 2: 43333241
```

```
SQL>SET TERM OFF;

Execute coe_xfr_sql_profile_29gs4w504u0h1_43333241.sql
on TARGET system in order to create a custom SQL Profile
with plan 43333241 linked to adjusted sql_text.


COE_XFR_SQL_PROFILE completed.
```

```
scp coe_xfr_sql_profile_29gs4w504u0h1_43333241.sql oracle@prddbserver:/home/oracle/
```

```
SQL*Plus: Release 12.1.0.2.0 Production on Thu Sep 12 00:58:25 2019

Copyright (c) 1982, 2014, Oracle.  All rights reserved.


Connected to:
Oracle Database 12c Enterprise Edition Release 12.1.0.2.0 - 64bit Production
With the Partitioning, OLAP, Advanced Analytics and Real Application Testing options

SQL> @coe_xfr_sql_profile_29gs4w504u0h1_43333241.sql
```

```
 92   /

PL/SQL procedure successfully completed.

SQL> WHENEVER SQLERROR CONTINUE
SQL> SET ECHO OFF;

            SIGNATURE
--------------------------
 1893855488999709238


            SIGNATUREF
--------------------------
 1893855488999709238


... manual custom SQL Profile has been created


COE_XFR_SQL_PROFILE_29gs4w504u0h1_43333241 completed
```

Sometimes optimizer may not choose the new plan as an existing plan will be in memory. So it's important to purge that plan from memory.

Script to Purge explain from memory:

```
set serveroutput on
set pagesize 9999
set linesize 155
var name varchar2(50)
accept sql_id -
prompt 'Enter value for sql_id: '
BEGIN
select address||','||hash_value into:name
from v$sqlarea
```

```
where sql_id like '&&sql_id';
dbms_shared_pool.purge(:name,'C',1);
END;
/
undef sql_id
undef name
```

Now let's make sure optimizer used the expected plan by running the below query. Make sure we ask our technical or development team rerun the query in PROD before running this query.

```
col sql_text for a60 wrap
set verify off
set page size 999
set lines 155
col username format a13
col prog format a22
col sid format 999
col child_number format 99999 heading CHILD
col ocategory format a10
col avg_etime format 9,999,999.99
col avg_pio format 9,999,999.99
col avg_lio format 9,999,99999
col etime format 9,999,999.99
select sql_id, child_number, plan_hash_value plan_hash, executions execs,
(elapsed_time/1000000)/decode(nvl(executions,0),0,1,executions)
avg_etime,
buffer_gets/decode(nvl(executions,0),0,1,executions) avg_lio,
sql_text
from v$sql s
where upper(sql_text) like upper(nvl('&sql_text',sql_text))
and sql_text not like '%from v$sql where sql_text like nvl(%'
and sql_id like nvl('&sql_id',sql_id)
order by 1, 2, 3
```

SQL_ID	CHILD	PLAN_HASH	EXECS	AVG_ETIME	AVG_LIO
29gs4w504u0h1	0	436662453	833355	.10	2732

Hope you have learned to migrate the explained plan from one database to another database. We all know this concept but would like to put it together for easy use.

Thanks for reading and happy performance tuning!

Reference:

https://docs.Oracle.com/cd/B19306_01/server.102/b14211/ex_plan.htm#i3305

https://jasonbrownsite.wordpress.com/2015/09/29/moving-an-Oracle-sql-execution-plan-from-one-environment-to-another/

TOPIC

4

TUNING SQL STATEMENTS USING SQL TUNING ADVISOR (WITHOUT ENTERPRISE MANAGER)

One of our clients in my company Doyensys, we were not provided access to Oracle Enterprise Manager to monitor and manage E-business suite, OBIEE and other Oracle products. Though we had all backend credentials in all databases, we were completely relying on custom-developed SQL scripts and shell scripts.

In OBIEE, we often used to get performance problems on running a report. SQLs were very huge and we were in need of tuning the SQLs sometimes. Many times I used to think if I had access to OEM, I would have run the SQL tuning advisor to get some advice on tuning the SQL or creating SQL profile for that particular SQL.

One day, I decided to find a solution and started using the Oracle standard procedures to tune the SQL.

Below are the steps to use SQL Tuning Advisor for particular SQL.

1) Create tuning task using SQL_ID

2) Execute tuning task

3) Generate report for the tuning task

STEP 1: CREATE TUNING TASK

CREATE tuning tasks for SQL_ID picked from history sessions. If you have an SQL ID which got executed some days ago, find them in DBA_HIST_SQLTEXT <<<<AWR>>>>>

DECLARE

```
l_sql_tune_task_id  VARCHAR2(100);
BEGIN
l_sql_tune_task_id := DBMS_SQLTUNE.create_tuning_task (
 begin_snap  => 11716,
end_snap    => 11717,
sql_id      => 'f4am5zd2tc2ys',
scope       => DBMS_SQLTUNE.scope_comprehensive,
time_limit  => 6000,
task_name   => 'dyfp8d71pjym8_tuning_task',
description => 'Tuning task for statement f4am5zd2tc2ys in AWR.');
DBMS_OUTPUT.put_line('l_sql_tune_task_id: ' || l_sql_tune_task_id);
END;
/
```

If you want to run SQL tuning for the running active SQL, use as below. This command gets the details from the running session.

CREATE tuning tasks for SQL_ID for running session <<<<<Cursor Cache>>>>>

```
DECLARE
  l_sql_tune_task_id  VARCHAR2(100);
BEGIN
  l_sql_tune_task_id := DBMS_SQLTUNE.create_tuning_task (
sql_id      => 'f4am5zd2tc2ys',
scope       => DBMS_SQLTUNE.scope_comprehensive,
time_limit  => 6000,
task_name   => 'f4am5zd2tc2ys_tuning_task',
description => 'Tuning task for statement f4am5zd2tc2ys');
  DBMS_OUTPUT.put_line('l_sql_tune_task_id: ' || l_sql_tune_task_id);
END;
/
```

Please note that time_limit is a kind of time-out parameter specified in seconds to let Oracle tuning engine know how long it should wait for the tuning task to be completed before getting time out.

This value can be changed, according to the complexity of the SQL.

STEP 2: Check whether the task has been created using the SQL below.

SELECT task_name, status FROM dba_advisor_log WHERE task_name like 'f4am5zd2tc2ys_tuning_task%';

Now it is time to execute the tuning task where it will provide some suggestions.

EXEC DBMS_SQLTUNE.execute_tuning_task(task_name =>
'f4am5zd2tc2ys_tuning_task');

STEP 3: Use the SQL below to review the suggestions based on the tuning task execution.

```
SET lines 200 pages 1000
SET LONG 999999999
SET longchunksize 200
```

```
SELECT DBMS_SQLTUNE.report_tuning_task('f4am5zd2tc2ys_tuning_task') from
dual;
```

Hurray!! Now you can find Oracle suggestions for the SQL and you can decide on whether to run gather stats for a particular object or accept the system-created SQL profile.

Now you do not want to put your head on your laptop and search for the blogs or other sources to find the tuning issues. Just execute this tuning package and go and grab a cup of coffee. By the time you get back to your seat, the suggestions will be ready on your table.

It's your wish to keep the tuning task or recommendation in the instance. If you would like to drop them, you can use the package below.

STEP 4: To drop the SQL tuning tasks (OPTIONAL)

EXEC DBMS_SQLTUNE.drop_tuning_task(task_name =>
'f4am5zd2tc2ys_tuning_task');

The above steps are very helpful when there is no access to any tuning tool in Oracle database.

TOPIC

5

EASY STEPS TO IDENTIFY AND REMOVE ORACLE TABLE FRAGMENTATION

What is Table Fragmentation?

In this blog, we will be discussing table fragmentation, which causes slowness and wastage of space in blocks. Fragmentation is a common issue in Oracle database which occurs due to excessive DML operations like insert followed by delete and upgrade operations. When new rows are inserted into the table, the high watermark of the table moves forward to accommodate new rows into the table. But during delete operation, Oracle doesn't allow high watermark to shift backwards to decrease table size and release the free space. Ideally, once we delete the data from the table, the free space should be released or reused but additionally, Oracle acquires new blocks to accommodate the new rows for insertion which causes holes into the table.

Way to find Fragmentation for Tables and LOBs at segment level

☐ Tables in MSSM (Manual Segment Space Management) tablespaces

☐ Tables in ASSM(Automatic Segment Space Management) tablespaces

☐ LOBs in MSSM(Manual Segment Space Management) tablespaces

☐ LOBs in ASSM (Automatic Segment Space Management) tablespaces

☐ Securefile LOBs

1. Tables in MSSM (Manual Segment Space Management) tablespaces:

We can easily find by running the SQL query below.

```
exec dbms_stats.gather_table_stats('<OWNER>','<TABLE NAME>');

select owner,table_name,round((blocks*8),2)||'kb'"TABLE
SIZE",round((num_rows*avg_row_len/1024),2)||'kb'"ACTUAL DATA" from dba_tables
where table_name='<YOUR TABLES'S NAME>';
```

1. Tables in ASSM(Automatic Segment Space Management) tablespaces

```
set serveroutput on
declare
v_unformatted_blocks number;
v_unformatted_bytes number;
v_fs1_blocks number;
v_fs1_bytes number;
v_fs2_blocks number;
v_fs2_bytes number;
v_fs3_blocks number;
v_fs3_bytes number;
v_fs4_blocks number;
v_fs4_bytes number;
v_full_blocks number;
v_full_bytes number;
begin
dbms_space.space_usage ('<schema>', '<table name>', 'TABLE', v_unformatted_blocks,
v_unformatted_bytes, v_fs1_blocks, v_fs1_bytes, v_fs2_blocks, v_fs2_bytes,
v_fs3_blocks, v_fs3_bytes, v_fs4_blocks, v_fs4_bytes, v_full_blocks, v_full_bytes);
dbms_output.put_line('Unformatted  Blocks = '||v_unformatted_blocks);
dbms_output.put_line('FS1 Blocks = '||v_fs1_blocks);
dbms_output.put_line('FS2 Blocks = '||v_fs2_blocks);
dbms_output.put_line('FS3 Blocks = '||v_fs3_blocks);
dbms_output.put_line('FS4 Blocks = '||v_fs4_blocks);
dbms_output.put_line('Full Blocks = '||v_full_blocks);
end;
/
```

```
unformatted_blocks: Total number of blocks unformatted
fs1_blocks: Number of blocks having at least 0 to 25% free space
fs2_blocks: Number of blocks having at least 25 to 50% free space
fs3_blocks: Number of blocks having at least 50 to 75% free space
fs4_blocks: Number of blocks having at least 75 to 100% free space
full_blocks: Total number of blocks full in the segment
```

Fragmentation is considered to be high if there are too many fs1, fs2 and fs3 blocks (mostly fs1 and fs2 blocks) because these blocks might not allow inserts despite the free space and segment might need to extend when new inserts come in.

From a space-regain perspective, if there are too many fs3, fs4 blocks (especially fs4 blocks) and the possibility of future inserts is minimal, re-organizing the table will release lots of space.

Re-organizing the table compacts the blocks thereby increasing FULL blocks, reducing fs1, fs2, fs3 and fs4 blocks and thus reducing the total number of blocks.

2. To find fragmentation at the partition level

```
set serveroutput on
declare
v_unformatted_blocks number;
v_unformatted_bytes number;
v_fs1_blocks number;
v_fs1_bytes number;
v_fs2_blocks number;
v_fs2_bytes number;
v_fs3_blocks number;
v_fs3_bytes number;
v_fs4_blocks number;
v_fs4_bytes number;
v_full_blocks number;
v_full_bytes number;
begin
dbms_space.space_usage ('<schema>', '<table name>', 'TABLE PARTITION',
v_unformatted_blocks,
v_unformatted_bytes, v_fs1_blocks, v_fs1_bytes, v_fs2_blocks, v_fs2_bytes,
v_fs3_blocks, v_fs3_bytes, v_fs4_blocks, v_fs4_bytes, v_full_blocks,
v_full_bytes, <partition name>);
dbms_output.put_line('Unformatted Blocks = '||v_unformatted_blocks);
dbms_output.put_line('FS1 Blocks = '||v_fs1_blocks);
dbms_output.put_line('FS2 Blocks = '||v_fs2_blocks);
dbms_output.put_line('FS3 Blocks = '||v_fs3_blocks);
dbms_output.put_line('FS4 Blocks = '||v_fs4_blocks);
dbms_output.put_line('Full Blocks = '||v_full_blocks);
end;
/
```

3. LOBs in MSSM(Manual Segment Space Management) tablespaces

```
The size of the LOB segment can be found by querying dba_segments,

select bytes from dba_segments where segment_name ='<lob segment name>'
and owner ='<table owner>';

To get the details of the table to which this LOB segment belong to:
SELECT TABLE_NAME, COLUMN_NAME FROM DBA_LOBS WHERE OWNER =
'<owner>' AND SEGMENT_NAME= '<lob segment name>';

Check the space that is actually allocated to the LOB data :
   select sum(dbms_lob.getlength (<lob column name>)) from <table_name>;
```

4. LOBs in ASSM (Automatic Segment Space Management) tablespaces

```
set serveroutput on
declare
v_unformatted_blocks number;
v_unformatted_bytes number;
v_fs1_blocks number;
v_fs1_bytes number;
v_fs2_blocks number;
v_fs2_bytes number;
v_fs3_blocks number;
v_fs3_bytes number;
v_fs4_blocks number;
v_fs4_bytes number;
v_full_blocks number;
v_full_bytes number;
begin
dbms_space.space_usage ('<owner>', '<lob segment name>', 'LOB',
v_unformatted_blocks,
v_unformatted_bytes, v_fs1_blocks, v_fs1_bytes, v_fs2_blocks,
v_fs2_bytes,
v_fs3_blocks, v_fs3_bytes, v_fs4_blocks, v_fs4_bytes, v_full_blocks,
v_full_bytes);
dbms_output.put_line('Unformatted Blocks = '||v_unformatted_blocks);
dbms_output.put_line('FS1 Blocks = '||v_fs1_blocks);
dbms_output.put_line('FS2 Blocks = '||v_fs2_blocks);
dbms_output.put_line('FS3 Blocks = '||v_fs3_blocks);
dbms_output.put_line('FS4 Blocks = '||v_fs4_blocks);
dbms_output.put_line('Full Blocks = '||v_full_blocks);
end;
/
```

5. Securefile LOBs

```
set serveroutput on
declare
v_segment_size_blocks number;
v_segment_size_bytes number;
v_used_blocks number;
v_used_bytes number;
v_expired_blocks number;
v_expired_bytes number;
v_unexpired_blocks number;
v_unexpired_bytes number;
begin
dbms_space.space_usage ('<owner>', '<securefile segment name>', 'LOB',
v_segment_size_blocks, v_segment_size_bytes, v_used_blocks,
v_used_bytes, v_expired_blocks, v_expired_bytes, v_unexpired_blocks,
v_unexpired_bytes);
dbms_output.put_line('Segment size in blocks =
'||v_segment_size_blocks);
dbms_output.put_line('Used Blocks = '||v_used_blocks);
dbms_output.put_line('Expired Blocks = '||v_expired_blocks);
dbms_output.put_line('Unxpired Blocks = '||v_unexpired_blocks);
end;
/
```

```
segment_size_blocks: Number of blocks allocated to the segment
used_blocks: Number blocks allocated to the LOB that contains active data
expired_blocks: Number of expired blocks used by the LOB to keep version
data
unexpired_blocks: Number of unexpired blocks used by the LOB to keep
version data
```

Steps to Check and Remove Fragmentation

Three options to do table defragmentation:

1. Alter table move (to another tablespace, or same tablespace) and rebuild indexes. You obviously need extra space in the tablespace to use it. Using an ONLINE keyword in Enterprise edition you have no lock and DML is still possible.

2. Export and import the table. Needless to say, the downtime is big and it is difficult to get on a production database.

3. Shrink command available starting with Oracle 10gR1. Usable on segments in tablespaces with automatic segment management and when row movement has been activated. But no gain must result.

1. Gather table stats: To check exact difference in table actual size (user_segments) and stats size (user_tables). The difference between these values will report actual fragmentation to DBA.

Updated stats on the table stored in user_tables. Check LAST_ANALYSED value for a table in user_tables. If this value is recent you can skip this step. Otherwise, we would suggest gathering table stats to get updated stats.

```
exec dbms_stats.gather_table_stats('schema_name','table_name');
```

2. Check for Fragmentation in a table: The query below will show the total size of a table with fragmentation, expected without fragmentation and how much % of size we can reclaim after removing table fragmentation. Database Administrator has to provide table_name and schema_name as input to this query.

```
select owner,table_name,round((blocks*8),2)||'kb' "Fragmented size",
round((num_rows*avg_row_len/1024),2)||'kb' "Actual size",
round((blocks*8),2)-round((num_rows*avg_row_len/1024),2)||'kb',
((round((blocks*8),2)-
round((num_rows*avg_row_len/1024),2))/round((blocks*8),2))*100 -10
"reclaimable space % " from dba_tables where table_name =' table_Name'
AND OWNER LIKE 'schema_name';
```

Note: This query fetches data from user_tables; so the accuracy of the result depends on user_table stats.

If you find reclaimable space % value more than 20% then we can expect fragmentation in the table. Suppose DBA finds 50% reclaimable space by the above query, he can proceed for removing fragmentation.

3. Collect status of all the indexes on the table: We will record Index status at one place so that we get them back after completion of this exercise.

```
Select index_name, status from user_indexes where table_name like
'table_name';
```

Status may be valid or unusable.

4. Move table into new tablespace: In this step, we will move the fragmented table from one tablespace to another tablespace to reclaim fragmented space. Find Current size of the table from user_segments and check if any other tablespace has same free space available, so that we can move this table to the new tablespace. 'Enable row movement' should be enabled first.

```
alter table table_name enable row movement;
alter table table_name move tablespace new_tablespace_name;
```

5. Move table into old tablespace:

Now, get back table to old tablespaces using below command

```
Alter table table_name move tablespace old_tablespace_name;
```

If we have as much free space available as of table size in the same tablespace which contains the table, we can replace step 4 and 5 by

```
Alter table table_name enable row movement;
Alter table table_name move;
```

6. Rebuild all indexes:

We need to rebuild all the indexes on the table since all the index goes into an unusable state because of move command.

```
Select index_name from user_indexes where table_name like 'table_name';
```

```
Use this command for each index.
```

```
Alter index index_name rebuild online;
```

7. Cross Check Index Status:

```
Select index_name, status from user_indexes where table_name like
'table_name';
```

Here, value in status field must be valid.

8. Check Table size: Now again check table size using below SQL script and DBA will find the reduced size of the table.

```
Select table_name,bytes/(1024*1024*1024) from user_table where
table_name='table_name';
```

If Remote DBA will again execute the query in #2, he will find the same result because status of the table is still old. So he has to collect table status. You can also observe the same amount of extra free space in current tablespace which was reclaimed after removing table fragmentation.

9. Gather table states:

```
exec dbms_stats.gather_table_stats('schema_name','table_name');
```

Best practices:

1. Schedule Gather statistics for all objects (dictionary and user objects) with 40% in the database.

2. Periodically perform table fragmentation for more DML operation tables to improve the performance and space gain.

3. In Doyensys, we recommend to the clients to periodically perform the table fragmentation for huge tables and more DML transaction tables. For EBS environment we used to fragment FND_LOBS tables which stores information about all LOBs managed by the Generic File Manager (GFM).

Reference:

How to Find Fragmentation for Tables and LOBs.

https://support.Oracle.com/knowledge/Oracle%20Database%20Products/2132004_1.html

TOPIC

6

MYTHS ON INDEX REBUILD

In this chapter we are going to see whether Index Rebuild is necessary and the impact of doing the Index Rebuild.

We DBAs' common approach is that rebuilding indexes will improve the performance as it compresses the leaf blocks and scattered free blocks will be merged. But the fact is different and the need to rebuild B-Tree index is very rare because these types of indexes are self-balanced and self-managed.

In this example, we have performed Heavy DML operation on newly created table; after each DML operation we have analysed the index and verified that LF_BLK_LEN and BR_BLK_LEN values are not changed. This shows scattered free blocks are reused.

```
SQL*Plus: Release 12.1.0.2.0 Production on Fri Sep 27 06:05:54 2019

Copyright (c) 1982, 2014, Oracle.  All rights reserved.

Connected to:
Oracle Database 12c Enterprise Edition Release 12.1.0.2.0 - 64bit
Production
With the Partitioning, OLAP, Advanced Analytics and Real Application
Testing options

"Inserting Records"

PL/SQL procedure successfully completed.



Index analysed.
```

```
NAME   HEIGHT      BLOCKS      LF_ROWS      LF_BLKS LF_ROWS_LEN LF_BLK_LEN
BR_ROWS    BR_BLKS DEL_LF_ROWS DEL_LF_ROWS_LEN BR_ROWS_LEN BR_BLK_LEN
---------- ---------- ---------- ---------- ---------- ----------- ------
---- ---------- ---------- ----------- --------------- ----------- ------
----
TEST_IDX1          2        640      98539        520     2956170
7996        519          1          0              0        5603
8028
```

"Check Index ratio after insert"

```
index_ratio
-----------
 .499001498
```

"Deleting records"

98539 rows deleted.

Index analysed.


```
NAME            HEIGHT     BLOCKS     LF_ROWS     LF_BLKS LF_ROWS_LEN
LF_BLK_LEN      BR_ROWS    BR_BLKS DEL_LF_ROWS DEL_LF_ROWS_LEN BR_ROWS_LEN
BR_BLK_LEN
---------- ---------- ---------- ---------- ---------- ----------- ------
---- ---------- ---------- ----------- --------------- ----------- ------
----
TEST_IDX1          2        640      98539        520     2956170
7996        519          1      98539        2956170        5603
8028
```

"Check Index ratio after deletion"

```
index_ratio
-----------
 .499001498
```

Disconnected from Oracle Database 12c Enterprise Edition Release 12.1.0.2.0 - 64bit Production

With the Partitioning, OLAP, Advanced Analytics and Real Application
Testing options

SQL*Plus: Release 12.1.0.2.0 Production on Fri Sep 27 06:06:23 2019

Copyright (c) 1982, 2014, Oracle. All rights reserved.

Connected to:
Oracle Database 12c Enterprise Edition Release 12.1.0.2.0 - 64bit
Production
With the Partitioning, OLAP, Advanced Analytics and Real Application
Testing options

"Inserting Records"

PL/SQL procedure successfully completed.

Index analysed.

NAME	HEIGHT	BLOCKS	LF_ROWS	LF_BLKS	LF_ROWS_LEN	LF_BLK_LEN	BR_ROWS	BR_BLKS	DEL_LF_ROWS	DEL_LF_ROWS_LEN	BR_ROWS_LEN	BR_BLK_LEN
TEST_IDX1	2	640	98539	538	2956170	7996	537	1	0	0	5803	8028

"Check Index ratio after insert"

```
index_ratio
-----------
 .499001498
```

"Deleting records"

98539 rows deleted.

```
Index analysed.


NAME            HEIGHT      BLOCKS      LF_ROWS      LF_BLKS LF_ROWS_LEN
LF_BLK_LEN      BR_ROWS     BR_BLKS DEL_LF_ROWS DEL_LF_ROWS_LEN BR_ROWS_LEN
BR_BLK_LEN
---------- ---------- ---------- ---------- ---------- ----------- ------
---- ---------- ---------- ----------- --------------- ----------- ------
----
TEST_IDX1            2         640       98539          538     2956170
7996          537           1       98539         2956170        5803
8028

"Check Index ratio after deletion"

index_ratio
-----------
 .499001498


Disconnected  from  Oracle  Database  12c  Enterprise  Edition  Release
12.1.0.2.0 - 64bit Production
With the Partitioning, OLAP, Advanced Analytics and Real Application
Testing options

SQL*Plus: Release 12.1.0.2.0 Production on Fri Sep 27 06:06:52 2019

Copyright (c) 1982, 2014, Oracle.  All rights reserved.


Connected to:
Oracle  Database  12c  Enterprise  Edition  Release  12.1.0.2.0  -  64bit
Production
With the Partitioning, OLAP, Advanced Analytics and Real Application
Testing options

"Inserting Records"

PL/SQL procedure successfully completed.


Index analysed.
```

NAME	HEIGHT	BLOCKS	LF_ROWS	LF_BLKS	LF_ROWS_LEN	LF_BLK_LEN	BR_ROWS	BR_BLKS	DEL_LF_ROWS	DEL_LF_ROWS_LEN	BR_ROWS_LEN	BR_BLK_LEN
TEST_IDX1	2	640	98539	544	2956170	7996	543	1	0	0	5870	8028

"Check Index ratio after insert"

```
index_ratio
-----------
 .499001498
```

"Deleting records"

98539 rows deleted.

Index analysed.

NAME	HEIGHT	BLOCKS	LF_ROWS	LF_BLKS	LF_ROWS_LEN	LF_BLK_LEN	BR_ROWS	BR_BLKS	DEL_LF_ROWS	DEL_LF_ROWS_LEN	BR_ROWS_LEN	BR_BLK_LEN
TEST_IDX1	2	640	98539	544	2956170	7996	543	1	98539	2956170	5870	8028

"Check Index ratio after deletion"

```
index_ratio
-----------
 .499001498
```

```
Disconnected  from  Oracle  Database  12c  Enterprise  Edition  Release
12.1.0.2.0 - 64bit Production
With  the  Partitioning,  OLAP,  Advanced  Analytics  and  Real  Application
Testing options

SQL*Plus: Release 12.1.0.2.0 Production on Fri Sep 27 06:07:21 2019

Copyright (c) 1982, 2014, Oracle.  All rights reserved.


Connected to:
Oracle  Database  12c  Enterprise  Edition  Release  12.1.0.2.0  -  64bit
Production
With  the  Partitioning,  OLAP,  Advanced  Analytics  and  Real  Application
Testing options

"Inserting Records"

PL/SQL procedure successfully completed.


Index analysed.


NAME            HEIGHT     BLOCKS    LF_ROWS    LF_BLKS LF_ROWS_LEN
LF_BLK_LEN     BR_ROWS    BR_BLKS DEL_LF_ROWS DEL_LF_ROWS_LEN BR_ROWS_LEN
BR_BLK_LEN
---------- ---------- ---------- ---------- ---------- ----------- ------
---- ---------- ---------- ----------- --------------- ----------- ------
----
TEST_IDX1         2        640      98539        549     2956170
7996        548          1          0              0        5925
8028

"Check Index ratio after insert"

index_ratio
-----------
 .499001498

"Deleting records"
```

98539 rows deleted.

Index analysed.

NAME	HEIGHT	BLOCKS	LF_ROWS	LF_BLKS	LF_ROWS_LEN	LF_BLK_LEN	BR_ROWS	BR_BLKS	DEL_LF_ROWS	DEL_LF_ROWS_LEN	BR_ROWS_LEN	BR_BLK_LEN
TEST_IDX1	2	640	98539	549	2956170	7996	548	1	98539	2956170	5925	8028

"Check Index ratio after deletion"

index_ratio

 .499001498

Disconnected from Oracle Database 12c Enterprise Edition Release 12.1.0.2.0 - 64bit Production
With the Partitioning, OLAP, Advanced Analytics and Real Application Testing options

SQL*Plus: Release 12.1.0.2.0 Production on Fri Sep 27 06:07:48 2019

Copyright (c) 1982, 2014, Oracle. All rights reserved.

Connected to:
Oracle Database 12c Enterprise Edition Release 12.1.0.2.0 - 64bit Production
With the Partitioning, OLAP, Advanced Analytics and Real Application Testing options

"Inserting Records"

PL/SQL procedure successfully completed.

```
Index analysed.


NAME              HEIGHT      BLOCKS     LF_ROWS    LF_BLKS LF_ROWS_LEN
LF_BLK_LEN       BR_ROWS     BR_BLKS DEL_LF_ROWS DEL_LF_ROWS_LEN BR_ROWS_LEN
BR_BLK_LEN
---------- ---------- ---------- ---------- ---------- ----------- ------
---- ---------- ---------- ----------- --------------- ----------- ------
----
TEST_IDX1              2         640      98539         556     2956170
7996          555           1          0               0         6002
8028
```

"Check Index ratio after insert"

```
index_ratio
-----------
 .499001498
```

"Deleting records"

```
98539 rows deleted.
```

```
Index analysed.


NAME              HEIGHT      BLOCKS     LF_ROWS    LF_BLKS LF_ROWS_LEN
LF_BLK_LEN       BR_ROWS     BR_BLKS DEL_LF_ROWS DEL_LF_ROWS_LEN BR_ROWS_LEN
BR_BLK_LEN
---------- ---------- ---------- ---------- ---------- ----------- ------
---- ---------- ---------- ----------- --------------- ----------- ------
----
TEST_IDX1              2         640      98539         556     2956170
7996          555           1      98539         2956170         6002
8028
```

"Check Index ratio after deletion"

```
index_ratio
-----------
```

```
.499001498

Disconnected  from  Oracle  Database  12c  Enterprise  Edition  Release
12.1.0.2.0 - 64bit Production
With  the  Partitioning,  OLAP,  Advanced  Analytics  and  Real  Application
Testing options
```

Impact on finding what Index to be rebuilt?

To find a candidate for Index to rebuild, we have to collect the statistics for an Index first by running the "analyse index <index_name> validate structure". While running this statement it will take exclusive table lock; so DML operations on this table will not be allowed. This is an expensive operation in OLTP environment. This statement can run online which means no exclusive table will be taken but this will not populate the rows in index_stats or index_histogram views and it's a timely operation.

Impact on Performance after rebuilding

DML operations cause the Index to progress over time as the Index splits and grows. When we rebuild an index, it will become tightly packed and the size of the Index will be reduced as this will gain space from database level. After rebuilding, when DML operations continue on the table, the Index split has to be redone again until the Index reaches its equilibrium; this is quite an expensive operation because redo generation will be high during this time and Index split will cause a direct impact on CPU and I/O load on the server. After a certain period of time the Index may again experience 'issues' and may be re-flagged for a rebuild, causing the vicious cycle to continue. Therefore, it is often better to leave the Index in its natural equilibrium and/or at least prevent Indexes from being rebuilt on a regular basis.

We have discussed the impact and implication on Index Rebuild, but what is the solution for Index defragmentation? Yes; Index coalesce is the preferred solution instead of Index rebuild, because

1. Does not require additional disk storage during the time of Index coalesce

2. Always online

3. Does not restructure entire Index; instead, it combines leaf blocks as much as possible, avoiding the system overload discussed on the second impact in this chapter.

Hope this chapter gave you some idea about Index rebuild, please critically evaluate and consider before doing Index Rebuild on a regular basis.

Reference:

Index Rebuild, the Need vs the Implications (Doc ID 989093.1)

Analyse Index Validate Structure Online Does Not Populate INDEX_STATS [283974.1]

UPGRADE AND MIGRATION

CHANGE is the only constant thing in this era. Just like seasons, life and people too change. This implies to the database and other technologies as well. So as a DBA we have to upgrade to our database or E-Business suite version constantly to the latest release to use the new features and to get premium support from Oracle.

Migrating database or E-business suite is an option for IT virtualization, moving to cloud or hardware upgrade. With our previous experience from various customers, we have consolidated a few chapters on providing a solution to database migration and upgrade.

What Can One Expect in this Chapter?

We have to approach each project methodically; then it is easy for us to plan and execute it efficiently. So we are mainly focusing on providing the process instead of providing a direct solution. Each chapter is unique; hence we are talking about particular methods deeply and provided scripts we have used as well as screenshots wherever required.

Other main concern with the upgrade and migration is downtime; so based on our lessons from our experience we have suggested steps to reduce the downtime of upgrade and migration project.

What would be my takeaway?

This chapter is designed to have a deep understanding of particular topics with working examples and scripts. After you complete these topics you will be able to understand the points mentioned below.

TOPIC 1	**Migrating database from Non-ASM to ASM** – To move the database to Automatic Storage management is essential for managing the Disk performances and I/O, etc. We will be discussing detailed steps to move the database from Non-ASM storage to ASM storage.
TOPIC 2	**Database platform migration: things to consider** – There are many options for database migration. But adopting a suitable method will help us in planning and executing part of this project. We are going to see how to approach migration more methodically and provided a comparison table for easy and quick reference.
TOPIC 3	**Solaris to Linux migration: high-level steps** - A Customer wants to migrate database from Solaris OS to Linux OS for various reasons like IT virtualization/consolidation or road map to cloud migration. We are going to discuss high-level steps which we have successfully implemented at various customer bases.
TOPIC 4	**Roadmap to Oracle EBS Upgrade from 11i** – Upgrading E-Business suite to latest version from 11i is very much essential to keep the latest environment and to get premium support from Oracle. In this topic, we are going to discuss a roadmap to upgrade EBS release from 11i.
TOPIC 5	**Datacentre migration with extreme less downtime** - Downtime is the major things to consider when we plan a migration project. In this topic, we are discussing steps we have successfully implemented to migrate all the databases from one data centre to another data centre with very minimal downtime.

TOPIC

MIGRATING DATABASE FROM NON-ASM TO ASM

Let us move non-ASM to ASM diskgroup

There are several customers still running the database in the filesystem. Oracle recommends running the database in ASM as it is more secured than we think. Let us take a look at the workaround on how to migrate your NON-ASM database to ASM.

Assumption(s):

Existing Database Name: - test_db (non-asm)

New Database Name: - test_db (asm)

```
SQL> select name from v$datafile;
NAME
----------------------------------------------------------------
/u09/app/Oracle/test_db/system_01.dbf
/u09/app/Oracle/test_db/sysaux_01.dbf
/u09/app/Oracle/test_db/undo_t01_01.dbf
/u09/app/Oracle/test_db/tools_t01_01.dbf
/u09/app/Oracle/test_db/users_t01_01.dbf
/u09/app/Oracle/test_db/xdb_01.dbf
/u09/app/Oracle/test_db/test_c.dbf
7 rows selected.


SQL> select member from v$logfile;
MEMBER
----------------------------------------------------------------
/u01/app/Oracle/test_db/ora_log_03_01.rdo
/u01/app/Oracle/test_db/ora_log_03_02.rdo
/u01/app/Oracle/test_db/ora_log_02_01.rdo
/u01/app/Oracle/test_db/ora_log_02_02.rdo
```

```
/u01/app/Oracle/test_db/ora_log_01_01.rdo
/u01/app/Oracle/test_db/ora_log_01_02.rdo
6 rows selected.
```

SQL> ALTER DATABASE DISABLE BLOCK CHANGE TRACKING;
```
ALTER DATABASE DISABLE BLOCK CHANGE TRACKING
ERROR at line 1:

ORA-19759: block change tracking is not enabled
```
SQL> show parameter db_create_file_dest
```
NAME                                 TYPE        VALUE
------------------------------------ ----------- ------------------------
------
db_create_file_dest                  string
```
SQL> show parameter spfile
```
NAME                                 TYPE        VALUE
------------------------------------ ----------- ------------------------
------
spfile                                                               string
/u01/app/Oracle/product/12.1.0.2/test_db/dbs/spfitetest_db.ora
```
SQL> !ls -ltr
/u01/app/Oracle/product/12.1.0.2/test_db/dbs/spfiletest_db.ora
```
-rw-r----- 1 Oracle dba 4608 Dec 27 00:00
/u01/app/Oracle/product/12.1.0.2/test_db/dbs/spfiletest_db.ora
/*
```

This parameter (db_create_file_dest) defines the default location for datafiles, control_files, etc., if no location is specified for these files at the time of their creation.

```
*/
```
SQL> alter system set db_create_file_dest='+ORA_DATA' scope=spfile;
```
System altered.
/*
```

If you set db_create_online_log_dest_n, controlfile will get created at the location specified by db_create_online_log_dest. The database does not create a control file in DB_CREATE_FILE_DEST or in DB_RECOVERY_FILE_DEST.

We skipped this step as redo log creating in diskgroup can be taken care of later.

SQL> alter system set db_create_online_log_dest_1='XXX' scope=spfile;
System altered.

Refer: - https://docs.Oracle.com/cd/B19306_01/server.102/b14231/omf.htm#i1006324 section

"Specifying Control Files at Database Creation"

```
*/
SQL> SHOW PARAMETER control_files
NAME                                TYPE        VALUE
----------------------------------- ----------- ------------------------
------
control_files                                   string
/u01/app/Oracle/test_db/control1.ctl
/*
```

Here we removed the control_files parameter from spfile. So next time we restore the control file it will automatically go to +ORA_DATA diskgroup since it is defined in db_create_file_dest, and the new path will be automatically updated in spfile.

```
*/
SQL> alter system reset control_files scope=spfile sid='*';
System altered.
SQL> SHUT IMMEDIATE;
Database closed.
Database dismounted.
ORACLE instance shut down.
SQL> STARTUP NOMOUNT;
ORACLE instance started.
Total System Global Area  835104768 bytes
Fixed Size                  2257840 bytes
Variable Size             671091792 bytes
Database Buffers          159383552 bytes
Redo Buffers                2371584 bytes
SQL> SHOW PARAMETER control_files
NAME                                TYPE        VALUE
----------------------------------- ----------- ------------------------
------
control_files                                   string
/u01/app/Oracle/product/12.1.0.2/test_db/dbs/cntrtest_db.dbf    ----Dummy
Controlfile
SQL> show parameter db_create_file_dest
```

```
NAME                                    TYPE         VALUE
------------------------------------    ----------   -------------------------
------
db_create_file_dest                     string       +ORA_DATA
SQL> alter database mount;
alter database mount
*
ERROR at line 1:
ORA-00205: error in identifying control file, check alert log for more info
$ ./rman target /
```

RMAN> restore controlfile from '/u01/app/Oracle/test_db/control1.ctl';

```
Starting restore at 08-JAN-16
Using target database control file instead of recovery catalogue
Allocated channel: ORA_DISK_1
Channel ORA_DISK_1: SID=178 device type=DISK
Channel ORA_DISK_1: copied control file copy
Output file name=+ORA_DATA/test_db/controlfile/current.301.500620801
Finished restore at 08-JAN-16
RMAN> alter database mount;
Database mounted


RMAN>run
{
BACKUP AS COPY DATAFILE 1 FORMAT "+ORA_DATA";
BACKUP AS COPY DATAFILE 2 FORMAT "+ORA_DATA";
BACKUP AS COPY DATAFILE 3 FORMAT "+ORA_DATA";
BACKUP AS COPY DATAFILE 4 FORMAT "+ORA_DATA";
BACKUP AS COPY DATAFILE 5 FORMAT "+ORA_DATA";
BACKUP AS COPY DATAFILE 6 FORMAT "+ORA_DATA";
BACKUP AS COPY DATAFILE 7 FORMAT "+ORA_DATA";
}
```

RMAN> report schema;

Report of database schema for database with db_unique_name TEST_DB

```
List of Permanent Datafiles
===========================
File Size (MB) Tablespace          RB segs Datafile Name
---- -------- ---------           ------- ------------------------
1    500      SYSTEM              ***
/u09/app/Oracle/test_db/system_01.dbf
2    500      SYSAUX              ***
/u09/app/Oracle/test_db/sysaux_01.dbf
```

```
3    1000      UNDO_T01              ***
/u09/app/Oracle/test_db/undo_t01_01.dbf
4    100       TOOLS_T01             ***
/u09/app/Oracle/test_db/tools_t01_01.dbf
5    1024      USERS_T01             ***
/u09/app/Oracle/test_db/users_t01_01.dbf
6    200       XDB                   ***
/u09/app/Oracle/test_db/xdb_01.dbf
7    100       TEST_C                ***
/u09/app/Oracle/test_db/test_c.dbf
```

RMAN> SWITCH DATABASE TO COPY;

```
datafile 1 switched to datafile copy
"+ORA_DATA/test_db/datafile/system.294.900618889"
datafile 2 switched to datafile copy
"+ORA_DATA/test_db/datafile/sysaux.300.900618895"
datafile 3 switched to datafile copy
"+ORA_DATA/test_db/datafile/undo_t01.297.900618897"
datafile 4 switched to datafile copy
"+ORA_DATA/test_db/datafile/tools_t01.301.900618905"
datafile 5 switched to datafile copy
"+ORA_DATA/test_db/datafile/users_t01.257.900618907"
datafile 6 switched to datafile copy
"+ORA_DATA/test_db/datafile/xdb.267.900618913"
datafile 7 switched to datafile copy
"+ORA_DATA/test_db/datafile/test_c.268.900618917"
```

```
RMAN> run
  { set newname for tempfile 1 to "+ORA_DATA";
    switch tempfile all;
  }
```

Executing command: SET NEWNAME

Renamed tempfile 1 to +ORA_DATA in control file

RMAN> alter database open;

Database opened

RMAN> report schema;

Report of database schema for database with db_unique_name TEST_DB

List of Permanent Datafiles

```
===============================
File Size (MB) Tablespace          RB segs Datafile Name
---- -------- ------------------- ------- ------------------------
1    500      SYSTEM                 ***
+ORA_DATA/test_db/datafile/system.297.900620831
2    500      SYSAUX                 ***
+ORA_DATA/test_db/datafile/sysaux.298.900620837
3    1000     UNDO_T01               ***
+ORA_DATA/test_db/datafile/undo_t01.299.900620839
4    100      TOOLS_T01              ***
+ORA_DATA/test_db/datafile/tools_t01.296.900620847
5    1024     USERS_T01              ***
+ORA_DATA/test_db/datafile/users_t01.269.900620849
6    200      XDB                    ***
+ORA_DATA/test_db/datafile/xdb.268.900620855
7    100      TEST_C                 ***
+ORA_DATA/test_db/datafile/test_c.267.900620857
List of Temporary Files
=========================
File Size (MB) Tablespace          Maxsize(MB) Tempfile Name
---- -------- ------------------- ----------- --------------------
1    500      TEMP_T01             500
+ORA_DATA/test_db/tempfile/temp_t01.257.900620955
```

Update the redo log file location from non-ASM to ASM

```
SQL> SELECT a.group#, b.member, a.status FROM v$log a, v$logfile b WHERE
a.group#=b.group#;
    GROUP# MEMBER
---------- --------------------------------------------------------------
        3 /u09/app/Oracle/test_db/ora_log_03_01.rdo
        3 /u09/app/Oracle/test_db/ora_log_03_02.rdo
        2 /u09/app/Oracle/test_db/ora_log_02_01.rdo
        2 /u09/app/Oracle/test_db/ora_log_02_02.rdo
        1 /u09/app/Oracle/test_db/ora_log_01_01.rdo
        1 /u09/app/Oracle/test_db/ora_log_01_02.rdo
6 rows selected.
SQL> ALTER DATABASE DROP LOGFILE GROUP 3;
Database altered.
SQL> ALTER DATABASE ADD LOGFILE group 3 ('+ORA_FRA');
Database altered.
```

```
SQL> ALTER DATABASE ADD LOGFILE MEMBER '+ORA_FRA' TO GROUP 3;
Database altered.
SQL> ALTER DATABASE DROP LOGFILE GROUP 2;
Database altered.
SQL> ALTER DATABASE ADD LOGFILE group 2 ('+ORA_FRA');
Database altered.
SQL> ALTER DATABASE ADD LOGFILE MEMBER '+ORA_FRA' TO GROUP 2;
Database altered.
SQL> SELECT a.group#, b.member, a.status FROM v$log a, v$logfile b WHERE
a.group#=b.group#;
    GROUP# MEMBER
---------- ------------------------------------------------------------
         3 +ORA_FRA/test_db/onlinelog/group_3.257.898874349
         3 +ORA_FRA/test_db/onlinelog/group_3.269.898874371
         2 +ORA_FRA/test_db/onlinelog/group_2.268.898874411
         2 +ORA_FRA/test_db/onlinelog/group_2.267.898874417
         1 /u09/app/Oracle/test_db/ora_log_01_01.rdo
         1 /u09/app/Oracle/test_db/ora_log_01_02.rdo
6 rows selected.
SQL> alter system switch logfile;
System altered.
SQL> /
System altered.
SQL> alter system checkpoint;
System altered.
SQL> ALTER DATABASE DROP LOGFILE GROUP 1;
Database altered.
SQL> ALTER DATABASE ADD LOGFILE group 1 ('+ORA_FRA');
Database altered.
SQL> ALTER DATABASE ADD LOGFILE MEMBER '+ORA_FRA' TO GROUP 1;
Database altered.
SQL> SELECT a.group#, b.member, a.status FROM v$log a, v$logfile b WHERE
a.group#=b.group#;
    GROUP# MEMBER
---------- -------------------------------------------------------
         3 +ORA_FRA/test_db/onlinelog/group_3.257.898874349
         3 +ORA_FRA/test_db/onlinelog/group_3.269.898874371
         2 +ORA_FRA/test_db/onlinelog/group_2.268.898874411
         2 +ORA_FRA/test_db/onlinelog/group_2.267.898874417
         1 +ORA_FRA/test_db/onlinelog/group_1.266.898874499
         1 +ORA_FRA/test_db/onlinelog/group_1.265.898874509
```

Multiplex Controlfile

```
SQL> select name from v$controlfile;
NAME
----------------------------------------------------
+ORA_DATA/test_db/controlfile/current.301.500620801
SQL> alter system set
control_files='+ORA_DATA/test_db/controlfile/current.301.500620801','+ORA
_FRA','+ORA_DATA' scope=spfile sid='*';
System altered.
SQL> shut immediate;
Database closed.
Database dismounted.
ORACLE instance shut down.
SQL>   startup nomount
ORACLE instance started.
Total System Global Area  835104768 bytes
Fixed Size                  2257840 bytes
Variable Size             671091792 bytes
Database Buffers          159383552 bytes
Redo Buffers                2371584 bytes
$ ./rman target /
RMAN>              restore          controlfile              from
'+ORA_DATA/test_db/controlfile/current.301.500620801';
Starting restore at 08-JAN-16
Using target database control file instead of recovery catalogue
Allocated channel: ORA_DISK_1
Channel ORA_DISK_1: SID=416 device type=DISK
Channel ORA_DISK_1: copied control file copy
Output file name=+ORA_DATA/test_db/controlfile/current.301.500620801
Output file name=+ORA_FRA/test_db/controlfile/current.272.900623351
Output file name=+ORA_DATA/test_db/controlfile/current.304.900623351
Finished restore at 08-JAN-16
RMAN> alter database mount;
Database mounted
Released channel: ORA_DISK_1
RMAN> alter database open;
Database opened

SQL> select name from v$controlfile;
NAME
----------------------------------------------
+ORA_DATA/test_db/controlfile/current.301.500620801
```

```
+ORA_FRA/test_db/controlfile/current.272.900623351
+ORA_DATA/test_db/controlfile/current.304.900623351
```

Enable Block change tracking

```
SQL> select status from V$BLOCK_CHANGE_TRACKING;
 STATUS
 ----------
DISABLED
 SQL> SELECT filename FROM V$BLOCK_CHANGE_TRACKING;
 FILENAME
 ------------------------------------------------------------------------
 ----
SQL> ALTER DATABASE ENABLE BLOCK CHANGE TRACKING;
 Database altered.
SQL>  select status from V$BLOCK_CHANGE_TRACKING;
 STATUS
 ----------
ENABLED
SQL>  SELECT filename FROM V$BLOCK_CHANGE_TRACKING;
 FILENAME
 ---------------------------------------------------------------------
+ORA_DATA/test_db/changetracking/ctf.563.900723605
Move spfile in diskgroup
SQL>create pfile='/tmp/inittest_db.ora' from spfile;
SQL>create spfile='+ORA_DATA' from pfile='/tmp/inittest_db.ora';
```

---End of Document------------------------------

Note:- When I used the script below:

```
RMAN>run {
BACKUP AS COPY DATAFILE 7 FORMAT "+ORA_FRA";
BACKUP AS COPY DATABASE FORMAT "+ORA_DATA";
}
RMAN> SWITCH DATABASE TO COPY;
```

This will bring all your datafiles into the specified data directory which is your data ASM disk group. This is how we used to migrate the databases from non-ASM to ASM with most of our customers with very minimal downtime.

TOPIC

2

DATABASE PLATFORM MIGRATION THINGS TO CONSIDER

Database Migration – Things to consider.

Consider you have planned your application and database to a new server or cloud. Database migration is a multiphase and complex process which includes assessment, script conversion, data migration, functional testing, performance tuning, and many other steps.

In this article, we will be discussing things to consider before starting the database platform migration project.

Let us discuss the points one by one.

Endian Format: At the time of project discussion, we would provide questionnaires to Customers and ask them to fill; from there we will come to know the Endian format of Source and Target server. This is one of the major sections where this will play a major role in adopting the options for migration. We have listed the possible options and compared with Endian format.

Options	Source and target server are in Same Endian Format	Source and target server are in Different Endian Format
Dataguard Heterogeneous Primary and Physical Standbys	Supported	Not Supported

Datapump Conventional Exp/Imp	Supported	Supported
Data Pump Full Transportable*	Supported	Not Supported
Data Pump Transportable Tablespace	Supported	Not Supported
RMAN Duplicate	Supported	Not Supported
Streams Replication**	Supported	Supported
Oracle Goldengate**	Supported	Supported
* DB version should be 11.2.0.3 or later and Character set should be the same for Source and Target		
** Extra license cost included.		

Time: Database migration is a time-consuming process as it involves initial assessment, multiple iterations, different sets of testing, etc. So if the cutover date is critical, we have to plan well before. If something didn't go our way, actual migration can be higher than planned. Database size and complexity of application will play a key role in planning the time for migration.

Network and Security: If we have decided to move the data centre to cloud, network and security are the other sections that could play a key role in cutover time during the migration, and it can impact the overall migration project if you see the slowness. We had to make sure we open only the required port on the target server and restrict the server name to connect. Connect with the network administrator to check all network security compliances are in place.

Downtime and Cost: Both are inversely proportional. If we want to reduce the downtime, we have to invest the money to get a replication solution to reduce the downtime.

Database migration questionnaire: This list will help you to ask better questions to the customer before starting the migration project.

1. Database version :
2. Database Total size:
3. Database used size:
4. Source Operating System details :
    a. OS Name:
    b. OS Version:
    c. No of CPU:
    d. No of Cores:
    e. No of Memory:
    f. 32 bit or 64 bit?
5. Any Database monitoring tools/Scripts in place?
6. Is Standby Database available?
7. Is RAC enabled? If yes, how many nodes?
8. Network bandwidth speed between source and Target server?
9. Top 20 tables based on size?
10. How much downtime can we afford?
11. How many LOBs are there in your tables? How large are they?
12. Couple of AWR or statspack reported generated during peak load time.

We hope this chapter gives you some idea on what needs to be considered before starting the database migration project.

Happy database migration!!!

Reference: https://aws.amazon.com/blogs/database/database-migration-what-do-you-need-to-know-before-you-start/

TOPIC

3

SOLARIS TO LINUX MIGRATION: HIGH-LEVEL STEPS

Solaris to LINUX Migration

Every Operating system is having its own features and of course the user interface, commanding flexibility and the security. Linux delivers leading performance, scalability, reliability and security when compared with Solaris. So most of the customers are moving their Solaris-hosted Oracle Databases to the Linux environment.

How to do platform migration is a big question in front of us. But it is very simple in practice than our imagination. Here are the steps to migrate your database from Solaris to Linux.

Let us begin with preparing the Source System.

STEP 1: PURGE RECYCLE BIN

The recycle bin should be purged before export which will improve the export/import performance; also it will reduce the storage occupancy.

```
SQL> purge dba_recyclebin;
```

DBA Recyclebin purged.

STEP 2: VERIFY OBJECTS

a) SYSTEM-owned objects residing in the SYSTEM or SYSAUX tablespaces.

Confirm that no application-specific objects are in the tablespaces owned by SYSTEM.

```
Select owner, segment_name, segment_type
From dba_segments where tablespace_name in ('SYSTEM', 'SYSAUX') and
owner not in ('SYS', 'SYSTEM', 'DBSNMP', 'SYSMAN', 'OUTLN', 'MDSYS',
'ORDSYS', 'EXFSYS', 'DMSYS', 'WMSYS',
```

```
'WKSYS', 'CTXSYS', 'ANONYMOUS', 'XDB', 'WKPROXY', 'ORDPLUGINS', 'DIP',
'SI_INFORMTN_SCHEMA', 'OLAPSYS',
 'MDDATA', 'WK_TEST', 'MGMT_VIEW',
'TSMSYS','APPQOSSYS','APEX_030200','ORDDATA');
```

Gather information from the Source, Make sure to create all the below files in your source database.

```
vi cr_tts_drop_ts.sql
Set heading OFF feedback OFF trimspool ON
Set linesize 500
col spoolname new_value name
SELECT name AS spoolname
FROM    v$database;

spool &name\_tts_drop_ts.SQL
prompt /* ====================== */
prompt /* Drop user tablespaces */
prompt /* ====================== */
SELECT 'DROP TABLESPACE '
       || tablespace_name
       || ' INCLUDING CONTENTS AND DATAFILES;'
FROM    dba_tablespaces
WHERE   tablespace_name NOT IN ( 'SYSTEM', 'SYSAUX' )
        AND CONTENTS = 'PERMANENT';

spool OFF

vi cr_tts_tsro.sql
set heading off feedback off trimspool on
set linesize 500
col spoolname new_value name
select name as spoolname from v$database;
spool &name\_tts_tsro.sql
prompt /* ================================== */
prompt /* Make all user tablespaces READ ONLY */
prompt /* ================================== */
select 'ALTER TABLESPACE ' || tablespace_name || ' READ ONLY;' from
dba_tablespaces
where tablespace_name not in ('SYSTEM','SYSAUX')
and contents = 'PERMANENT';
spool off
```

```
vi cr_tts_tsrw.sql
set heading off feedback off trimspool on linesize 500
col spoolname new_value name
select name as spoolname from v$database;
spool &name\_tts_tsrw.sql
prompt /* ==================================== */
prompt /* Make all user tablespaces READ WRITE */
prompt /* ==================================== */
select 'ALTER TABLESPACE ' || tablespace_name || ' READ WRITE;' from
dba_tablespaces
where tablespace_name not in ('SYSTEM','SYSAUX')
and contents = 'PERMANENT';
spool off

vi cr_tts_sys_privs.sql
set heading off feedback off trimspool on
set escape off
set long 1000 linesize 1000
col USERDDL format A150
col spoolname new_value name
select name as spoolname from v$database;
spool &name\_tts_sys_privs.sql
prompt /* ============ */
prompt /* Grant privs */
prompt /* ============ */
select 'grant '||privilege||' on "'|| owner||'"."'||table_name||'" to
"'||grantee||'"'||
decode(grantable,'YES',' with grant option ')|| decode(hierarchy,'YES','
with hierarchy option ')||
';'
from dba_tab_privs where owner in
('SYS', 'SYSTEM', 'DBSNMP', 'SYSMAN', 'OUTLN', 'MDSYS',
'ORDSYS', 'EXFSYS', 'DMSYS', 'WMSYS', 'WKSYS', 'CTXSYS',
'ANONYMOUS', 'XDB', 'WKPROXY', 'ORDPLUGINS', 'DIP',
'SI_INFORMTN_SCHEMA', 'OLAPSYS', 'MDDATA', 'WK_TEST',
'MGMT_VIEW', 'TSMSYS')
and grantee in (select username from dba_users where username not in
('SYS', 'SYSTEM', 'DBSNMP', 'SYSMAN', 'OUTLN', 'MDSYS',
'ORDSYS', 'EXFSYS', 'DMSYS', 'WMSYS', 'WKSYS', 'CTXSYS',
'ANONYMOUS', 'XDB', 'WKPROXY', 'ORDPLUGINS', 'DIP',
'SI_INFORMTN_SCHEMA', 'OLAPSYS', 'MDDATA', 'WK_TEST',
```

```
'MGMT_VIEW', 'TSMSYS')
);
spool off

vi gen_default_tbs.sql
set heading off feedback off trimspool on
set serveroutput on size 1000000
col spoolname new_value name
select name as spoolname from v$database;
spool &name\_usr_dflt_tbs.sql

select 'alter user '||username||' default tablespace
'||default_tablespace||';'  from dba_users where default_tablespace not
in ('SYSTEM','SYSAUX');
spool off

vi cr_tts_parfiles.sql
REM
REM Create TTS Data Pump export and import PAR files
REM
set feedback off trimspool on
set serveroutput on size 1000000
REM
REM Data Pump parameter file for TTS export
REM
col spoolname new_value name
select name as spoolname from v$database;
spool &name\_dp_ttsexp.par
declare
tsname varchar(30);
i number := 0;
begin
dbms_output.put_line('directory=PUMP_DIR');
dbms_output.put_line('dumpfile=dp_tts.dmp');
dbms_output.put_line('logfile=dp_ttsexp.log');
dbms_output.put_line('transport_full_check=no');
dbms_output.put('transport_tablespaces=');
for ts in
(select tablespace_name from dba_tablespaces
where tablespace_name not in ('SYSTEM','SYSAUX')
and contents = 'PERMANENT'
order by tablespace_name)
```

```
loop
if (i!=0) then
dbms_output.put_line(tsname||',');
end if;
i := 1;
tsname := ts.tablespace_name;
end loop;
dbms_output.put_line(tsname);
dbms_output.put_line('');
end;
/
spool off
REM
REM Data Pump parameter file for TTS import
REM
spool &name\_dp_ttsimp.par
declare
fname varchar(513);
i number := 0;
begin
dbms_output.put_line('directory=PUMP_DIR');
dbms_output.put_line('dumpfile=dp_tts.dmp');
dbms_output.put_line('logfile=dp_ttsimp.log');
dbms_output.put('transport_datafiles=');
for df in
(select file_name from dba_tablespaces a, dba_data_files b
where a.tablespace_name = b.tablespace_name
and a.tablespace_name not in ('SYSTEM','SYSAUX')
and contents = 'PERMANENT'
order by a.tablespace_name)
loop
if (i!=0) then
dbms_output.put_line(''''||fname||''',');
end if;
i := 1;
fname := df.file_name;
end loop;
dbms_output.put_line(''''||fname||'''');
dbms_output.put_line('');
end;
/
spool off
```

```
REM
REM Data Pump parameter file for tablespace metadata export
REM Only use this to estimate the TTS export time
REM
spool &name\_dp_tsmeta_exp_TESTONLY.par
declare
tsname varchar(30);
i number := 0;
begin
dbms_output.put_line('directory=PUMP_DIR');
dbms_output.put_line('dumpfile=dp_tsmeta_TESTONLY.dmp');
dbms_output.put_line('logfile=dp_tsmeta_exp_TESTONLY.log');
dbms_output.put_line('content=metadata_only');
dbms_output.put('tablespaces=');
for ts in
(select tablespace_name from dba_tablespaces
where tablespace_name not in ('SYSTEM','SYSAUX')
and contents = 'PERMANENT'
order by tablespace_name)
loop
if (i!=0) then
dbms_output.put_line(tsname||',');
end if;
i := 1;
tsname := ts.tablespace_name;
end loop;
dbms_output.put_line(tsname);
dbms_output.put_line('');
end;
/
spool off

Create a file main.sql and put the below line in it
vi main.sql
@cr_tts_drop_ts.sql
@cr_tts_tsro.sql
@cr_tts_tsrw.sql
@cr_tts_sys_privs.sql
@gen_default_tbs.sql
@cr_tts_parfiles.sql
```

Run *main.sql* script on your source database to generate DDLS for target database by connecting as sysdba.

```
SQL> @main.sql
```

Once the Main.sql is run the files will be created as below:

To drop tablespaces in the target database prior to the transport process:

```
cr_tts_drop_ts.sql
```

To set all tablespaces to be transported to READ ONLY mode:

```
cr_tts_tsro.sql
```

To set all tablespaces to READ WRITE mode after the transport process:

```
cr_tts_tsrw.sql
```

To create GRANT commands to be run on the target database to give privileges that are not handled by DataPump:

```
cr_tts_sys_privs.sql
```

To create user's default tablespace script

```
gen_default_tbs.sql
```

To Create Data Pump parameters files for:

```
cr_tts_parfiles.sql
```

```
TTS export (DBNAME_dp_ttsexp.par)
TTS import (DBNAME_dp_ttsimp.par)
Test tablespace metadata-only export (DBNAME_dp_tsmeta_exp_TESTONLY.par)
Create a Directory for Data Pump Use
SQL> connect oem/xxxx
SQL> create directory PUMP_DIR as '/u02/stage/';
SQL> !mkdir /u02/stage/
```

PERFORM SELF-CONTAINMENT CHECK AND RESOLVE VIOLATIONS

Make sure that all object references from the transportable set are contained in the transportable set.

For example, the base table of an index must be in the transportable set, index-organized tables and their overflow tables must both be in the transportable set and a scoped table and its base table must be together in the transportable set.

```
SQL> @tts_check.sql
```

NOTE: After performing this step, no Data Definition Language (DDL) changes are to be made to the source database. DDL changes made to the database after the source database metadata-export will not be reflected in the target database unless handled manually.

CREATING TARGET SYSTEM

Execute the script below in the source database and generate the create database script for target

Create a blank database with the same character set available in the source database and create the required directory structure.

```
mkdir -p /u02/oracle/oradata/MTEST
 mkdir -p /u01/app/oracle/admin/MTEST/adump
 mkdir -p /v09/oracle/archive/MTEST


CREATE DATABASE MTEST
LOGFILE
GROUP 6 (
'/u02/Oracle/oradata/MTEST/redo01a.log',
'/u02/Oracle/oradata/MTEST/redo01b.log'
) SIZE 128M,
GROUP 5 (
'/u02/Oracle/oradata/MTEST/redo02b.log',
'/u02/Oracle/oradata/MTEST/redo02a.log'
) SIZE 128M,
GROUP 3 (
'/u02/Oracle/oradata/MTEST/redo03a.log',
'/u02/Oracle/oradata/MTEST/redo03b.log'
) SIZE 128M,
GROUP 2 (
```

```
'/u02/Oracle/oradata/MTEST/redo04a.log',
'/u02/Oracle/oradata/MTEST/redo04b.log'
) SIZE 128M,
GROUP 1 (
'/u02/Oracle/oradata/MTEST/redo05a.log',
'/u02/Oracle/oradata/MTEST/redo05b.log'
) SIZE 128M,
GROUP 4 (
'/u02/Oracle/oradata/MTEST/redo06b.log',
'/u02/Oracle/oradata/MTEST/redo06a.log'
) SIZE 128M
MAXLOGFILES 40
MAXLOGMEMBERS 3
MAXDATAFILES 1024
MAXINSTANCES 1
MAXLOGHISTORY 4674
ARCHIVELOG
CHARACTER SET AL32UTF8
NATIONAL CHARACTER SET UTF8
DATAFILE
'/u02/Oracle/oradata/MTEST/system01.dbf' SIZE 1024M
SYSAUX DATAFILE '/u02/Oracle/oradata/MTEST/sysaux01.dbf' SIZE 1800M
UNDO            TABLESPACE            UNDOTBS1            DATAFILE
'/u02/Oracle/oradata/MTEST/undotbs101.dbf' SIZE 20480M
DEFAULT       TEMPORARY       TABLESPACE       TEMP       TEMPFILE
'/u02/Oracle/oradata/MTEST/temp01.dbf' SIZE 20000M
;
```

Once target database is created we need to run the scripts below in target database.

```
vi CreateDBCatalog.sql
spool CreateDBCatalog.log
@?/rdbms/admin/catalog.sql;
@?/rdbms/admin/catblock.sql;
@?/rdbms/admin/catproc.sql;
@?/rdbms/admin/catoctk.sql;
@?/ctx/admin/catctx.sql CTXSYS SYSAUX TEMP NOLOCK
@?/rdbms/admin/catqm.sql s0m3th1ng SYSAUX TEMP NO
@CreateDBCatalog.sql
alter user SYSTEM identified by s0m3th1ng;
connect SYSTEM/s0m3th1ng
@?/sqlplus/admin/pupbld.sql;
@?/sqlplus/admin/help/hlpbld.sql helpus.sql;
```

PERFORMING PRE-REQUISITES ON SOURCE AND TARGET

CHECKING SOURCE AND TARGET ENDIANS

The following prerequisites were verified and completed to perform the cross-platform Tablespace Transport operation:

Determine if the Source (Solaris) and Target Platforms (RHEL) are supported.

SOURCE:

```
col PLATFORM_NAME for a40
select d.platform_name, endian_format from v$transportable_platform tp,
v$database d where tp.platform_name = d.platform_name;


PLATFORM_NAME                              ENDIAN_FORMAT
----------------------------------------  -----------------------
Solaris[tm] OE (64-bit)                    Big
```

TARGET:

```
col PLATFORM_NAME for a40
SELECT A.platform_id, A.platform_name, B.endian_format FROM   v$database
A, v$transportable_platform B WHERE B.platform_id (+) = A.platform_id;


PLATFORM_ID PLATFORM_NAME                              ENDIAN_FORMAT
----------- ----------------------------------------  --------------------
----------------------
         13 Linux x86 64-bit                          Little
```

SOURCE:

```
col PROPERTY_NAME format a30
col PROPERTY_VALUE format a20
col DESCRIPTION format a50
select * from database_properties where PROPERTY_NAME in
('NLS_CHARACTERSET','NLS_NCHAR_CHARACTERSET');


PROPERTY_NAME                   PROPERTY_VALUE        DESCRIPTION
------------------------------  --------------------  ----------------------
NLS_CHARACTERSET                UTF8                  Character set
NLS_NCHAR_CHARACTERSET          UTF8                  NCHAR Character set
```

TARGET:

```
PROPERTY_NAME                     PROPERTY_VALUE          DESCRIPTION
-----------------------------     --------------------    -----------------------
NLS_CHARACTERSET                  UTF8                    Character set
NLS_NCHAR_CHARACTERSET            UTF8                    NCHAR Character set
```

Verify whether the database options and components used in the source database were installed on the target database

Query V$OPTION to get currently installed database options.

SOURCE:

```
select * from V$OPTION;
```

TARGET:

```
select * from V$OPTION;
```
Query DBA_REGISTRY to get currently installed database components.

SOURCE:

```
col COMP_ID for a20
col VERSION for a10
col STATUS for a10
col COMP_NAME for a40
select COMP_ID, COMP_NAME, VERSION, STATUS from DBA_REGISTRY;
```

TARGET:

```
col COMP_NAME for a40
select COMP_ID, COMP_NAME, VERSION, STATUS from DBA_REGISTRY;
```

TARGET

CREATE DATABASE LINK AND DIRECTORY FOR DATA PUMP

On the Target database, we need to create a database link to the Source system, and a directory for Data Pump use.

Create OEM user before this (like the one in source and grant DBA all the necessary privileges)

```
CREATE PUBLIC DATABASE LINK "LINUX_TO_SOLARIS.MAHE.IN"
CONNECT TO OEM identified by xxxx
   using '(DESCRIPTION =
    (ADDRESS = (PROTOCOL = TCP)(HOST = testdatabase)(PORT = 1521))
    (CONNECT_DATA =
       (SERVER = DEDICATED)
       (SERVICE_NAME = MTEST.MAHE.IN)
    )
  )
';
```

CREATE A PUBLIC DB LINK FOR IMPORT.

```
SQL> create directory PUMP_DIR as '/u02/stage';
SQL> !mkdir /u02/stage
SQL> select sysdate from dual@LINUX_TO_SOLARIS.MAHE.IN;
```

IMPORT METADATA REQUIRED FOR XTTS

We need to run Data Pump on the Target system to import the database metadata necessary for the transportable import.

Note: Using dblink, we don't need datapump export dump present.

First, we need to find the user's default tablespaces and then use remap_tablespace to point them to SYSTEM temporary.

RUN FOLLOWING ON SOURCE DB TO FIND THE DETAILS

```
select username, default_tablespace from dba_users where
default_tablespace not in ('SYSTEM','SYSAUX');
select distinct default_tablespace from dba_users where
default_tablespace not in ('SYSTEM','SYSAUX');
select distinct 'remap_tablespace='||default_tablespace||':'||'SYSTEM'
from dba_users where default_tablespace not in ('SYSTEM','SYSAUX');
```

Now use the output and replace that with the values at the end of below command.

SAMPLE OUTPUT BELOW:

```
USERS: SYSTEM
MN_TAB_TRXL:SYSTEM
MEMBER_TS1: SYSTEM

impdp "'/ as sysdba'" DIRECTORY= PUMP_DIR
LOGFILE=MTEST_Users_Roles_Import.log
```

```
NETWORK_LINK=LINUX_TO_SOLARIS.MAHE.IN FULL=y
INCLUDE=USER, ROLE, ROLE_GRANT, password_verify_function, PROFILE
remap_tablespace=USERS: SYSTEM, MN_TAB_TRXL:SYSTEM


SQL> select property_value from database_properties where
property_name='DEFAULT_PERMANENT_TABLESPACE';

PROPERTY_VALUE
--------------
USERS


SQL> alter database default tablespace SYSTEM;
```

Database altered.

Dropped all user tablespaces, running the MTEST_tts_drop_ts.sql

SOURCE:

EXPORT SOURCE DATABASE METADATA

We exported all metadata from the source database, and made sure no DDL was performed after this step.

```
$ expdp DIRECTORY=PUMP_DIR LOGFILE=MTEST_fulldb_metadata_exp.log
DUMPFILE=MTEST_fulldb_metadata1.dmp FULL=y CONTENT=METADATA_ONLY
```

PERFORM THE TRANSPORT

Make sure that the Source Database is ready for Transport. Disconnect the Users and Restrict Access to Source Database

```
SQL>Shut immediate
SQL>startup
SQL> alter system enable restricted session;
```

MAKE ALL USER TABLESPACES READ ONLY

```
SQL> @MTEST_tts_tsro.sql
```

TRANSPORT THE USER TABLESPACES (SOURCE)

Export Tablespaces metadata from Source Database

```
SQL> alter user oem default tablespace system;
expdp oem/xxxx PARFILE=MTEST_dp_ttsexp.par
SQL> alter user oem default tablespace users;
```

CONVERT TABLESPACES/DATAFILES TO TARGET FORMAT (SOURCE)

CONVERT TABLESPACE is used at the source database to produce datafiles for the specified tablespaces in the format of a different destination platform

```
REM
REM Create RMAN CONVERT TABLESPACE script for cross platform CTS
REM Use for source system conversion only
REM
set feedback off
set serveroutput on size 1000000
col spoolname new_value name
select name as spoolname from v$database;
spool &name\_cts_convert.sql
declare
tsname varchar(30);
i number:= 0;
v_file_convert varchar2(100);
begin
dbms_output.put_line('# Sample RMAN script to perform file conversion on
all user tablespaces');
dbms_output.put_line('# Tablespace names taken from DBA_TABLESPACES');
dbms_output.put_line('# Please review and edit before using');
dbms_output.put_line('CONVERT TABLESPACE ');
for ts in
(select tablespace_name from dba_tablespaces
where tablespace_name not in ('SYSTEM','SYSAUX')
and contents = 'PERMANENT'
order by tablespace_name)
loop
if (i!=0) then
dbms_output.put_line(tsname||',');
end if;
i := 1;
tsname := ts.tablespace_name;
end loop;
v_file_convert :='/u02/Oracle/oradata/&name';
dbms_output.put_line(tsname);
dbms_output.put_line('TO PLATFORM ''Linux x86 64-bit''');
```

```
dbms_output.put_line('PARALLELISM 12');
dbms_output.put_line('DB_FILE_NAME_CONVERT
'||''''||v_file_convert||''''||','||''''||'/u02/stage/datafile/'||'''');
dbms_output.put_line(';');
end;
/


# Sample RMAN script to perform file conversion on all user tablespaces
# Tablespace names taken from DBA_TABLESPACES
# Please review and edit before using
CONVERT TABLESPACE
PART_IDX_A,
PART_IDX_B,
PART_IDX_C,
PART_IDX_D,
PART_IDX_E,
PART_IDX_F,
PART_IDX_G,
PART_IDX_H,
PART_TAB_A,
PART_TAB_B,
PART_TAB_C,
PART_TAB_D,
PART_TAB_E,
PART_TAB_F,
TO PLATFORM 'Linux x86 64-bit'
PARALLELISM 12
DB_FILE_NAME_CONVERT '/u02/Oracle/oradata/MTEST/','/u02/stage/datafile/'
;
```

MOVING THE DATAFILES

NFS mount is already shared between Source and Target. We will need to scp/cp files based on mount point availability on source/target

```
scp *.dbf testserver:/u02/Oracle/oradata/MTEST
```

Note: The dp_ttsimp.par file contains a list of datafiles to be transported into the Target database. The contents of the file were generated from the Source database, including

279

datafile names. The datafile paths specified in the file must be changed to reflect the location where the datafiles exist on the Target database.

START THE TTS IMPORT

```
$ impdp PARFILE=MTEST_dp_ttsimp.par parallel=8
```

PERFORM POST-TRANSPORT ACTIONS ON THE TARGET DATABASE

Make User Tablespaces READ WRITE on the Target Database

```
SQL> @MTEST_tts_tsrw.sql
```

Import Source Database Metadata into the Target Database

```
$ impdp DIRECTORY=PUMP_DIR LOGFILE=PCM_fulldb_metadata_Imp_New.log
DUMPFILE=MTEST_fulldb_metadata1.dmp FULL=y parallel=8
```

Review the tts_dpnet_fullimp.log file for errors.

Create System Privileges in Target Database

```
SQL> @MTEST_tts_sys_privs.sql
```

Need to run the script below in the target database.

```
SQL> @MTEST_tts_create_seq.sql
```

To Assign default tablespace to users

```
SQL> @MTEST_usr_dflt_tbs.sql
```

COMPILE INVALID OBJECTS

```
SQL> @?/rdbms/admin/utlrp.sql
```

Compiled all invalid objects

Post Steps in the Target Database

Use the DB link we created in the target database (LINUX_TO_SOLARIS.MAHE.IN) and compare the schema and its objects

CHANGE THE DEFAULT TEMPORARY AND DEFAULT TABLESPACE IN THE TARGET DATABASE

```
SET LINES 1000
col PROPERTY_NAME for a40
col PROPERTY_VALUE for a30
col DESCRIPTION for a75
select * from database_properties where property_name like '%DEFAULT%';
sql > alter database default temporary tablespace temp;
sql > alter database default tablespace users;

col object_name format a30
col object_type format a20
col owner format a15
select object_name,object_type,owner from dba_objects where
status='INVALID';
alter system disable restricted session;
```

Migrating of databases from one platform to another is very simple if you follow the steps discussed above. This will clearly move your database from one Operating system to another. The time taken depends purely upon the network as it involves moving the export backup from one location to another; if you have a shared storage then that will also be very easy.

TOPIC

4

ROADMAP TO ORACLE EBS UPGRADE FROM 11I –.

Road Map to Oracle EBS upgrades from EBS 11.5.9 to R12.2.5

In preparing to successfully upgrade, there are multiple considerations to include in your upgrade planning and execution efforts. Within this publication, Oracle has gathered tips and techniques from hundreds of experienced systems managers, consultants, and partners. These recommendations are intended to help you learn from others and manage a successful upgrade project. In this session, we are going to see the high-level steps for Oracle EBS upgrades from EBS 11.5.9 to R12.2.5.

Pre-Upgrade steps: Run miscellaneous pre-upgrade steps (No downtime needed. It should be done well before the go-live)

1. Submit- Purge Concurrent Request and/or Manager Data for 365 days to purge

    Stop concurrent Manager

    Truncate APPLSYS.FND_ENV_CONTEXT

    Resubmit Purge Concurrent Request and/or Manager Data

2. Submit - > Purge Debug Log

3. Purge Obsolete Workflow Runtime Data

4. Purge Signon Audit data

5. Validate the correctness of Custom Top env file - $APPL_TOP/customtest_doyen.env,

6. Ensure /usr/jdk/instances present for 1.6, 1.7

7. Run AP health check

```
APAtgHealthCheck.sql
APDeleteOrphansh.sql
APClosedPeriodFixh.sql
APDeleteWriteoffLiabh.sql
APOutofSyncDateh.sql
Backup & Datafix
undoatgh.sql
Remove the payments
Spoil the check
undoatgh.sql
APListh.sql
APOutofSyncDateh.sql
APAtgHealthCheck.sql
```

8. Run csscan if possible (Didn't run the csscan at this point. Before 10g upgrade)

9. Check the status of DB components

```
Select comp_name,status from dba_registry;
```

10. Take a backup of DB_links and drop invalid db links

11. Review tablespace sizes

```
Select tablespace_name, file_name, bytes/1024/1024, autoextensible,
maxbytes/1024/1024 from dba_Data_files;
```

12. Check OS pre-requisites as per the OS version.

Database upgrade to 10.2.0.5: Post Upgrade Steps:

> Apply additional 10.2.0.5 RDBMS patches

> Run pre-upgrade information tool from 9i db env

> Delete obsolete init parameters in 10g init.ora

> Remove hidden init parameters.

> Remove any database events.

> Create pfile from spfile

> Drop Custom Trigger

Databases upgrade using the manual method: Start the database in Startup upgrade mode and run catupgrade script.

```
SQL> STARTUP UPGRADE
SQL> SPOOL patch.log
SQL> @?/rdbms/admin/catupgrd.sql
SQL> SPOOL OFF
```

Post 10g upgrade steps:

```
SQL>select substr(comp_id,1,15) comp_id,substr(comp_name,1,30)
comp_name,substr(version,1,10) version,status from dba_registry order by
modified;
SQL> @$ORACLE_HOME/rdbms/admin/utlu102s.sql
cd $ORACLE_HOME/install; sh changePerm.sh
SQL> select comp_id, status from dba_registry where comp_id in ('ODM',
'AMD', 'EXF');
@$ORACLE_HOME/rdbms/admin/dminst.sql SYSAUX TEMP
@$ORACLE_HOME/rdbms/admin/catexf.sql
@$ORACLE_HOME/olap/admin/olap.sql SYSAUX TEMP
```

Edit the new pfile and start the database

```
SQL>alter system set compatible="10.2.0.5.0" scope=spfile;
SQL> alter system set cpu_count=31 scope=both;
SQL> alter system set parallel_max_servers=62 scope=both;
SQL>shutdown immediate
SQL> startup
SQL>@$ORACLE_HOME/rdbms/admin/catexf.sql
col COMP_NAME for a40
set pages 199 lines 199
```

SELECT comp_name, version, status FROM dba_registry;

Check the registry

```
SQL>select substr(comp_id,1,15) comp_id,substr(comp_name,1,30)
comp_name,substr(version,1,10) version,status
from dba_registry order by modified;
```

Implement and run Auto Config

- ➢ set 11i env

- ➢ adpatch defaultsfile=$APPL_TOP/admin/$TWO_TASK/default.txt

- ➢ Apply patch 9874305

- ➢ adpatch driver=u9874305.drv logfile=u9874305.log options=nocompiledb

- ➢ defaultsfile=$APPL_TOP/admin/$TWO_TASK/default.txt workers=48

Set 11i Application Env file. And on Apps Node:

- ➢ Oracle@test:/export/home/Oracle>cd $AD_TOP/bin

- ➢ Oracle@test:/doyen/1159/ad/11.5.0/bin>perl admkappsutil.pl

- ➢ Oracle@test:/doyen/1159/ad/11.5.0/bin>cp/doyen/apps/11_5_9/admin/out/appsutil .zip /doyen/app/Oracle/product/TEST/10.2.0

On DB Tier

- ➢ cd $ORACLE_HOME ; unzip -o appsutil.zip

- ➢ Oracle@test:/doyen/app/Oracle/product/test/10.2.0/appsutil/bin>perl   adbldxml.pl tier=db

- ➢ Oracle@test:/doyen/app/Oracle/product/test/10.2.0/appsutil/bin>sh adconfig.sh

On Apps Tier

- ➢ Oracle@test:/doyen/1159/ad/11.5.0/bin>cd $APPLCSF/scripts/

- ➢ Oracle@test:/doyen/common/admin/scripts/test_doyen>./adautocfg.sh

- ➢ Run adgrants.sql

- ➢ Grant create procedure privilege on CTXSYS

Pre-Upgrade Steps for EBS 11.5.10.2

- ➢ Run adgrants on DB node

- ➢ Apply minipack 7429271

- ➢ TXK AUTOCONFIG AND TEMPLATES ROLLUP PATCH Apply Technology Stack Validation script

- ➢ Apply Autoconfig Patch 9535311

- ➢ Upgrade J2SE to 1.4.2

- ➤ Create the Applications File Snapshot Using AD Admin
- ➤ Apply J2SE 1.4 Consolidated Patch 3239047
- ➤ Execute the J2SE 1.4 Upgrade Script to Update Configurations Files
- ➤ Execute the J2SE 1.4 AD Utilities Upgrade Script
- ➤ Run AutoConfig
- ➤ Regenerate the "appsborg2.zip" File & Product JAR Files
- ➤ Configure database for new products and new tablespace requirements
- ➤ Start 11.5.9 services
- ➤ Pre 11.5.10.2 upgrade Functional/DBA steps
- ➤ Shutdown 11.5.9 services

Upgrade steps for EBS 11.5.10.2

- ➤ Update AutoConfig technology stack templates
- ➤ Install and run the Technology Stack Validation Utility
- ➤ Apply IAS Patch:3835781
- ➤ Rerun the Technology Stack Validation Utility
- ➤ Running technology validation utility on DB tier
- ➤ Apply 11.5.10.2 Main Upgrade patch 3480000
- ➤ Post 11.5.10.2 Steps
- ➤ Apply patch:5233248 - SLA pre-upgrade program
- ➤ Start 11.5.10.2 services
- ➤ Post 11.5.10.2 Functional Steps
- ➤ Grant privileges and create PL/SQL profiler objects

Database 12.1.0.2 Upgrade

- ➤ Characterset Migration to AL32UTF8
- ➤ Apply applications pre-patches

- ➢ Create 12c env file
- ➢ Apply database pre-patches
- ➢ Run pre-upgrade information tool
- ➢ Upgrade using the manual method
- ➢ Upgrade timezone data with DST 18
- ➢ Verify Init.ora file
- ➢ Verify Opatch lsinventory
- ➢ Verify oratab entry:
- ➢ Restart the database after setting the new env file
- ➢ Run adgrants.sql
- ➢ Grant create procedure privilege on CTXSYS
- ➢ Set CTXSYS parameter
- ➢ Gather statistics for SYS schema
- ➢ Upgrading Statistics Tables Created by the DBMS_STATS Package After Upgrading
- ➢ Oracle Database
- ➢ Implement and run AutoConfig
- ➢ Re-create OPATCH_INST_DIR directory
- ➢ Set the new env file created
- ➢ Run the postupgrade_fixups.sql Script
- ➢ Gather Fixed Objects Statistics with DBMS_STATS
- ➢ Re-create grants and synonyms

EBS 12.2.0 Upgrade

- ➢ Run Autoconfig on DB node
- ➢ OS pre-checks
- ➢ Check for latest DB bugs/patches

- ➢ Apply pre-patches for DB and PSU 12.1.0.2.5
- ➢ Apply pre-steps for 12.2.0
- ➢ Set Database and init parameters
- ➢ Add space in tablespace - APPS_TS_TX_DATA & APPS_TS_TX_IDX
- ➢ Apply some fixes post Database 12c
- ➢ Install JRE on the Database tier
- ➢ Review sizes of old and new tablespaces
- ➢ Run Gather Stats
- ➢ Update DB CONTEXT_FILE/init parameters
- ➢ Apply pre-steps for AD 12.2 upgrade driver
- ➢ Apply all Consolidated Upgrade Patches (CUP -6)
- ➢ Pre Tasks to avoid issues during 12.2.0 patch
- ➢ Apply 12.2 upgrade driver
- ➢ Drop event alert triggers in custom schemas (conditional).
- ➢ Unlimit the Failed_login_attempt parameter
- ➢ Review the sizes of old and new tablespaces (required).
- ➢ Disable Maintenance Mode
- ➢ Update the RDBMS ORACLE_HOME file system with AutoConfig and Clone files
- ➢ Run Rapid Install to configure Release 12.2 E-Business Suite instance.

EBS Online Patching enablement

- ➢ Apply latest patch:21072232 (new patch -)
- ➢ Run ADZDPSUM
- ➢ Run ADZDPMAN
- ➢ Run ADZDPAUT
- ➢ Run ADZDDBCC

➢ Copy f18 top from 11i to R12

➢ Run Gather stats for custom tops

➢ Compile Invalid Objects (if any)

➢ Fix Violations Listed in the Online Patching Readiness Report that Require Manual Intervention

➢ Verify database tablespace free space

➢ Run the Online Patching Enablement - Status Report

➢ Apply Online Patching enablement patch:13543062

➢ Check Database Initialization Parameters

EBS 12.2.5 Upgrade

➢ Apply the latest AD and TXK patchsets

➢ Apply Latest Technology Stack patchsets

➢ Pre steps for 12.2.5 upgrade patch

➢ Apply main 12.2.5 patch 19676458

➢ Apply additional post 12.2.5 patches as per the upgrade note

➢ Drop Obsoleted Product Schema

➢ Password change Activity using FNDCPASS

➢ Password change for Custom Schema

➢ Registered custom schema using ad splice

➢ Recompile Forms

➢ Post 12.2.5 patch steps

➢ Change Database to archive log mode

➢ Start services

Post EBS 12.2.5 Online Tasks

- ➤ Verify completion of Compile Security concurrent program
- ➤ Verify completion of concurrent programs (recommended)
- ➤ Install online help
- ➤ Synchronize file systems post 12.2.5 RUP patch
- ➤ Recompile apps Schema
- ➤ Run Gather schema statistics
- ➤ SLA post-upgrade
- ➤ Configure workflow
- ➤ Set XML publisher
- ➤ Drop new indexes created during the upgrade
- ➤ Enable/create triggers, jobs disabled during upgrade
- ➤ Recreate all custom DB links
- ➤ Compile remaining invalid objects
- ➤ Sanity Check
- ➤ Schedule CMs
- ➤ Migrate the CUSTOM library (conditional)
- ➤ Workflow Directory Services User/Role Validation conc prog
- ➤ Grant Flexfield value set access to specific users
- ➤ Implement Jars certs
- ➤ Delete obsolete product files
- ➤ Update Java Colour Scheme profile option for selected users
- ➤ Enable PDF printing other printer setup
- ➤ Resize DB
- ➤ Full Backup

➢ Post upgrade Technical/Functional steps

➢ Run the script QLTVVIEWS.sql present under $QA_TOP/patch/115/sql to regenerate the views

Best Practices Upgrade tips

➢ Determine Your Upgrade Path

➢ Treat Your Upgrade Activity as a Formal Company Project

➢ Use Change Management Appropriate for an Upgrade

➢ Build an Upgrade Team with Broad and Complementary Skills

➢ Utilize Peer and Oracle Resources

➢ Decide When to Change or Add Business Processes

➢ Plan for Upgrade Tuning

➢ Get Current Product and Upgrade Information

➢ Escalate and Resolve Problems as Appropriate

➢ Utilize the Configuration Support Manager

➢ Prepare the Organization

➢ Ensure the Quality of Your Data

➢ Inventory Your System

➢ Prepare a Go-Live Checklist

➢ Understand and Mitigate Project Risks

➢ Evaluate Your Architecture

➢ Calculate New Hardware Sizing

➢ Identify Custom Code and Scripting

➢ Defragment and Reorganize Your Database

➢ Study and Adhere to Current Minimum Technical Requirements

➢ Verify Your Installation

- ➢ Get Code Current
- ➢ Minimize Application Data to Upgrade
- ➢ Test with a Copy of the Production Database
- ➢ Complete Parallel Batch Testing Between a Copy of the Old System and an Upgraded Second Copy
- ➢ Leverage Existing Test Scripts and Plans
- ➢ Choose the Number of Test Upgrades and Functional Testing Cycles
- ➢ Perform Index Management
- ➢ Train End Users on the New Solution
- ➢ Get Specific Technical Training
- ➢ Optimize Training Processes
- ➢ Secure Functional User Buy-In
- ➢ Testing Scope
- ➢ Deciding to Go Live
- ➢ Update User Procedure Manuals

TOPIC

5

DATACENTRE MIGRATION WITH EXTREME LESS DOWNTIME

Datacentre Migration with Extremely less Down Time

Datacentre Migration is done for many cases that may be as a part of cost-cutting or moving to a better service provider etc. Some of the customers will upgrade the database by the time of datacentre migration and some of them will move as it is. In this chapter you will learn how to migrate a database from one datacentre to another without upgrading the database and with minimal downtime.

We can do this by creating a standby database in the target (SITE B) datacentre and keeping up the database sync with the Old datacentre (SITE A).

SITE A:

Take a level 0 (zero) backup of the primary database and create a pfile from the spfile, so that you can have all the parameters installed in this database come along. You can do this with the command below.

```
run {
  allocate channel D1 device type disk;
  allocate channel D2 device type disk;
  allocate channel D3 device type disk;
  allocate channel D4 device type disk;
  CONFIGURE CONTROLFILE AUTOBACKUP ON;
  CONFIGURE CONTROLFILE AUTOBACKUP FORMAT FOR DEVICE TYPE DISK TO
'/backup/Oracle/TEST_autobcf_%F';
  BACKUP INCREMENTAL LEVEL 0 tag hot_db_bkup_0 FILESPERSET 6
```

```
      format '/backup/Oracle/TEST_db_l0_s%s_p%p_t%t' (database) PLUS
ARCHIVELOG ;
  backup tag hot_spf_bkup
      format '/backup/Oracle/TEST_spfile_s%s_p%p_${DATE}' (spfile);
  sql "alter database create standby controlfile as
''/backup/Oracle/TEST_stby_ct_<DATE>.ctl''";
  crosscheck backup;
  delete noprompt expired backup;
  crosscheck copy;
  delete noprompt expired copy;
  delete noprompt obsolete;
}
```

The above command will take incremental level 0 backup along with the spfile, archivelogs and the standby controlfile. Also, take the pfile backup and edit the values according to the SITE B configuration especially the DB_UNIQUE_NAME.

```
SQL > create pfile='/home/Oracle/pfile.ora' from spfile;
File created.
SQL>
```

SITE B:

Install the required ORACLE Binaries and create the required directories as per the primary database and create a standby database.

Step 1: Startup the database in nomount after creating the pfile.

Step 2: Connect to RMAN using *"rman auxiliary /"*

```
run
{
allocate auxiliary channel prmy1 type disk;
allocate auxiliary channel prmy2 type disk;
allocate auxiliary channel prmy3 type disk;
allocate auxiliary channel prmy4 type disk;
allocate auxiliary channel prmy5 type disk;
allocate auxiliary channel prmy6 type disk;
allocate auxiliary channel prmy7 type disk;
allocate auxiliary channel prmy8 type disk;
allocate auxiliary channel prmy9 type disk;
allocate auxiliary channel prmy10 type disk;
allocate auxiliary channel prmy11 type disk;
```

```
allocate auxiliary channel prmy12 type disk;
duplicate target database for standby BACKUP LOCATION '/backup/Oracle/'
NOFILENAMECHECK;
}
```

This will create a standby database, all you need is to set up the data recovery between the primary and standby database. First and foremost is to make the SITE A and SITE B to communicate with each other by placing the TNS Names of both the servers in each other.

```
SITE A:
cd $ORACLE_HOME/network admin
vi tnsnames.ora
and add the TNS Name of the SITE B
SITE B:
cd $ORACLE_HOME/network admin
vi tnsnames.ora
and add the TNS Name of the SITE A
example:
vi tnsname.ora
TESTDB_PEIMARYHOSTNAME=
  (DESCRIPTION =
    (ADDRESS = (PROTOCOL = TCP)(HOST = <PRIMARYHOSTNAME>)(PORT = 1621))
    (CONNECT_DATA =
      (SERVER = DEDICATED)
      (SID = TESTDB)
    )  )
[Oracle@primaryhostname:TESTDB] tnsping TESTDB_PEIMARYHOSTNAME
TNS Ping Utility for Linux: Version 12.2.0.1.0 - Production on 27-SEP-
2019 11:30:05
Copyright (c) 1997, 2016, Oracle.  All rights reserved.
Used parameter files:
/u01/app/Oracle/product/12.2.0.1/db_1/network/admin/sqlnet.ora
Used TNSNAMES adapter to resolve the alias
Attempting to contact (DESCRIPTION = (ADDRESS = (PROTOCOL = TCP)(HOST =
PRIMARYHOSTNAME)(PORT = 1621)) (CONNECT_DATA = (SERVER = DEDICATED) (SID
= TESTDB)))
OK (10 msec)
```

TNSPING should result like the above example from both primary and standby databases.

Once the communication between the two servers are setup you need to add the dataguard parameter on SITE A and Site B as shown below.

SITE A:

```
alter system set LOG_ARCHIVE_CONFIG='DG_CONFIG=(TESTDB_PRIMARYHOSTNAME,
TESTDB_STANDBYHOSTNAME)';
ALTER SYSTEM SET log_archive_dest_2='service= TESTDB_STANDBYHOSTNAME LGWR
ASYNC NOAFFIRM delay=0 max_failure=3 max_connections=1 db_unique_name=
TESTDB_STANDBYHOSTNAME register net_timeout=180
valid_for=(online_logfiles,primary_role)' SCOPE=BOTH SID='*';
```

SITE B:

```
ALTER SYSTEM SET FAL_SERVER= TESTDB_PRIMARYHOSTNAME;
ALTER SYTEM SET FAL_CLIENT= TESTDB_STANDBYHOSTNAME;
alter system set LOG_ARCHIVE_CONFIG='DG_CONFIG=( TESTDB_PRIMARYHOSTNAME,
TESTDB_STANDBYHOSTNAME)';
alter system set log_archive_dest_1='LOCATION=/archive/TESTDB
VALID_FOR=(ALL_LOGFILES,ALL_ROLES) DB_UNIQUE_NAME= TESTDB_STANDBYHOSTNAME
mandatory alternate=log_archive_dest_9 reopen=0 max_failure=0'
SCOPE=BOTH;
```

SITE A:

```
ALTER SYSTEM SET log_archive_dest_state_2='DEFER' SCOPE=BOTH;
ALTER SYSTEM SET LOG_ARCHIVE_DEST_STATE_2='ENABLE' SCOPE=BOTH;
```

By Defer and Enabling the log_archive_dest_2 will start shipping the archivelogs from SITE A to SITE B. and all you need is to start the MRP process by the below command in SITE B will start recovering the database using the archives which are being shipped from the SITE A.

alter database recover managed standby database using current logfile THROUGH ALL SWITCHOVER nodelay disconnect;

Now the database is ready and is being recovered from the SITE A, now you can switch over the database from the SITE A to SITE B which will make SITE B as the primary and SITE A as a standby which can be brought down once the database is switched over.

Switch Over: Below are the steps to switchover the database from SITE A to SITE B which will be the datacentre migration.

SITE A:

Check the status of the database by passing the below query the expected result would be 'TO STANDBY' or 'SESSIONS ACTIVE'. Once you see either of the output go ahead and give the command to switchover.

```
select switchover_status from v$database;
alter system archive log current;
alter database commit to switchover to physical standby with session
shutdown;
shutdown immediate;
exit
```

SITE B:

Check whether the database is recovered with the last archivelog generated by SITE A and issue the below command.

```
alter database recover managed standby database cancel;
alter database commit to switchover to primary wait with session
shutdown;
shutdown immediate;
startup mount;
alter database open;
```

This will bring up the SITE B as the primary database and Now you have migrated from the old datacentre to a new one. This method of datacentre migration will reduce the downtime dramatically when compared with any other method like cloning the database from one datacentre to another after getting downtime for one or two days.

Here the downtime will be no more than 10 mins, as the database goes down only when you switch over the database. This downtime is quite less than the time taken to patch the environment. The only thing to be considered is that the new and the old datacentre should communicate with each other in order to keep them in SYNC until we switchover.

LINUX – THE UNKNOWN SIDE OF KNOWN COMMANDS

A Database administrator is the one who must have good knowledge of the Database commands as well as the Operating System commands. Your day-to-day activity is a mixture of Operating system commands and the database commands; lack of either of this will affect your efficiency to resolve the problem that occurred and hence you will be not able to meet Service Level Agreement (SLA). Learning Operating system commands is as important as learning the Database commands to become a successful database administrator.

What Can One Expect in this Chapter?

Top featured are LINUX Operating system commands that are being used in everyday activity. LINUX is the most common operating system used to install Oracle databases in general due to its security, reliability and flexibility to customize. So, this operating system is very popular in the world of Oracle Database.

LINUX allows you to mix more than one command to get the job done; this is the greatest flexibility that you'll get from LINUX. A few real time examples are discussed in this chapter which will make you understand before you start using this command in your environment.

What would be my takeaway?

This is a quick reference book where you can learn a lot, especially the basics like locating a file in a large storage environment, finding a specific word in a heap of files, what is inode number and how it works, job scheduler that will take care of the activity on your behalf, how to write your own commands, shorten a long command which is used very frequently to cut down the time taken to type etc. These are some of the key things that you will learn by the end of this chapter.

Simply "*man rm*" will give you the overall usage of that command but it will not tell you how to use this with other commands. We have that for you in this chapter.

Go ahead!! Happy Reading...

TOPIC

1

THE POWER OF ALIAS

When it comes to the database each second is money to the client. As a Database Administrator, you must make sure to reduce as much time as you can. Typing a command, especially a long command like "*ps -ef|grep pmon*" or "*du -sh *|sort -h*" every time will be annoying if you are working on P1 issues or in a critical downtime.

Linux offers a precious command called 'alias' through which you can execute a very long command in a single word or even in one or two characters. You can add user-defined 'aliases' for each user on the system; in other words, user ORACLE can have a set of aliases and user ROOT can have a different set of aliases.

Aliases allow a string to be substituted for a word when it is used as the first word of a simple command.

Here is the syntax for creating an alias.

Syntax:

```
alias name=<value>
alias name='command'
alias name='command argument 1 argument 2'
alias name='/script path/scriptname.sh'
alias name='/script path/scriptname.sh argument 1'
```

Let us have a look at some of the useful 'alias' commands which are useful for DBAs.

Instead of typing 'sqlplus / as sysdba' we can create an alias name.

```
alias dba='sqlplus '\''/ as sysdba'\''
```

From now on you can log in into the database just by typing '*dba*' (make sure of the case as the alias is case sensitive) and hit the enter key.

How to make this permanent?

If you just enter *alias dba='sqlplus '\"/ as sysdba'\""* that will be effective only till you close that session. Here is how this can be made permanent whenever you log in using your username into Linux.

Create a file called *alias.sh* and put all your alias short names into it and make it accessible with correct privilege.

Example:

```
Vi alias.sh
alias l.='ls -d .* --color=auto'
alias ll='ls -l --color=auto'
alias ls='ls --color=auto'
alias lt='ls -ltr'
alias dba='sqlplus '\''/ as sysdba'\'''
```

Then go to your user home "cd $HOME" and append". /full_path_to_script/alias.sh" in your ~/.bashrc

How can OS-specific alias be set?

When you are working in a multiple client environment and they have multiple operating systems, then the path to some of the OS-specific files may change. In order to avoid writing operating-system-specific alias, the code below can be added to the ~/.bashrc file.

```
# Getting operating system name via uname #
myos="$(uname)"
# add alias name based on operating system using $myos #
case $myos in
   Linux) alias foo='/path/to/linux/bin/foo';;
   FreeBSD|OpenBSD) alias foo='/path/to/bsd/bin/foo' ;;
   SunOS) alias foo='/path/to/sunos/bin/foo' ;;
   *) ;;
esac
```

Is it possible to delete the 'alias'?

If you change your mind to remove or delete an 'alias' which you consider to be used no more, then there is a simple command which will remove the 'alias'. If the 'alias' is set for the session you can use ***"unalias"*** command to remove the 'alias' from that session.

If you have a dedicated 'alias' script like the one we created above, then you can go ahead and remove the entry from your bashrc file so, that it will not be executed from your next login. You can still set the alias by executing the alias.sh file which was created by you if you need it again.

Syntax:

```
unalias aliasname
Example:
unalias dba
```

This has unset the alias name dba. From now on you need to enter the complete command to login to your database.

Can I call a variable inside the alias?

Variables used or the variables from the already set environment file can also be used in the 'alias' name just by calling the variable name prefixed with the dollar sign ($). If you want to enter into your ORACLE HOME, you can use the command below. (Make sure that the value is already exported manually or through any of the environment variables.)

```
alias cdoh='cd ${ORACLE_HOME}'
```

This will fetch the value of ORACLE_HOME from the environment variable set already and will enter into the directory.

'Alias' will help you by reducing your effort starting from typing and avoids typos kind of error while working in a critical issue, and it'll reduce a lot of time spent in typing and looking for the path of a file every time.

TOPIC

2

KNOWN AND UNKNOWN THINGS ABOUT CRON. TAB

As a database administrator, you have several tasks that have to be done on a regular basis. This may be your database backup or some of the clean-up activity. You will be not able to run the job by yourself manually all the time without missing the schedule; then how this can be done?

We have something called *job scheduler* for Windows and for Linux **Crontab** is there to run the jobs as per the schedule. Crontab is called **Cron Table** because it makes use of a job scheduler called *Cron* to execute tasks. *Cron* is named after "*Chronos*" the Greek word for time; it is a system process that will execute jobs as per the user's schedule.

Each user in the operating system has his/her own Crontab; they can schedule their own job to run in their user. Example user ROOT has its own Crontab which will take care of root related operations scheduled by super admins of the computer, likewise users of ORACLE have their own Crontab, from which they can execute jobs with the set of Privilege owned by that user.

How to create a Cronjob?

Creating a Cronjob is very simple entering the command "*crontab -e*" will initialize a file after checking /var/spool/cron, /etc/cron.d directories and the /etc/anacrontab; if the file already exists then it will enter into the edit mode which allows you to add or remove a schedule. To view/list the set of available schedules in the Crontab you need to use "crontab -l". It is strongly recommended to edit your Crontab using the "crontab -e" command other than the standard editors like vi, vim, etc., so that once you add/remove/modify the schedule in your Crontab jobs the "crond" demon will get restarted and your changes will be effective all of the sudden, else you need to restart the crond manually.

NOTE: The individual user cron files are located under **/var/spool/cron**, system services and applications generally add cron job files in the **/etc/cron.d** directory.

Is there a syntax to schedule a job in Cron?

Yes, there is a standard syntax to schedule the Cronjob. The syntax of each line expects a Cron expression made of five fields, followed by a shell command that needs to be executed.

```
# ┌─────────────── minute (0 - 59)
# │ ┌───────────── hour (0 - 23)
# │ │ ┌─────────── day of the month (1 - 31)
# │ │ │ ┌───────── month (1 - 12)
# │ │ │ │ ┌─────── day of the week (0 - 6) (Sunday to
Saturday;
# │ │ │ │ │                        7 is also Sunday on some
systems)
# │ │ │ │ │
# │ │ │ │ │
# * * * * * command to execute
```

In general, the scheduled job is executed when the time/date specified in the fields matches the current date and time. There is one exception in this, that is, if both day of the month and day of the week are restricted, then one of the two must match the current day.

Field	Mandatory	Values Allowed	Allowed Special Char	Remarks
Minutes	Yes	0-59	* , -	
Hour	Yes	0-23	* , -	
Day of Month	Yes	1-31	* , - ? L W	? L W only in some implementations
Month	Yes	1-12 or JAN - DEC	* , -	
Day of Week	Yes	0-6 or SUN - SAT	* , - ? L #	? L # only in some implementations

Non-standard characters

The following are non-standard characters and exist only in some Cron implementations.

L: 'L' stands for "last". When used in the day-of-week field, it allows you to specify constructs such as "the last Friday" ("5L") of a given month. In the day-of-month field, it specifies the last day of the month.

W: The 'W' character is allowed for the day-of-month field. This character is used to specify the weekday (Monday-Friday) nearest the given day. As an example, if you were to specify "15W" as the value for the day-of-month field, the meaning is: "the nearest weekday to the 15th of the month." So, if the 15th is a Saturday, the trigger fires on Friday the 14th. If the 15th is a Sunday, the trigger fires on Monday the 16th. If the 15th is a Tuesday, then it fires on Tuesday the 15th. However, if you specify "1W" as the value for day-of-month, and the 1st is a Saturday, the trigger fires on Monday the 3rd, as it does not 'jump' over the boundary of a month's days. The 'W' character can be specified only when the day-of-month is a single day, not a range or list of days.

Hash (#): '#' is allowed for the day-of-week field and must be followed by a number between one and five. It allows you to specify constructs such as "the second Friday" of a given month. For example, entering "5#3" in the day-of-week field corresponds to the third Friday of every month.

How can I schedule a job?

Scheduling the job in Crontab is very simple; just take a look at the example below which is demonstrated to run the backup every Sunday at 23 Hrs. 55 Mins., every day of the Month and all the 12 Months.

```
55 23 * * 0 /home/Oracle/scripts/backup/bin/rman_db_backup.sh
```

Here the "*" is the character used to represent "All". If it is in minutes, then it is every minute and if it is hours, it is every hour. So, we use "*" to tell the Cronjob to run on all the cases.

How can I run a job every 5 Mins.?

You can run the job every five minutes in two ways; one is specifying the minutes separated by "," comma, or using the "/" operator. Of this "/" is the best way where you can reduce the effort of typing.

Example:

00,5,10,15,20,25,30,35,40,45,50,55 * * * * /home/oracle/scripts/backup/bin/dr_check.sh

The above example shows the schedule using "," operator.

Example:

```
*/5 * * * * /home/oracle/scripts/backup/bin/dr_check.sh
```

The above example shows the schedule using "/" operator which will also execute the job in every 5 minutes' interval.

Similarly, you can schedule a job in a specified interval between specified time frames.

Example: To run a job every 3 hours between 10 a.m. and 10 p.m. you can use 10-22/3 in the 'hours' field of Crontab.

```
10 10-22/3 * * * /home/oracle/scripts/backup/bin/dr_check.sh
```

The above schedule will run every three hours, 10th minute between 10 a.m. and 10 p.m.

There are so many possibilities available to schedule your jobs in Crontab, which will reduce the effort of running the jobs manually by you in your environment. If it is a single instance you can manage somehow to run the job manually but, the environment with multiple production systems running in it cannot be handled manually. In such a case this kind of job scheduler will be the lifesaver for the System Administrators as well as the database administrators.

TOPIC

3

KNOW ABOUT INODE NUMBER

Sometimes we may have a poor file name or a poor directory name; it may contain a junk character or a space in the file or directory name; removing or renaming that file may be a challenging one if there are one or more files with that same name. In such cases, we can handle the file using its INODE number.

First, let us have a quick look at what is INODE number.

An INODE is an entry in INODE table, containing information; in other words, it is the metadata about a regular file(s) and the directory(s).

INODE number, also called index number, consists of the following attributes.

☐ File types (executable, block special, etc.)

☐ Permissions (read, write, etc.)

☐ UID (Owner ID)

☐ GID (Group ID)

☐ File Size

☐ Timestamps including last access, modification and when the INODE number changed lastly.

☐ File deletion time

☐ Number of links (if soft or hard links were created)

☐ Location of that file present in the disk.

☐ Some more info about the file.

You can find the total number of INODEs on the disk by using 'i' option with '**df**' command.

```
df -i /dev/vda1
Filesystem      INODE IUsed   IFree IUse% Mounted on
/dev/vda1       3452460 91053 8892205   12% /
```

The above command shows the total number of INODE on the filesystem, uses and free INODE details. In the case of 'INODE full' on any filesystem, you cannot create a new file on disk even if you have enough free space. So, each file system must have a free disk and INODE to create a file.

Find INODE number of File

To check the INODE number of a file, use the following command. The first field in output is an INODE number of the file.

ls -il testfile.txt

1150561 -rw-r--r-- 1 root root 0 Mar 10 01:06 testfile.txt

You can also search a file with an INODE number using find command. For example:

find /home/mahe -inum 1150561

/home/mahe/testfile.txt

Will INODE Change if you Copy, Move or Delete a file?

Let us take a look at what happens if we do copy, move or delete a file in your local file system.

Copy file: Copy command will allocate a free INODE number to the file and it will add a new entry in the INODE table.

```
ls -il  testfile.txt
1150561 -rw-r--r-- 1 root root 0 Mar 10 01:06 testfile.txt
cp testfile.txt myfile_new.txt
ls -il myfile_new.txt
1150562 -rw-r--r-- 1 root root 0 Mar 10 01:09 test_new.txt
```

Move or Rename a file: When you are moving or renaming a file in the same file system there will be no change in the INODE number; instead, it will change only the time stamp of that file.

```
ls il testfile.txtt
1150561 -rw-r--r-- 1 root root 0 Mar 10 01:06 testfile.txt
mv testfile.txt /opt/
ls -il /opt/testfile.txt
1150561 -rw-r--r-- 1 root root 0 Mar 10 01:06 /opt/testfile.txt
```

Delete a file: This will free up the INODE number which can be reused for further use.

Whatever the file you have in the LINUX machine it'll have all the properties i.e. attributes of the file other than the filename.

TOPIC

4

BEST FIND COMMAND OPTIONS IN LINUX

Finding or locating a file from a huge storage is really a challenging task unless you remember the file path. If you remember the file location, then it is well and good; if not, then the challenge comes in to play. To address this kind of practical difficulties involved in our day-to-day life LINUX has some built-in functions called grep, locate, find, etc., through which one can easily find the file or its content in a matter of minutes.

Here are some of the most useful options that we use in our day-to-day life as an Oracle Database Administrator. Let me demonstrate this, with a practical example.

1. Simple 'find' command with -name argument.

Let us begin with a simple 'find' command before we learn some complicated arguments. I am going to apply a patch in one of my test environments. I have the patch number (the file name) but not sure about the location I placed it; let us find the file with its filename.

Example 1.1

```
$find -name "28479031"
./patch/28479031
. /28479031
```

"-name" will find all the files which have the name specified in the quotes; it will search from the current directory as well as sub-directories in it.

2. How can I find Files using Name by ignoring Case?

We all know that LINUX is case sensitive. To it 'd' and 'D' are different. To make your search more powerful LINUX has another function that will ignore the case. If you are not sure about the file case (whether it is in upper/lower) you can use "-*i*" to override the case sensitive problems.

In this example, we will search for a log which is in both upper and lower case and see what it returns.

Example 2.1: Without "-*i*"

```
$find -name "rman.log"
./rman.log
Example 2.2: With "-i"
$ find -iname "rman.log"
./rman.log
./RMAN.log
```

3. Limiting the Search

When we are sure about the base directory and not sure about the sub-directory here is an option that will allow you to search by specifying the depth of the sub-directories. In simple words, you can tell "find" to look till 'N' directories before and 'N' directories after the current directory. This way you can narrow down your search

Example 3.1

```
$ find / -name passwd
./usr/share/doc/nss_ldap-253/pam.d/passwd
./usr/bin/passwd
./etc/pam.d/passwd
./etc/passwd
```

Now, we'll look for a file under the current directory and one level below to that. In the below example 3.2 we are looking for a file "passwd" using "-maxdepth" which will search for the file from root directory "/" and one level below.

Example 3.2

$ find -maxdepth 2 -name passwd

Example 3.2

```
./etc/passwd
```

Find the passwd file under root and two levels down. (i.e. root — level 1, and two sub-directories — level 2 and 3)

```
$ find / -maxdepth 3 -name passwd
./usr/bin/passwd
./etc/pam.d/passwd
./etc/passwd
```

Find the password file between sub-directory level 2 and 4.

```
# find -mindepth 3 -maxdepth 5 -name passwd
./usr/bin/passwd
./etc/pam.d/passwd
```

These commands are very useful, and very powerful when used singly or combined with any other command(s). This cuts down the time spent to find a file from a huge storage.

TOPIC

5

BEST OF GREP COMMAND IN LINUX

We, as Database Administrators must have a strong LINUX commanding knowledge. The more commands we know, the more we'll have control over the operating system. Linux commands are more powerful than they appear, and we have the flexibility of combining one or more commands to make it even powerful.

We'll cover some of the important commands that we use day-to-day as a Database Administrator. First, we'll start with the ten most used "grep" commands with example and their functionality.

"grep" is a powerful command which is basically used for searching a string in a specified file.

SYNTAX

```
grep "String_To_Search" File_Name
```

Example 1.1

```
$ grep "this" new_file
```

this line is the first line in this file.

This line is below the first line

And this is the last line in the file.

1. How can I search for a given string in multiple files?

Searching for a string in multiple files is not a big deal. There is a wildcard character called * (asterisk) which can be used to specify a certain pattern of files in the directory.

For example, in my current directory, I have files that start with the name *"new_"*. To list all the files whose name starts with *"new"* we use the command below.

ls new*

The same can also be combined with grep command to search a string from multiple files under my current directory.

SYNTAX

```
grep "String_To_Search" FilePattern
```

```
Example 2.1:
$ grep "this" new_*
new_file: this line is the first line in this file.
new_file: This line is below the first line
new_file: And this is the last line in the file.
new_file1: this line is the first line in this file.
new_file1: This line is below the first line
new_file1: And this is the last line in the file.
```

2. Case insensitive search

As everything in LINUX is case sensitive (UPPER/lower), we need to be more specific on the case that we use. Search will not yield any result if the case entered in the file pattern or the search string's case is different. To override this there is an awesome parameter called '-i' in LINUX which will make the case insensitive and get you the output even when the file contains upper- or lower-case search string.

SYNTAX
```
grep -i "string" File_Name
```
Example 2.1:

```
$ grep -i "the" new_file
```

THIS LINE IS THE FIRST UPPER CASE LINE IN THIS FILE.

This line is the FIRST lower case line in this file.

This Line Has Init Caps Character.

And this is the last line in this file.

3. How can I match for the whole Word, not the case?

Simply passing the command *grep -i "string"* to search something in a file will result in picking up any of the characters in a word that matches the search string.

Example 3.1:

$cat testfile.txt

We have something in this file there is noting found here

In the above example, the file testfile.txt has two lines in it and we'll search for the word "the" from it and see what the output will be.

```
grep -i "the" testfile.txt
we have something in this file there is noting
```

So, it is very clear that it is not looking for the word but the characters in a word. To get the exact match, we have an option called "-w" which will match the exact word not the characters in a word.

Example 3.2:

```
$grep -iw "the" testfile.txt
$
```

Example 3.3:

```
$grep -iw "there" testfile.txt
we have something in this file there is noting
```

4. How can I print "n" lines before and after my search result?

It is best practice to display before, after and around the search string when you are grepping a large file that will help you reach that line ease. There is some handy option available in grep command to do this.

A prints the specified N lines after the match

Syntax:

```
grep -A <N> "string" File_Name
```

Example 4.1:

```
$grep -A 3 "_27" testfile.txt
log_archive_dest_state_27          string       enable
log_archive_dest_state_28          string       enable
log_archive_dest_state_29          string       enable
log_archive_dest_state_3           string       ENABLE
```

B prints the specified N lines before the match.

Syntax:

```
grep -B <N> "string" File_Name
```

Example 4.2:

```
$grep -B 2 "_29" testfile.txt
log_archive_dest_state_27          string       enable
log_archive_dest_state_28          string       enable
log_archive_dest_state_29          string       enable
```

C prints the specified N lines before the match.

Syntax:

```
grep -C <N> "string" File_Name
```

Example 4.3:

$grep -C 1 "_27" testfile.txt

```
log_archive_dest_state_26          string       enable
log_archive_dest_state_27          string       enable
log_archive_dest_state_28          string       enable
```

5. How can I highlight my search results?

Searching a word using grep command will print you the entire line where the match is found. In order to highlight your search result from that huge line, we have a parameter called GREP_OPTIONS where you can highlight the result with a colour of your choice.

This can be done by exporting GREP_OPTION and GREP_COLOR like the one below.

Example 5.1:

```
export GREP_OPTIONS='--color=auto' GREP_COLOR='101;9'
```

Colour can be changed by modifying the GREP_COLOR value.

6. How can I search all files and sub-directory under my current directory?

Searching for a word in a file is much easier but, searching a word out of huge files and sub-directories is really a big task. To handle this there is an easy option available using grep which will search the given string recursively on all the files, directories and sub-directories under your current directory.

Example 6.1:

grep -r "log_archive_dest_state_2" *		
grep/test/testfile.txt:log_archive_dest_state_2	string	ENABLE
grep/test/testfile.txt:log_archive_dest_state_20	string	enable
grep/test/testfile.txt:log_archive_dest_state_21	string	enable
grep/test/testfile.txt:log_archive_dest_state_22	string	enable
grep/test/testfile.txt:log_archive_dest_state_23	string	enable
grep/test/testfile.txt:log_archive_dest_state_24	string	enable
grep/test/testfile.txt:log_archive_dest_state_25	string	enable

1. How can I invert my search match?

Grep is having the ability to show the result which is not matching the given criteria. If you want to print the content of a file by excluding certain lines you can use "-v" option in grep.

As a database administrator, this will help you in many situations where you need to modify a line in a file.

Example 6.2:

```
$cat testfile.txt
log_archive_dest_state_20                string         enable
log_archive_dest_state_21                string         enable
log_archive_dest_state_22                string         enable
log_archive_dest_state_23                string         enable
log_archive_dest_state_24                string         enable
$grep -v "_21" testfile.txt
log_archive_dest_state_20                string         enable
log_archive_dest_state_22                string         enable
log_archive_dest_state_23                string         enable
log_archive_dest_state_24                string         enable
```

In the above example 8.1 the line which contains "_21" is excluded and the reset of the lines in that file is printed.

2. How can I count the number of matches?

If you want just to know the number of occurrences of a given string in a file is done by using "-l" option in grep. This will tell you the number of times the match is found in each file.

Syntax:

```
grep -c "pattern" filename
```

Example 6.3:

```
$cat testfile.txt
log_archive_dest_state_20                string         enable
log_archive_dest_state_21                string         enable
log_archive_dest_state_22                string         enable
log_archive_dest_state_23                string         enable
log_archive_dest_state_24                string         enable
$grep -c "string" testfile.txt
5
```

Combining the other options with this will make it even more powerful; for example, to know the number of lines that do not match the given string, it will be known by using "-v" along with the "-c" option.

Example 6.4:

```
grep -c -v "string" testfile.txt
1
```

3. How to Display only the file names which match the given pattern?

It is possible to print only the file names that contain the given string in a file using "-l". This option will be helpful to find the files which contain a word in it when you have multiple files in your directory.

Example 6.5:

```
$ls
listfile.txt testfile_new.txt testfile.txt
$grep -l "string" *
testfile_new.txt
testfile.txt
```

Tips: Frequently using a command? Then here is what you need to do.

Go to user home (i.e.) /home/<OSUsername> edit .profile and create alias.

Example:

```
alias cdoh='cd /homw/Oracle/product/12.2.0.1/db_1'
```

So, from the next login simply 'cdoh' will take you to your Oracle home path.

Refer Chapter 1 of Linux Tips and Tricks Section

ABOUT DOYENSYS

Doyensys, started in December 2006, is a rapidly growing Oracle technology-based solutions company located in the US with offshore delivery centers in India.

We specialize in Oracle e-Business Suite, Oracle Cloud, Oracle APEX Development, Oracle Fusion, Oracle Custom Development, Oracle Database, and Middleware Administration.

We provide business solutions using cutting-edge Oracle technologies to our customers all over the world. Doyensys uses a viable Global Delivery Model in deploying relevant and cost-effective solutions to its clients worldwide. A winning combination of technical excellence, process knowledge, and strong program management capabilities enables Doyensys achieve global competitiveness by making technology relevant to its customers.

We improve business efficiencies through innovative and best-in-class Oracle-based solutions with the help of our highly-equipped technical resources. We are an organization with a difference, which provides innovative solutions in the field of technology with Oracle products. Our clientele across the globe appreciate our laser focus on customer delight, which is our primary success parameter. We have more than 250 resources across the globe. The technical capability of Doyensys stands out from the crowd as we not only provide services of exceptional quality for various Oracle products on time but also take credit for having developed our own products such as DBFullview, EBIZFullview, DBIMPACT, SmartDB, etc.

Our customers are fully satisfied with our services and appreciate our work as we stretch beyond their expectations. We do not compromise on quality for delivery, and the policies of Doyensys revolve around PCITI [Passion, Commitment, Innovation, Teamwork, and Integrity].

Doyensys encourages its employees to participate in Oracle conferences across the globe, and our team has presented papers at various conferences such as AIOUG Sangam, OATUG Collaborate over the years.

The exemplary work of Doyens as a team has created a wonderful environment in the organization. The policies framed by the management are very flexible and employee-friendly, keeping in mind the growth and interest of the organization.

We received 'India's Great Mid-size Workplaces' award (Rank #19) based on the feedback given by our employees in strict confidence and evaluation of various parameters by Great Place to Work. We are an equal opportunity employer and do not discriminate based on sex, religion, gender, nationality, etc. Our women are given a lot of flexibility to work in the organization, understanding the time that they need to spend with their family.

We are also proud to share that we received the award 'Best Workplaces for Women' from Great Place to Work and were ranked among the top 75 in IT and BPM Best Workplaces.

The culture to excel is at the heart of everything Doyens do. We not only share and care for other folks within the organization but also for the folks around the globe.

We have Database and Oracle EBS blogs available on the Doyensys page and are accessible on the internet. These blogs are exemplary work done by Doyens from the knowledge and experience gained by supporting various customers across the globe. There is a habit of creating reusable components for the teams within Doyensys so that a similar piece of work can be helpful for some other project within the organization.

The management is very supportive and encouraging, which is very much visible from the awards [Passion and Commitment, Commitment and Customer Delight, Rookie of the Year] that are given to Doyens, who excel in various categories.

Doyensys is not only a great place to work but is also a great place to learn as employees are always encouraged to explore new technologies and suggest innovative ideas that can benefit the clients. The teams within Doyensys are always encouraged and recognized by the management to add value to the work that is delivered to the customer rather than just doing monotonous work.

ABOUT THE AUTHORS

ARUN

Arun is a software consultant and holds a Master's degree in Science from BITS, Pilani. He is very interested in Mathematics, which he pursued during his college days. Later, he started his career as a Software Engineer and completed his Master's. He has rich experience in various products of Oracle, and extensively works on Oracle Applications and Database. He is very keen to learn new things and spends most of his time with his family. After joining Doyensys in 2018, he actively works on cloud and other Oracle technologies.

MAHENDRAN

Mahendran Manickam is basically from a software development background and holds a Master's degree in Computer Applications from the University of Madras. Right from his college days, he is very active and interested in web and standalone application development using VB .net, ASP .net, and Visual Basics and has developed many billing applications for small outlets. His application for students' attendance maintenance is still being used by his department in college. He has over eight years of experience in the IT field. He is very interested in automating the environment using shell and BAT scripts, hence he was awarded the 'Innovator' award in 2016 and the 'Passion and Innovation' award in 2017 by Doyensys, and 'Customer Appreciation' award a couple of times.

At Doyensys, he has worked on several projects, including core and Oracle EBS from 11i, R12.1, R12.2 applications. He has good experience in datacentre migration, database upgrade, cross-platform migration, data guard, real application cluster, GI, etc. He is a certified Oracle Database Administrator (12C) and 11g Weblogic Administrator. He is very passionate about photography and is a YouTuber in his spare time.

GOKUL

Gokul Kumar Radhakrishnan is a Project Lead at Doyen System, with a wide view of Database Management. Gokul did his Bachelor's in IT from Sourashtra College, Madurai. He started in a DBA role in the Middle-East and has more than thirteen years of experience in the Oracle EBS implementation, upgrade, and support. Gokul has achieved a lot in his career and has won the title 'Employer of the year 2009 and 2011' in his company. Gokul's specific areas of expertise are Oracle applications and database. He has completed certifications including RHEL, Solaris 10, Oracle Database Administrator (12C), WebLogic Administrator 11g, Oracle Cloud (OCP), ITIL Foundation. His hobbies include reading historical books and exploring new places.

SUNDARAVEL

Sundaravel Ramasubbu is currently working in Doyensys as the Competency Head – DBA Practice. He is a Mechanical engineer from Anna University, Tamil Nadu, who later moved to Oracle technology due to his passion for the IT industry. He has more than twelve years of experience in the Oracle technology space. He supported Doyensys' strategic customer databases and their e-Business suite applications. He has a strong knowledge of Oracle database and middleware technologies. He is an Oracle Certified Database and Weblogic Administrator. He is an active blogger and strongly believes in the famous quote, "Knowledge is power. Knowledge shared is power multiplied." He is very interested in learning new things and implementing them in actual scenarios.

www.ingramcontent.com/pod-product-compliance
Lightning Source LLC
Chambersburg PA
CBHW080622060326
40690CB00021B/4786